MASTERING THE CHAOS OF
MERGERS AND
ACQUISITIONS

MASTERING THE CHAOS OF
MERGERS AND ACQUISITIONS

HOW TO PLAN, NEGOTIATE, AND IMPLEMENT ALLIANCES AND PARTNERSHIPS IN A COMPLEX WORLD

J. GARRETT RALLS, JR.
AND KIMBERLY A. WEBB

Cashman Dudley
An imprint of Gulf Publishing Company
Houston, Texas

MASTERING THE CHAOS OF
MERGERS AND
ACQUISITIONS

Cashman Dudley
An imprint of Gulf Publishing Company
P. O. Box 2608 ☐ Houston, Texas 77252-2608

10 9 8 7 6 5 4 3 2 1

Library of Congress Cataloging-in-Publication Data

Ralls, J. Garrett.
    Mastering the chaos of mergers and acquisitions :
how to plan, negotiate, and implement alliances and partner-
ships in a complex world / J. Garrett Ralls, Jr. and Kimberly
A. Webb.
       p.   cm.
    Includes index.
    ISBN 0-87719-365-7 (alk. paper)
    1. Consolidation and merger of corporations—
Management.   2. Strategic alliances (Business)—
Management.   3. Partnershp.   I. Webb, Kimberly A.
II. Title.
HD58.8.R345   1999
658.1′6—dc21   99-36244
                                               CIP

Printed in the United States of America.
Printed on acid-free paper (∞).

For My Family
Francia, Little Justy, and Jeff
With Love,
J. R.
(aka Daddy)

For My Husband and Family
With Love,
Kimberly

We would also like to express our appreciation and gratitude
to the editorial assistance of Debbie Markley.

A portion of this book's royalties is dedicated to the Epilepsy
Foundation of Southeast Texas and its Camp Spike 'n' Wave,
a camp for children with seizure disorders.

EPILEPSY
FOUNDATION
SOUTHEAST TEXAS

2650 Fountain View, Suite 316
Houston, Texas 77057
(713) 789-6295
(713) 789-5628 Fax
Web page: www.efset.org
E-mail: hboyd@efset.org

Contents

A Sketch:
The Landscape
of the Book

Globalization is not a phenomenon. It is not just some passing trend. Today it is the overarching international system. . . . To begin with, the globalization system . . . is not static, but a dynamic ongoing process: globalization involves the inexorable integration of markets, nation-states and technologies to a degree never witnessed before—in a way that is enabling individuals, corporations and nation-states to reach around the world farther, faster, deeper and cheaper than ever before, and in a way that is also producing a powerful backlash from those brutalized or left behind by this new system. . . . The defining document of the globalization system is "The Deal."

— Thomas L. Friedman, author of
The Lexus and the Olive Tree

The deal is the essence of business today. A deal by itself is not enough. A deal might not close. It may fall apart or be diluted by the nature of chaos in business. A deal may focus on the here and now, and fail to provide growth for the future. Distractions half a world away may accumulate into a contagion spread through markets and ultimately defeat a deal. Successful deals unfold across their business landscape over time and deliver material wealth.

Value emerges from business relationships—partnerships, alliances, acquisitions, and other investments—only when after the closing of the deal, value extraction is orchestrated with care and precision. Care implies attention to what is happening and the flexibility to treat changing circumstances. Precision is accuracy in the knowledge about the business play, as well as an insight for executing in the complexity of globalization.

Broad acceptance by stakeholders—shareowners, customers, employees, value chain partners, community—is the precursor to success. Success is material wealth gauged by cash flows and proven again and again in market space share and net income. Success is also, however, a life worth living at work with a quality of home life that renews, energizes, and fulfills.

Value is influenced by how we prepare to do a deal, how we negotiate, and how we manage the complexity in business growth. Mastering orchestration—from deal preparation, to closing, and to extraction of the promised value—is an art that escapes most business leaders and their firms. Too many of us are still caught up in yesterday's models of success. Despite the rhetoric, boards, management, and employees avoid the reality of globalization or fail to grasp how interdependent the world has become. In globalization, we must see the business landscape, appreciate all the interactions on it, optimize against diminishing returns, and create pathways for new, ever-increasing returns. Putting it together takes thought. Adapting and emerging with success requires the intent to make things happen.

Orchestrating everything to extract value is the business challenge of the new millenium. The process is non-linear, capable of moving in many directions. More attention must be given to the business landscape to achieve any success. Purposeful action and the ability to lace actions together in a certain direction is important. Continuous performance and innovation are hallmarks for successful firms in globalization.

This book is about what it takes to orchestrate value extraction. The way in which value emerges in business is explained. The interdependent nature of influences and events found in "globalized" value chains are revealed. In doing so, the mystery of creating economic value is unveiled. Templates and coaching tips are offered to guide preparation, action planning, and implementation. Case illustrations provide benchmarks and help in understanding what may happen in building strategic business relationships.

Part One: Orchestrating Value Extraction is an essay on how to put things into motion. It appeared as the final chapter in our first book, *The Nature of Chaos: Using Complexity to Foster Successful Alliances and Acquisitions*. We begin where we left off because this book provides the detailed process and templates for orchestration. Part One concludes with a review of how to prepare.

Part Two: Entering Negotiations is not just another approach to negotiation. It addresses dealing with irresponsible behavior and how to move to a level of trust in which data about performance determines valuation. What it really takes to achieve win-win is defined. Transparency is treated not as an absolute but as a series of states in a process wherein sharing information affects trust.

Part Three: Making it Happen covers the broad range of topics that lead to value extraction. Implementation strategies, application of new systems and technologies, and stewardship are discussed with suggestions and recommendations. Part Three concludes with a statement on what leadership must be in the new era of globalization.

Our Roots

The book has its foundation in two basic views of the world: Chaos Theory and its Complexity Principles, and the Building Blocks for Trust. Intertwined, these concepts provide an organic view of how work takes place. They are not linear, but are based on assumptions about nature as it is. Firms, deals, and work practices are viewed as life systems. Even many of our technologies are viewed as taking on characteristics of life systems.

As Kevin Kelly says in his recent book, *New Rules for the New Economy* (Viking, 1998), "Technology has become our culture, our culture technology. . . . Technology has been able to infiltrate into our lives to the degree it has because it has become more like us. It's become organic in structure. Because network technology behaves more like an organism than like a machine, biological metaphors are far more useful than mechanical ones in understanding how the network economy runs."

Why is it important to be organic? The natural view better represents reality and encourages us to envision all the key influences in relationships and value offerings as well as how these influences and offerings interact among themselves. Like watching a bee hive, what seems at first to be chaos is better viewed as numerous pathways being pursued simultaneously in service to life.

Our old models for organization and deal transactions evolved from paradigms of command and control through hierarchy and forceful direction. Winners held power and authority when these models were born. On a planet of nearly six billion highly interactive people, power and authority remain important determinants of outcomes. Cooperation, acceptance and tolerance also function to determine success. The organic view opens our eyes to see how political, social, environmental, cultural and individual dynamics shape economic dynamics. These economic dynamics may be changes in ownership, cooperation across firms, collaboration within a team and across silos, or individual effort. These are the dynamics for orchestrating value extraction.

Chaos and Complexity

Chaos and complexity concepts help us to appreciate how circumstances may just happen in business. Some seem random or crazy. Certain circumstances can be so maddening as to distract from value or destroy it altogether. In recent years, the scientific community has challenged us to take the organic view and appreciate more the nature of nature. As we discussed in *The Nature of Chaos,* patterns evolve to a new order—whether by intention or adaptation, for good or bad. When shaped to create value, patterns are powerful economic tools. In chaos, there are two ways to access economic value. One is to emerge with patterns that create a new order for business. As patterns repeat across a business landscape, they begin to dominate. This is known as the principle of increasing returns in chaos. Optimization, that is, making systems, processes, or procedures as efficient, cost-effective, and productive as possible, is the other means for accessing value.

In the last quarter of the 20th century, we have optimized with information technology, reengineering projects, operations management, quality programs, and business consolidation through roll-ups and mergers. Once addressed, optimization against diminishing returns offers limited growth. Optimization will continue as privatization moves forward around the world, yet will offer less and less opportunity. What lies ahead in the next millenium is the challenge to create increasing returns. This means gleaning insights into the business landscape and setting pathways for growth with unlimited potential.

The trick is to understand the business landscape and to envision new pathways. Firms in the 21st century will emit catalysts that bond them to other enterprises. Partnering with resources, talent, and knowledge will better enable the intersection of forces that create commercial opportunities. Combining capabilities enhances:

- Access to new markets
- The bundling of old and new technologies to create still other product innovations

- The ability to attract capital
- Leverage in the use of infrastructures

Effective relations with communities and governments will heighten sensitivity for social responsibility and changing policy. Strategic business relations will establish and maintain pipelines for value creation.

Building Blocks for Trust

Trust is a function of our life experiences. How we are treated as a child by family, friends, teachers, and mentors shape whether we genuinely trust at all and how long it will take for us to trust another. All in all, trust is the underpinning to our feelings about others. It influences the choices we make about how much we depend on others, what energy and resources we will put into a relationship, and where we will go in the future with others.

The Essence of Trust

- Trust begins with the ability to predict what another will do. We want others to keep their promises.
- We draw on our childhood and adult life experiences to define trust.
- Trust strengthens as others act in our best interest.
- Most of us are fair; we do not expect self-sacrifice as proof of trustworthiness.
- Trust abounds when another acts at risk to self yet still proceeds in the direction of our own best interest.
- Caring proves others to be worthy of our greatest trust. They act on our behalf without waiting for circumstances to require a choice. Those displaying their caring may do so at a risk of losing our appreciation or affection. This is particularly true when a mirror must be held up to encourage reality in thinking.
- Transparency makes it easier to trust. Prediction is simpler. There is validation that choices made are a matter of free will. Hidden agendas for personal gain would be known.
- The presence of trust in a relationship makes work more efficient. People rely on one another and genuine team work takes place with less distraction. There is great power in teamwork based on trust.

Trust expedites and strengthens strategic business relationships. Understanding the elements for trust provides a blueprint of what it takes to create a capable partnership. We present the element of trust as four building blocks: *transparency, learning, civility,* and the *capability to envision the business landscape.* The building blocks are adaptive and interactive with one another. Trust is not found at the end of a linear progression. Trust dynamics are much like the processes in adaptive cognition—how we think and deal with the world. We used to think cognition worked liked this: sense, think, then act. We are now certain that sensing, thinking, and action are always happening and that these dynamics are always adapting to each other, i.e., thinking is shaped by actions, actions are shaped by what we sense, and so on. This is a continuous, interactive process. Trust, too, is a continuous, interactive process. What is accomplished in business relationships can be lost or strengthened as the dynamics within trust affect the status of the relationships.

The Lay of the Land

An intensive review of a business landscape integrates the complexity of a value proposition with appreciation for the trust dynamics in relationships. All key influences and their interactions among themselves and with value are examined as the business landscape. The business landscape must place the human landscape into focus with the other elements of the landscape: investor relations, all dimensions of the value chain, financial engineering, strategic direction and growth ambitions, the infrastructure for action (structure, learning, communication, and orchestration), partnering experience and philosophy, along with technology. This dynamic model of business provides precise analytics of a firm's movements in value.

A business landscape reveals how chaos affects value. Globalization and advancing technology heighten the intensity and overlap among competitive forces and market influences. The capabilities to see, predict, and test assumptions are competitive advantages in the complexity which results. The business landscape provides the means for you to capture waves of opportunity or emerge with your own pattern for success.

The Bottom Line in Value Extraction—Buy-Ins

The bottom line in value extraction is gaining the acceptance of those who can make things happen or successfully stand in the way.

Without buy-in by key stakeholders, whatever the value proposition is, it will take longer, cost more, have less a chance of performing well, and will seldom innovate.

We can determine the motivation to act with enthusiasm by understanding acceptance. In 1991, Dr. Ken Organski of the Center for Conflict Resolution at the University of Michigan addressed the Society of International Business Fellows in Dallas. He reported on a model for examining effectiveness based on his research of war and civil unrest since the beginning of the 19th century. For Organski, acceptance is a function of *understanding, preferences, salience,* and *power.*

In developing orchestration plans, it is important to poll these dimensions of attitude toward the partnering or project of your business intent with key stakeholders—customers, employees, owners, partners, and community. It will help you gauge what must be done. For example, if understanding is low, education and communication are your best bet to initiate acceptance. Where preferences are against action, an experimental project to demonstrate comparative benefits of your intent may help embolden support.

The more salient or important the issue is to a person, the more they are likely to react, positively or negatively, depending on how their preferences lie. For those who are most concerned, more time will be needed to persuade. For those aligned, they will be quick studies and powerful advocates. Among this latter group, you will find help. Other times, people will not act because they do not see themselves as powerful enough to make something happen. Empowerment and demonstration of their autonomy will be useful to progress. In some cases, people may misuse their power and block progress. In these cases, it is important to know how they are likely to use their power and pursue persuasion or compromise before endangering progress by inviting resistance. If they are misusing power, make their actions transparent to others having influence.

Orchestration is about making things happen. Coaching and templates guide you to ensure complete action. They aid the most in doing a thorough job of reviewing where value is. They remind you to give consideration to how people are feeling and are likely to react to your value proposition. In the end, focus and action to make your intent happen is what counts. Along the way, monitoring change and adapting quickly will foster value extraction for what is worthwhile now and in the future. This unleashes you from past assumptions and errors in forecasting.

Over the Rolling Hills and Through the Valleys

The landscape for the book unfolds in a linear fashion. Preparation focuses on selecting worthy partners and valuing a deal for what it is worth—avoiding paying premiums or failing to extract value because unrealistic values were set at the onset. Negotiations are discussed next, revealing the complexity of what may be included in value and the various financial and commercial forms value may take. The human processes of getting a shared view that motivates a seller to offer a deal and a buyer to agree to a deal are addressed for alliances, acquisitions, and other forms of partnering. Implementation dynamics are reviewed to detail what you must do to make things happen. Choices in communication, organizing, stewardship, and cooperation are made clear.

Any book follows some course and a step-by-step progression that makes sense. It can be disconcerting in application because things, which should come later, are suddenly important in the present. Not long ago, we were assisting in a corporate planning effort. Our client was moving along the linear progression when an acquisition opportunity surfaced because a competitor fell on hard times. The competitor was hurting because foreign sales were not realized and a public offering coincided with a sudden downturn in the IPO market. Our client had to choose between waiting until the planning was complete or acting in an ad hoc manner. They did the latter, yet kept moving on the corporate plan. Whenever possible, they linked the two efforts. On one hand, they learned how well their assumptions played in the real world. On the other hand, assumptions about the overall business guided valuation of the target.

Many times, events will drive what you do. It is important to read this entire book and utilize templates and suggestions as reminders for specific phases in which you find yourself. In the end, partnering and its orchestration are not linear processes. Making partnerships of any nature work is a complex, human enterprise. Like a beehive, it will appear chaotic to an outsider. If there is a sound process at work, pathways for increasing returns will emerge from the chaos. We call this "sweet success."

The picture of a business landscape is never complete in globalization. The landscape is in constant motion, driven by market turbulence, the choices of customers, the acts of competitors, and your progress in your strategy. At best, we have a sketch to guide us in extracting value. This book provides a detailed guide to understanding and conquering the chaos that accompanies mergers, acquisitions, and other alliances.

PART 1

Orchestrating Value Extraction

CHAPTER 1

Orchestration

UPSIDE

Orchestration is where the rubber meets the road in building a partnership. Brokers make money from the closing of a deal. If one of the parties goes fishing after the deal, as can happen in partnering involving acquisitions, that party may make money too. Usually stakeholders do not make money until the venture, whatever it is or however it is constituted, creates value. The outcomes for orchestration create revenues and make earnings possible. Orchestration is critical to success.

The excitement in orchestration is the wave of adaptation that can splash onto a business landscape. The challenge—to adapt to an opportunity, to resist being overwhelmed, or to prevent your strategy from being overshadowed—can be fierce. Good anticipation of forces requiring adaptation can facilitate orchestration. Flexibility to respond further enhances orchestration. The key to orchestration is emerging with your strategy and making it dominant, regardless of any interference.

In adaptation, orchestration influences your capability to exploit adaptive forces to serve your own ends. Dancing on your feet is an art, and it can add value. What you must do is foresee and be ready to act on the evolving advantage. Others may see it, but not act. Full and complete orchestration includes the capacity to turn a trend or an unanticipated event to your advantage.

War Story

The Global Cooperative

A good case illustration is the Saskatchewan Wheat Pool (SWP). SWP is the 54th largest corporation in Canada and the largest of the three western wheat pools. With sales over $4 billion (Canadian), SWP is a major force in agribusiness.

SWP is an aggressive player in its industry, with aspirations to be a 21st century leader. Both its adaptation and emerging strategies exemplify its approach. As deregulation invited change, SWP has responded in several ways. One is cost-efficiency efforts across its diverse businesses. Another is SWP's decision to consolidate across the prairies, acquiring businesses in other provinces in addition to its traditional marketplace. Technology is another example. SWP foresaw the aerospace technologies of global positioning and satellite sensing as important resources for the new agribusiness method, precision farming. The company could easily have ignored the wave of adaptation coming from aerospace, as did many other players in agribusiness. Instead, it added satellite sensing services to its portfolio.

Of greater importance to SWP are the emerging strategies for growth. SWP, in addition to consolidating, is investing through its Project Horizon in innovative farm service centers. SWP, as a cooperative, launched a favorable public offering of a Class B stock on the Toronto Stock Exchange. This insightful financial engineering is fueling the domestic growth noted and global expansion through partnerships in the U.S., Poland, Mexico, and elsewhere in the world. Setting the balance between the domestic agenda and new global ambition is a key task. In all, these emergent strategies fit with our notion of what business acumen will be in the 21st century:

- Grasping the business landscape and the impinging forces for adaptation
- Managing complexity for optimization and growth
- Leveraging strategic business relations in optimization and growth

Making bold and determined moves for value is a continuous process. Taking the breakaway position gets the ball rolling. Accomplishments to date are soon history. The future is the successful extension of the innovation process. For example, SWP will be challenged to maintain a domestic momentum and capture foreign growth aggressively. To realize these ambitions, the aggressive forward force cannot pause too long or wind down into complacency. Building processes for continuous improvement and innovation fuels progress.

DOWNSIDE

Many great partnerships are conceived and explored without results. Closing deals, making them work, and extracting value elude the best of businesspeople. Pessimism often dominates anticipation of partnerships. In interviews with executives, we asked if they prefer to do business in an alliance or as a single entity. Most cautioned against the use of a partnership to do business. They prefer direct control. They counsel ownership of at least 50 percent of a firm. Were there another way, they would avoid any form of partnering.

Why avoid partnering? It is more difficult to make work than a single entity. So why do these same executives continue to partner? There is no other way to capture the value. Someone else may own a talent, technology, or asset essential to success. The smartest or only way to gain access is to partner—or someone else may possess the wherewithal to finance the venture.

FIVE MAJOR SETTINGS FOR PARTNERING

Richard Pattarozzi, president of Shell Deepwater, began our interview with an important challenge: deal with the ambiguities in terminology. While his remarks focused on the supply chain, they have validity in all aspects of partnering. Everything is called an alliance. "Alliance" should not mean there is only a supplier relationship. "Alliance" should indicate when the relationship built on trust adds value, that is, where sharing intimate knowledge will reveal important opportunity and value-add. Pattarozzi's objective is to reduce cycle time and reduce cost *with* suppliers, not at their expense.

We are frustrated by the ambiguity that obscures the value in learnings. It is not clear what someone else's experience means in examining surveys of practitioners or comparing metrics. For this reason, we define major settings within the venues of strategic business relations.

In the chapter on orchestration, we distinguish among the five major settings for business partnering: **shared ownership** (such as partnering among individuals found in legal partnerships including more than one individual and between individuals and institutions such as limited liability corporations [LLCs], partnerships [LLPs], or joint ventures [JVs]), **value-chain partnering** (including supplier-customer action teams [SCATs]), **customer intimacy, employee partnerships,** and **passive investor relations.** In every case, the term "partner" or "partnership" is frequently used and refers to the joint human relationships in pursuit of a common business interest.

Figure 1-1 identifies the venues for strategic business relationships. **"Strategic business relationship (SBR)"** describes all partnering dynamics. A colleague of ours, Dr. Joe Vogel, coined the phrase. Hereafter, we use SBR to permit us to label characteristics which are common to all business partnering situations. When characteristics are unique, we use the specific label.

BUILDING SUCCESSFUL SBRS

What makes a successful strategic business relationship in many diverse situations? Our work over the years reveals, as essentials for success, the statements in Figure 1-2.

The size and scope of the partnership impact success. No guidelines exist as to what is a critical mass given the variety of influences and possibilities for partnership configuration. Likewise, there is no guarantee that size ensures progress.

The subject matter for partnering influences what the partnership accomplishes. A commodity transaction appears to require less thought or effort in the minds of executives accustomed to large value-chain partnerships or joint ventures. This is a popular yet naive view. What heretofore may have been a simple sales transaction can become complex. Today, suppliers may gain opportunity in the complexity of price, delivery, and finance. Eric Skilling at Enron earned a major career accomplishment by demonstrating that a company can manage commodities in a manner to differentiate value and bundle services. His organization introduced customized supply contracts in natural gas. Customers are able to tailor volume, terms, time, and price indices to suit their needs best.[1]

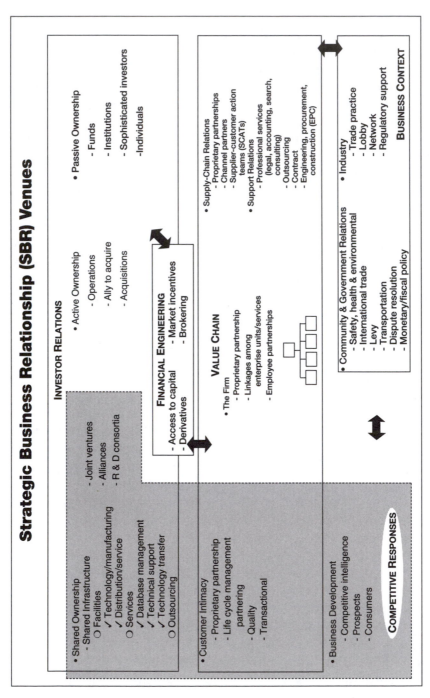

Figure 1-1. *Venues of strategic business relationships (SBRs).*

- A shared business objective validated by both a market for consuming products/services and investor interest in financing.
- Agreement on terms and conditions for operations and exit.
- Civility in the relationship as demonstrated by mutual respect, trust, and a bias to restore harmony (often called "chemistry").
- Teamwork in the pursuit of shared purpose . . . capability to marry different cultures.
- Sufficient investment to create the infrastructure/system of business (even if elements are shared with parents).
- Respect for any business unit as an entity—its own pursuit (an extension of the parents but distinct in destiny).
- Sponsorship for the relationship in formation, start-up, dispute resolution, and reinvestment.
- Metrics and the means for reward and recognition.
- Fun, celebration, and achievement . . . getting together is not enough in itself to motivate for high performance—the venture must be rewarding and fulfilling for stakeholders, in particular, those closest to the work being done.

Figure 1-2. Essentials of successful SBRs.

Additional success factors vary by their business settings, but the partnering process and the amount of work for the five major settings share some characteristics. There are important differences affecting workload, the issues and styles for planning, and terms and conditions.

Shared Ownership

There are several forms of shared ownership. Definitions are at best ambiguous. Joint ventures (JVs) bring to mind significant efforts, often requiring an operator organization independent of the owners and detailed legal agreements. This is not always the case. Some JVs refer to simple market sharing as we find in the airline industry where routes are shared. Another simpler form is a JV to share infrastructure.

Many companies are forming limited liability corporations (LLCs) or limited liability partnerships. These are popular in marketing supply chain partnering. Small enterprises with sales under $10 million are not uncommon. The objective is typically to bring together technology, talent, cash, or other assets owned by different parties for the purpose of creating a new enterprise. A good example is Southwest Convenience Stores, LLC, which melds the talents of Southwest Convenience Stores and Fina, the oil and petrochemical company.

Value-Chain Partnering

Value-chain partnering covers a plethora of SBRs. As noted in the discussion of shared ownership, supply chain linkages can be under the control of multiple owners. When cooperation is not held to an overview by shared owners, we think of alliances. Again there are exceptions wherein ownership is shared and the SBR is called an alliance.

Alliances take many forms. They can share a market, an infrastructure, an organization, a technology, or be more limited in focus to indicate a supply chain link such as a preferred provider, a sole source agreement, or a simple right of first refusal. Again, the vocabulary is ambiguous.

R&D alliances are normally called research consortia. The cost for invention and innovation is shared across an industry or among industry players, universities, and governments. The objective is to fund a breakthrough from which all parties benefit. Were it not for the concerted efforts of all parties, innovation would be too costly to consider.

Outsourcing is another form of alliance. An embellishment to the sole source agreement, outsourcing eliminates an internal service or step in the process. An outside contractor then takes responsibility for providing the activity. Often these are long-term agreements.

The advantages of outsourcing include sharing liabilities, in particular, environmental risks; having a career focus and training for operators shared among similar operations elsewhere (in place of being the odd fellows within a plant or site); efficiencies from sharing infrastructure and labor costs; and independent capitalization for necessary operations and their improvement or innovation. In outsourcing, you pay only for the service rendered.

Value-chain efforts are focused on optimizing against diminishing returns. Incremental improvement is the probable outcome, although the combination of two circumstances can produce impressive results. One of the pair is a long-standing value chain that has devolved into isolated segments and bureaucratic infighting. The other is the introduction of information technology to remedy and speed the process. Still, this is optimization and does not capture growth opportunity created by setting patterns that dominate a market. The elements of a value chain are listed in Figure 1-3.

We were benchmarking for an oil company when we discovered the following alliance. It is a good example of how an alliance can integrate strengths. An independent refiner and gasoline distributor, Holly, was able to access efficiencies in the supply chain. Fina benefited in capturing efficiencies and securing supply for its growth in the region. Different from larger oil companies, Fina offered its partner a tall vertical solution, which included oil exploration and production, refined products, storage, pipelines, and distribution. Most oil companies are establishing enterprise units in a particular segment of the value chain. As a result, compartmentalization sets in and the scope of optimization is then limited to a segment such as exploration and production, refining and manufacturing, pipelines, marketing/sales, or other logistics.

As you examine the value-chain elements in Figure 1-3, keep in mind there is little standardization in vocabulary used in value chains because vendors in consulting, software, and information architecture introduce their unique labels in attempts to differentiate among themselves and between generations of their own products.

Research on the value chain is limited by the variety of terms used to describe it. This is unfortunate given there is much to be learned about what works and what does not. We do not advocate standards and uniformity, but business researchers should make an effort to compare terms and their meanings carefully before drawing firm conclusions.

Customer Intimacy

Customer intimacy is the essential partnering dynamic in business. It involves a listening-sharing relationship that helps you understand customer needs and how you can best meet those needs. Shareholder value-add is best served by understanding a customer so well, and possessing close relations so strong, you are not only able to secure business but to increase it by leading customers to new products and services. Customer intimacy leverages a firm's competencies in trust, human communication, transparency in governance, rigorous business analytics, customer responsiveness, and teamwork. The goal is the pursuit of shared business objectives.

(text continued on page 12)

STRATEGY
- Fit (Vision, Understanding of Vision, Strategic Alignment Process (SAP), SAP+ or Architecture (Structure, Information Systems, Learning Systems, Strategic Relations)
- Planning and Monitoring
- Stewardship
- Joint Business Planning and Sponsorship
- Alignment of Rewards
- Metrics

TRANSACTIONS MANAGEMENT
- Transactions Minimization (Information Gathering, Negotiations, Contracting, Product Movement)
- Transactional Transparency (Costs, Problems and Opportunities for All Value-Chain Events)
- Transactional Databasing
- Order Management
- Forecast Fluctuation
- Customer Sales/Service
- Virtual Linkage (Head Office, Sales, etc.)

CUSTOMER INTIMACY
- Large Account Management
  - Percent of your target customers you have— and could have.
  - How do your customers behave? Do they buy all lines? Are they exclusive to you? Do they pay full price?
  - How long do customers last?
  - Share information with partner. Repeated for Supplier Rationalization
  - Follow industry standards (increase part or ingredient availability)
  - Common components/elements/subassembly or blends for manufacture/packaging (pool risk for stockouts)
  - Supplier sales force assists with:
    + Stocking
    + Technical training
    + Promotion
    + Limiting unnecessary shipment requests
    + Limiting high volume
    + Stopping abuse of performance-related advertising allowances
    + Avoiding delayed payments; extended dates; back orders; later delivery penalty fees
- Material Requirements Planning (MRP)
- Manufacturing Resource Planning (MRPII)
- Supplier Rationalization to Preferred Providers•• (Same Detail as Large Account Management Above)
- Supplier-Customer Action Teams (SCATs)
- Customer Sales/Service
- Life Cycle Management
- Customer Involvement in Product Development
- Customer/Carrier Optimization
- Customer Evaluation/Alliance: Carriers

PRODUCT DESIGN
- Customization or Design for Manufacturing (Software, Hardware or Both)
- Mass Customization
  - Transparent
  - Collaborative
  - Adaptive
  - Cosmetic
- Standardization (increase part or ingredient availability)
- Design for Localization
- Product Flexibility

CORE OPERATING EFFECTIVENESS
- Work Force Flexibility
- Leadership
- Batch/Continuous
- Product Change Over Time (Frequency often changes per month)
- Date of Last Major Rebuild/Turnaround
- Speed
- Net Output
- Average Crew Services
- Degree of Process Control Integration & CAM
- Breakdown Frequency
- Workforce Knowledge/Skill Base
- Work Flow Effectiveness
- Communication
- Network Management and Harvesting
- Cultural Due Diligence
- Cross Cultural Adaptive Capacity
- Experience Curve
- Right Investments Made to Sustain Operations
- Lower Tolerances
- Set Buffers
- Shorten Cycle Times
- Reduce Stepups

PACKAGING
- Naming
- Advertising & Promotion
- Labeling—Regulatory or Advertising
- Simplification: Reduce Products or Offerings
- Storability
- Serviceability
- Security
- Configurability to Material Handling
- Automated Material Handling (Movement, Inspection, Inventory Control Scans, Security Scans)

MISHAPS
- Defects
- Supply Defects
- Transportation & Storage Defects
- Delays
- Supplier Delays
- Transportation and Storage Delays
- Conflict Resolution and Harmony Restoration
- Dispute Resolution
- Inaccuracies in Sale-Forecasting
- Delays in Resolving Technical Disputes
- Lengthy or Frequent Maintenance
- Cost Estimate Variances (In what direction? At what frequency?)
- Engineering Change Orders
- Production Snags
- Demand Fluctuations
- Stockouts and Stock Not In Location

Figure 1-3. Elements of a value chain.

ISIT
- Architecture
  - Fit with business intent
  - Manageable, cost-effective infrastructure
  - Relational
  - Skill/use support
  - Vendor relations
  - Computer-assisted expert systems
- Security
  - Access
  - Reliability
  - Validity
  - Firewalls
  - Sandboxes
  - Policing
  - Repair/correction
- Intranets
- Web management
- Inventory control and monitoring
- Customer sales database
- Customer database (addressibility and store demographics with SMSA mapping and address books)
- Integrated scheduling systems

MARKETPLACE (PHYSICAL PRODUCT OR SERVICE)/MARKET SPACE (DIGITIZED DATA AND KNOWLEDGE)

OUTSOURCING
- Co-ownership
- Sustaining preeminent capabilities
- Operations only
- Skills and knowledge sharing
- Outplacement of assets or talent
- Risk management: loss of critical skills; develop wrong skills; loss of critical functions/control over suppliers

CHANNEL
- Value-adding services
- Incentives
- Forecasts
- Returns, warranty, and guarantee management
- Quality of service
- Material handling
- Delivery performance (distance to customers = transportation cost + delivery/coordination expense)
- Global positioning delivery support and inventory management
- Storage and responsible care
- Inventory tracking
- Technology development
- Packaging
- Adaptive channels

GROWTH AND OTHER OPPORTUNITY
- Pipeline agreements
- Co-investment
- R&D consortia
- Cultural due diligence for M&A
- Transnational expansion

TERMS AND CONDITIONS FOR LEGAL AGREEMENTS
- Intellectual property
- Joint business planning
- Conflict/dispute resolution
- Exit

- Sponsorship and stewardship

FINANCIAL ENGINEERING
- Credit
- Pricing models (experience curve pricing [supplier costs decrease with product life], price towers)
- Revenue structure (COGS—reserves for damaged/returned goods and discounts or allowances)
- Incentives
- ABC or activities-based costing (value drivers)
- Derivatives
- Collaborative ventures (alliances, JVs, research consortia, other shared ownership, etc.)
- Royalties and commissions
- Capital budget for value-chain improvements (physical site, human resources, technology)
- Business worthiness of potential partners/customers
- Risk management

SOVEREIGNTY LEVERAGE
- Levy
- Regulatory
- Intellectual property
- Trade agreement
- Research
- Dispute resolution

MARKET EVENTS
- International conflict
- Financial market disruption
- International disaster
- Local
- Regional
- Interregional
- Competitor play
- Customer play
- Consumer/user trend
- Your play
- Allied industry substitution play
- Disruptive technology
- Partnering play—inclusion
- Partnering play—exclusion
- Public attention

ASPIRATIONS AND OUTCOMES
- Just in Time (JIT) delivery
- Low inventory
- Zero defects
- Flexible production
- DFM (design for manufacturing . . . transgenics in food)
- Technical cooperation with suppliers
- Total quality
- Optimal exchange for customer—customer pays only for value they use
- Decrease costs
- Increase speed (delivery, time to introduce new products)
- Increase quality
- Increase flexibility

STAKEHOLDER ACCEPTANCE OF CHANGES
- Understanding
- Preferences
- Salience of changes
- Power to act on changes

Figure 1-3. Elements of a value chain (continued).

Once a firm determines a strategic intent in the marketplace, it defines its customers. The focus on customer expectations and feedback drives performance and planning for the future. Collaboration across the firm is aimed at customer satisfaction: leadership, technology, manufacturing/service operations, logistics/channel, marketing/sales, and finance.

Intimacy describes a relationship defined by a thorough understanding of the customer and superior rapport in interpersonal relations with decision makers (as well as those who shape the customer's view of you). Proactive communication and contact further enhance rapport and ensure timely information. This fosters adapting a customer strategy ahead of the market.

Intimacy is built across time in new relationships or by the renewal of a relationship. The latter may be more difficult to achieve if poor performance or indifference to customers is part of the first relationship. For past difficulty to be supplanted with a customer intimacy strategy, you will need to expend more time and resources for success.

The typical progression of events for building customer intimacy are:

- Research and planning
- Relationship building
- Customer intimacy implementation and operations
- Special events for dispute resolution, growth, or exit

Each process for customer intimacy development, implementation, operations, and growth is different. You build the most effective customer intimacy strategies on trust, transparency, and civility at all levels of your customer's organization and your firm.

Even when you initiate new business opportunity, the focus remains on the customer. An array of customers requires greater attention to your business landscape since forces requiring adaptation and emerging opportunities may necessitate choices among customer strategies.

Customer intimacy secures existing business by inviting continuous customer sales services; demonstrating responsiveness to customer feedback; introducing life cycle management commitments; inviting customer input to innovate services and products; and sharing public relations with the community, government, or trade agreement organization. Customer intimacy can improve financial performance by optimizing infrastructure in the value chain, levy, and intellectual property/trade agreement positions in partnerships.

Customer intimacy transforms commodity services and products into specialty revenue generators by bundling new services or products, infusing financial engineering (credit, derivatives, shared equity), obligating customers to technology development or shared channel investments, and pursuing joint ventures in expanding global markets.

The loss of customer focus happens when a product's specialty dilutes to a commodity or when the focus shifts from customer to self or a crisis. None of the aforementioned justifies the loss of customer focus or the diminished potential—if not a real-time decline—in value performance. Customer intimacy is a complex partnering process and is fragile. Continuous attention is necessary to sustain relations and to remain informed about customer views.

Employee Partnerships

Much has been said and written about employee partnering over the last 30 years. Various labels reflect a particular experience or differentiate among consulting products. In the early days, the term of favor was "organization development." Later that would be abandoned due to overuse and because it harkened back to too many efforts failing to produce results. With claims the entire organization would change and create a new order of business, early efforts met more often with failure than success. In addition, organization development was linked to group dynamics and interpersonal learnings many mainstream businesspeople perceived as outlandish. The term of favor became "quality of work" or "quality of work life." Companies aimed projects at improving productivity and life at work. Popular among union-management cooperative endeavors, few efforts produced financial results.

Disputes over the color of trash cans and other great dilemmas of the workplace diverted attention from real issues. W. Edwards Deming and Joseph M. Juran, interestingly, introduced a similar label yet a different agenda. "Quality circles" and the "total quality" movement were more successful at reaching a work team's efforts to plan and measure contribution. Deming brought back from Japan his quality concepts based on operations research optimization and old–fashioned teamwork. Since it was very successful in application to a hierarchical culture and the clean slate that World War II devastation made of Japanese business, executives heralded the quality movement as the answer.

Organization design reinforced or supplanted these efforts by taking a more holistic approach, reminiscent of the early paradigm of organization development. Companies changed the context in which quality teams functioned, thereby giving teams more freedom and rewards for accomplishments. Technology improvement, commercial pursuits, and organizational change co-evolved more frequently.

In an attempt to bring a stronger statement of change, organization design was relabeled as "transformation" or "revitalization" efforts. Indicating longer-term initiatives, the objective is the creation of a new work culture attuned to "incorporating employees fully into the process of dealing with business challenges," "leading from a different place," and "instilling mental disciplines."[2]

In their article "Changing the Way We Change," Richard Pascale, Mark Millemann, and Linda Gioja explain, "Done properly, these three interventions will create a landmark shift in an organization's operating state or culture by significantly altering the way people experience their own *power* and *identity* and the way they deal with *conflict* and *learning*."[3]

They observe further, "The problem is that the whole burden of change typically rests on so few people. In other words, the number of people at every level who make committed, imaginative contributions to organizational success is simply too small. More employees need to take a greater interest and a more active role in the business. More of them need to care deeply about success."[4]

In 20 years, we have seen both the partial attempts at change and the roaring successes. The difference is startling in business performance and the life worth living at work. Nonetheless, the history of linear, bureaucratic, and control-based models in business is much longer and supported by powerful devotees.

There are two interesting phenomena about employee partnering in an environment generally supportive of SBRs. One is akin to when parents treat their children better in public than in private. There is a concern for the perceptions of others. The second aspect of employee partnering is genuine behavior and more important to value. This is the recognition that those closest to the work influence partnering results. If employees are not aligned to partnering efforts, a company will suffer serious errors.

War Story

Don't Read My Lips Today

In a natural resources company, senior management and the marketing organization followed the lead of a marketing advisor. They created a life cycle management program to bundle services, secure share and premium price, and differentiate their commodity product. Of course, the cornerstone was environmental responsibility.

The CEO conveyed a mixed message to the organization. This new life cycle management—which he had not explained well enough to his direct reports—was not deemed as important as cutting costs. This led to one of his profit centers cutting costs so severely that numerous environmental violations were noted in a regulatory inspection.

To compound the problem, a program involving employees in the business turned down the employee middle management task force recommendation to fix the problem. The violations were repaired, but no one believed environmental responsibility was important to the business unless something was discovered by a regulator. A customer visit to prove that the regulator's concerns had been addressed met with disaster. One of the violations was repeated. This endangered the entire life cycle management program—with this customer and others. Competitors and the customer made the snafu known in the marketplace.

Later, management took the employee involvement process more seriously. The effort had to dig itself out of a hole in terms of credibility in the eyes of employees. As expected, the early interference slowed progress and diluted results. On the specific issue of the incidents, some upper managers denied the employee involvement effort helped in the cleanup. The subject became one that both sides agreed to disagree upon. How much further the effort might have gone with a more honest approach about the controversy!

On the other hand, employee partnering offers significant results:

War Story

A Plant Too Tough to Die

In what we later called the "Fayetteville" model, a plant by this name thwarted closure by achieving extraordinary results in quality, throughput, safety, and cost containment. They also pursued outsourcing, established partnering relations with utility suppliers to reduce the cost of inputs, plus partnered elsewhere within their own firm and with other firms to leverage excess storage space as a multipurpose distribution system—creating additional revenue streams. That was several years ago, and the plant is still in operation. From engineering to operations to maintenance to human resources to lab services and upper management, the commitment was to success.

The model was replicated in a union situation overseas in the Pacific Rim involving a sister unit. It succeeded in a like manner, taking a record three days to reach the appropriate labor accord, in contrast to the normal six or more months.

Passive Investor Relations

Some argue that there is no partnership between shareowners and the enterprise in which they possess stock. So passive is the ownership that boards and senior managers set the course with little regard for shareholders. Shareholder activism over the last decade and a half has helped to curb this, although the interaction has been more turbulent than productive.

This has begun to change greatly with the successes of firms like Batchelder and Partners of La Jolla, California. They secure a less-than-majority ownership and pursue relational investment. By relational investment, they mean securing a few board seats. They then establish rapport with other board members and management sufficient to set a more prosperous direction. They do not emphasize control or related turf disputes, but rather what needs to be done for enhancing shareholder value. They exercise the owner perogative typical to entrepreneurs; that is, they proactively offer their outsider's view as counsel to management and expect to be taken seriously because it is their and their investors' money at stake.

Selected by the powerful California Public Employees Retirement System (CalPERS), representing $127 billion in retirement monies of California state personnel, Batchelder and Partners manages a $700-million fund for underperforming companies. In a sharp departure from Dave Batchelder's earlier career days as corporate raider T. Boone Pickens' COO, Batchelder—along with his colleagues Joel Reed, Kathy Scott, and James Zehentbauer—now does not seek a takeover. They simply obtain a few board positions. In Batchelder and Partners' view, working with management by challenging them to value-add produces superior results with less hassle. They point to the quadrupling of stock value for their intervention at MacFrugal's Bargains-Close-Outs Inc. as proof. There, a collaboration with management among significant shareholders effected a turnaround. It is important to note that 1993 changes in SEC rules regarding collaboration by phone or mail among stock owners makes the passive influence process easier.[5]

CalPERS, long an activist fund, has succeeded on a grander scale. They "pushed directors to replace the underperforming leaders of General Motors Corp., Eastman Kodak Co., and International Business Machines Corp."[6] The direct use of board directors is something they do through funds in which they invest.

Do not expect there to be an overabundant application of passive board influence. Despite the success of Batchelder and Partners, fund managers are concerned about risks which may be inherent for activist roles in an investment. These include, according to Doug Willis of the Associated Press, "increased liability exposure, potential conflicts of interest and insider status—which could restrict . . . freedom to trade."[6] It seems that traditional operations managers are not the only ones who are risk-aversive.

Lost in the millions of shareholders, we have little impact by ourselves. Melding our resources with others in pension funds or mutual funds, we rely on professional money managers to pick board members and assert on our behalf. Passive ownership sheds us of entrepreneurial responsibility. When this happens, we steward our money's use less and react to abuse with an opportunistic sell—when the first opportunity presents itself.

Choosing responsible fund managers creates differentiation among them. Instead of entrusting your money to the guy who went to the right schools but did not learn, or was the son of someone but did not get the genes which count for finance, or entered the brokerage business because of the 1980s movies about big-time deal makers, pick passive representatives who ensure that management's choices serve shareholder value-add. This is the bond that counts to make the passive investor come alive in today's superstructures.

Before we will see a partnership between boards and management which truly challenges for shareholder value-add, there must be more worthy partners in the shareholder-to-fund manager-to-board bonds. We, the fund owners, own this selection problem. We, the shareowners, share in this.

IN THE END

Orchestration is complex. There are numerous settings in which partnering takes place. Each has its own agenda for implementation and successful operation. Orchestration is vital to extracting value from a deal for the owner. At the end of the day, owners are responsible for what happens to value along with the people they employ. The partnership between owners and their employees, managers, supervisors, or contributors is the cornerstone to all success. Even a partnership among firms rests on the abilities of the individual firms to fulfill commitments and encourage performance. There is no rocket science here, just fair play in hard work against a business intent.

REFERENCES

1. Tufano, Peter, "How Financial Information Can Advance Corporate Strategy," *Harvard Business Review,* January-February, 1996, pp. 138–139.
2. Pascale, Richard, Mark Millemann, Linda Gioja, "Changing the Way We Change," *Harvard Business Review,* November-December, 1997, pp. 127–139.
3. Pascale, R., et al., p. 128.
4. Pascale, R., et al., pp. 127–128.
5. Lubove, Seth, "The King Is Dead, Long Live the King," *Forbes,* July 15, 1996, p. 64.
6. Willis, Doug, "Major Pension Fund Downplays Policy on Board Representation," Associated Press, *Houston Chronicle,* Section C, December 27, 1997, p. 2.

CHAPTER 2

Preparation

Front-End Loading for Success

There is a film of a symphony orchestra preparing to perform *Bolero*. The filmmaker toured the concert hall during trials and practices. Players of common instruments gathered and played together. Alone, their performances sounded awkward and hollow. There was tension within various groups and, at times, among them. Based on what was seen, there was little hope of a decent performance. The final moments of the film is a lovely and near perfect recital. All the different instruments together created a music without comparison. The conductor simply opened doors for professionals flooding the room with their best performance. The orchestration was done.

The first step in managing complexity is valuing time to think about what is happening in the nature around you—whether it is a walk in the woods, a musical performance, or work in a commercial enterprise. The next step is advancing your perception of what is, with more thinking about what could be. Finally, a plan is conceived to get you from where you are now across the gap to where you need to be. The plan is simulated and practiced. Then it is put into action. Success does not just happen; it is made to happen.

We encounter most organizations at times when they are urgently in need of help in forming a partnership, or are in the panic of despair over a failing relationship. In either case, we begin by asking for the business plan.

A competent business plan is rare. We judge a business plan to be competent if it could be used successfully by an entrepreneur with no money to attract sophisticated investors for equity support or win a debt from a major bank without hesitation or serious reservation. The following components satisfy William Sahlman's criteria for a great business plan:[1]

- THE PEOPLE
  A profile of the men and women starting and running the venture, as well as the outside parties providing key services or important resources for it, such as its lawyers, accountants, and suppliers.
- THE OPPORTUNITY
  A profile of the business itself—what it will sell and to whom, whether the business can grow and how fast, what its economics are, as well as who and what stand in the way of success.
- THE CONTEXT
  A description of the big picture—the regulatory environment, interest rates, demographic trends, inflation, and the like—basically, factors that inevitably change but cannot be controlled by the entrepreneur.
- RISK AND REWARD
  An assessment of everything that can go wrong and right, and a discussion of how the entrepreneurial team can respond.

When we review business plans, we usually find one of four possibilities:

1. A competent plan—a rare occurrence.
2. The "business plan" doesn't really exist.
3. The business plan does not address important interdependencies—the landscape is not defined, and adaptive or emergent forces are not appreciated.
4. The business plan is not grounded in reality.

We read any business plan given to us so that we might learn where the client is, and how best to begin from his or her point of view. This is what we coach. Start the planning one step back with self-reflection. Implement an intensive review of your own business. Template 2-1 contains a list of questions to guide a thorough self-reflection called an intensive business review (IBR). Tier 1 inquiries provide information gathering. Tier 2 questions help discern patterns. Tier 1 and 2 questions are asked for each subject area in a business landscape: adaptive forces, investor relations, value chain management, financial engineering, direction and growth, learning and orchestration, partnering, and technology.

(text continued on page 26)

TEMPLATE 2-1: INTENSIVE BUSINESS REVIEW

ADAPTIVE FORCES: TIER 1: INFORMATION GATHERING

CUSTOMER
1. WHAT ARE YOUR CUSTOMER'S NEEDS AND DEMANDS?
   A. EXPRESSED REQUIREMENTS
   B. ASPIRATIONS FOR FUTURE
   C. NEEDS/OPPORTUNITIES YOU PERCEIVE (BUT CUSTOMER DOES NOT OR IS NOT ACTING UPON). LIST OPPORTUNITIES TO LEAD CUSTOMER TO NEW PRODUCTS/SERVICES
   D. BUSINESS VIABILITY OF CUSTOMER/CUSTOMER-OWNER
   E. WHO COULD BE A CUSTOMER AND WHY? REVIEW A–D ABOVE FOR REALISTIC PROSPECTS.
   F. IDENTIFY CUSTOMER TRENDS THAT ARE LIKELY TO INCREASE OR DECREASE USE OF YOUR SERVICES OR PRODUCTS.

REGULATOR & COMMUNITY
1. IDENTIFY ALL REGULATOR CONFORMANCE DEMANDS.
   A. INCLUDE ALL RELEVANT GLOBAL REQUIREMENTS.
   B. DESCRIBE RELATIONSHIPS WITH KEY REGULATORS AND OPPORTUNITY TO BUILD PARTNERING ALLIANCE.
2. IDENTIFY INDUSTRY ISSUES, LITIGATION AND PERFORMANCE TRENDS.
3. DESCRIBE COMMUNITY AMBITIONS AND POTENTIAL DISTRACTIONS.

COMPETITOR ANALYSIS
1. LIST KEY COMPETITORS AND RANK BY MATERIALITY FACTORS (MARKET SHARE AND NET INCOME).
2. DESCRIBE THEIR MARKETING/SALES METHODS AND CURRENT SALES PERFORMANCE.
3. DESCRIBE THEIR OPERATING METHODS, TECHNOLOGY, TECHNOLOGY DEVELOPMENT, R&D POTENTIAL AND COMPLIANCE WITH REGULATORS.
4. LIST THEIR APPARENT VULNERABILITIES.
5. IDENTIFY THEIR RECENT ACQUISITIONS AND ACQUISITION TARGETS.
6. DESCRIBE THEIR FINANCIAL ENGINEERING WITH AN ASSESSMENT OF WEAKNESS AND LEVERAGE OPPORTUNITY TO SUPPORT BUSINESS GROWTH.
7. EXAMINE THEIR IN-PROCESS OR POTENTIAL LEADER/OWNER TRANSITIONS.
8. OUTLINE THEIR ALLIANCES, JOINT VENTURES, PARTNERSHIPS, RETAINER POSITIONS.
9. MAP THEIR GEOGRAPHICAL PRESENCE ACROSS THE GLOBE.
10. DO THEY HAVE A "LIFE CYCLE" APPROACH?

ADAPTIVE FORCES: TIER II: PATTERN ANALYSIS

CUSTOMER
1. WHAT IS THE CATALYST FOR YOUR CUSTOMER'S CONSUMPTION OF YOUR SERVICES OR PRODUCTS?
2. IS THERE A CYCLE OR PATTERN TO CONSUMPTION?
3. DOES CONSUMPTION OCCUR IN INTERACTION WITH OTHER MARKET ELEMENTS?
4. LIST FORCES WITHIN YOUR CUSTOMER REQUIRING YOUR ADAPTATION.
5. LIST FORCES EMERGING FROM YOUR CUSTOMER FROM WHICH YOU CAN EXTRACT VALUE.
6. WITH WHAT STRATEGIES CAN YOU EMERGE TO LEAD YOUR CUSTOMER TO NEW VALUE?

REGULATOR & COMMUNITY
1. WHAT PATTERNS ARE EMERGING WHICH WILL AFFECT YOUR VALUE?
2. ARE THERE NEW PRODUCTS OR SERVICES YOU CAN OFFER TO TAKE ADVANTAGE OF THE ABOVE PATTERNS?

COMPETITOR ANALYSIS
1. WHAT ARE YOUR COMPETITORS LIKELY TO DO WHICH WOULD DISRUPT THE MARKET AND/OR IMPACT YOUR BUSINESS?
2. IDENTIFY SUBSTITUTION THREATS OR TRENDS WHICH WOULD REDUCE YOUR CUSTOMER'S USE OF YOUR SERVICES OR PRODUCTS.

(continued)

TEMPLATE 2-1: INTENSIVE BUSINESS REVIEW *(continued)*

3. ASSESS YOUR VULNERABILITIES AND DETERMINE LEVERAGE POINTS TO COUNTER YOUR VULNERABILITIES.
4. DEFINE ACTIONS YOU COULD TAKE IN THE MARKETPLACE TO PUT COMPETITORS AT A DISADVANTAGE.

INVESTOR RELATIONS: TIER I: INFORMATION GATHERING
1. IDENTIFY ALL MAJOR CONTRIBUTORS TO CAPITAL—DEBT HOLDERS AND INVESTORS.
    A. WHAT MEANS OF COMMUNICATIONS ARE USED TO INFORM, EDUCATE, AND SUBMIT FEEDBACK AND APPROVAL? WHO ARE THE KEY CONTACTS ON BOTH SIDES?
    B. WHICH PARTIES RESIST CHANGE?
    C. WHICH PARTIES ADVOCATE CHANGE?
    D. WHICH PARTIES HAVE THE CAPACITY TO FUND FUTURE PROJECTS?
    E. WHICH PARTIES ARE EXPERIENCING TURBULENCE AND MIGHT WITHDRAW SUPPORT?
    F. WHICH PARTIES ARE EXPERIENCING TURBULENCE AND WILL NOT BE VIABLE TO SUPPORT GROWTH?
    G. WHAT FREEDOM DO YOU HAVE TO PURSUE ALTERNATIVE FINANCING?
    H. FOR ALL SOURCES OF CAPITAL, CURRENT AND PROPOSED, WHAT IS THE ACTUAL COST OF CAPITAL—RATES AND TERMS?
    I. WHAT STEWARDSHIP IS CURRENTLY MADE BY INVESTORS AND DEBT HOLDERS OF YOUR FIRM? SCHEDULE? LEVEL OF DETAIL? AMOUNT OF TIME ON-SITE? DESCRIBE INFORMATION TECHNOLOGY LINK, IF ANY.
    J. IDENTIFY INDUSTRY ANALYSTS MAINTAINING DIRECT CONTACT WITH YOUR FIRM. DESCRIBE THE CURRENT RELATIONSHIP: WHAT DO YOU DO? WHAT DO THEY DO? WHAT IS MISSING FROM YOUR VANTAGE POINT?
    K. IDENTIFY AND DESCRIBE DOCUMENTS AND ELECTRONIC MEDIA USED IN INVESTOR RELATIONS.

INVESTOR RELATIONS: TIER II: PATTERN ANALYSIS
1. HOW DOES THE CURRENT PATTERN OF RELATIONSHIP WITH CAPITAL PROVIDERS AFFECT YOUR CURRENT OPERATIONS AND GROWTH POTENTIAL?
2. WHAT CAN BE DONE TO ESTABLISH A BETTER PATTERN OF SUPPORT AMONG BACKERS FOR CURRENT OPERATIONS AND GROWTH?
3. IS THERE A PATTERN EMERGING IN THE INVESTMENT COMMUNITY WHICH WOULD BETTER SUPPORT YOUR AMBITIONS? IF SO, HOW DO YOU CAPTURE THIS OPPORTUNITY?
4. WITH WHAT FINANCIAL ENGINEERING ALTERNATIVES CAN YOU EMERGE TO CREATE BETTER SUPPORT FOR YOUR AMBITIONS AMONG THE INVESTMENT COMMUNITY?

VALUE CHAIN MANAGEMENT: TIER I: INFORMATION GATHERING
1. EXAMINE CURRENT CUSTOMER RESPONSIVENESS.
    A. PRICE
    B. QUALITY: COMPLETENESS / RELIABILITY / DURABILITY / DELIVERY
    C. INNOVATION—"LEAD CUSTOMER TO WHAT IS NEXT"
    D. SUSTAIN INHERITANCE
    E. TIMELINESS
2. DESCRIBE CURRENT VALUE PERFORMANCE.
    A. FINANCIAL (CURRENT & FUTURE)
    B. SUPPLY CHAIN
    C. DEMAND CHAIN
    D. EMPLOYEE CAPABILITIES AND SUPPORT FOR MISSION
    E. R&D
3. ASSESS MARKET OPPORTUNITIES.
    A. NICHE DEMANDS
    B. CONSUMPTION TRENDS
    C. PROFIT POTENTIAL
    D. MARKETING/SALES METHODS
4. EXAMINE ORDER MANAGEMENT PROCESS FOR OPTIMUM FLOW AND DATABASING OF CUSTOMER EXPERIENCES FOR MARKETING/SALES.

TEMPLATE 2-1: INTENSIVE BUSINESS REVIEW *(continued)*

5. REVIEW LIFE CYCLE MANAGEMENT SOPHISTICATION.
6. EXAMINE WORK FLOWS FOR POTENTIAL IMPROVEMENTS.
   A. ASSESS VALUE-ADDED CONTRIBUTION FOR KEY ACTIVITIES TO DETERMINE CONTINUATION.
   B. EXAMINE TECHNOLOGY OPPORTUNITY SUCH AS AUTOMATION OR REENGINEERING OF WORK FLOW FOR COST EFFECTIVENESS, VALUE-ADDED CUSTOMER RESPONSIVENESS OR MARKET POSITIONING.
   C. IDENTIFY BARRIERS TO WORK PROGRESS.
   D. MONITOR WORK SCHEDULE FOR CYCLES.
   E. RANK-ORDER OPTIMIZATION PROJECTS BY SVA AND INITIAL CAPITAL REQUIREMENTS.
   F. INVESTIGATE OUTSOURCING RISKS AND BENEFITS.
   G. DETERMINE OPPORTUNITY FOR CONCURRENT EFFORT.

VALUE CHAIN MANAGEMENT: TIER II: PATTERN ANALYSIS

1. LIST THE OPTIMIZATION OPPORTUNITIES FOR OFFSETTING DIMINISHING RETURNS IN THE PHYSICAL WORK FLOW: SUPPLY CHAIN THROUGH TO DEMAND CHAIN.
2. LIST THE OPTIMIZATION OPPORTUNITIES FOR PAPER FLOW AND INFORMATION TECHNOLOGY IN THE ADMINISTRATION OF THE ENTIRE VALUE CHAIN.
3. DISCERN OVERLAP AND INTERACTION AMONG THE PREVIOUS TWO LISTS. THEN DEVELOP NO MORE THAN FIVE IMPROVEMENT AND INNOVATION PROJECTS, RANK-ORDER BY SVA AND TIME TO COMPLETE. AFTER COMPLETION, COMPLETE ANOTHER RANK-ORDER AND PURSUE THE NEXT FIVE CONTINUOUS IMPROVEMENT AND INNOVATION PROJECTS.
4. IDENTIFY MARKET FORCES OR PATTERNS YOU CAN CREATE FOR INCREASING RETURNS TO ACHIEVE DOMINANCE. EXAMINE INTERACTIONS AMONG VALUE CHAIN FACTORS.

FINANCIAL ENGINEERING: TIER I: INFORMATION GATHERING

1. ASSESS FINANCIAL ENGINEERING WEAKNESS AND LEVERAGE OPPORTUNITY TO SUPPORT BUSINESS GROWTH.
   A. NON-INDUSTRY GROWTH (CURRENCY, CREDIT, INTRAPRENEURING)
   B. CASH FLOW MANAGEMENT AND SVA* FORECAST
   C. PROPERTY MANAGEMENT AND LEASEBACK
   D. RISK ASSUMPTIONS/PRACTICES
   E. INSTRUMENTS/DERIVATIVES
   F. TAX POSITIONS
   G. CAPITAL EXPENDITURES AND MANAGEMENT
   H. ALLIANCES AND PARTNERSHIPS
   I. ACCOUNTING PRACTICES AND USE OF INNOVATIONS SUCH AS ACTIVITIES-BASED COSTING
   J. PROJECT AND MATERIAL PAYMENTS
   K. CONTRACTOR/VENDOR PAYMENTS
   L. ORDER MANAGEMENT—CUSTOMER RELATIONS TRACKING
   M. INVESTOR RELATIONS (INCLUDE SIGNIFICANT DEBT HOLDERS)
   N. COST IMPROVEMENT RETURNS
   O. OTHER INVESTMENTS AND TRADING

 * *Shareholder Value-Add*

FINANCIAL ENGINEERING: TIER II: PATTERN ANALYSIS

1. LIST FINANCIAL ENGINEERING SOLUTIONS WHICH OPTIMIZE THE USE OF MONEY.
2. EXAMINE FINANCIAL ENGINEERING ALTERNATIVES FOR INTERRELATIONSHIPS WHICH FORM PATTERNS FOR INCREASING RETURNS. FOR EXAMPLE, ARE THERE DERIVATIVES FOR SUPPLIERS IN YOUR VALUE CHAIN WHICH WOULD FUND ENTRY INTO ALTERNATIVE DISTRIBUTION PRACTICES, OR DOES IT MAKE SENSE TO FINANCE NON-INDUSTRY BUSINESSES TO FULLY UTILIZE EXISTING ASSETS SUCH AS FARMING AND RANCHING ON THE SURFACE LANDS OF UNDERGROUND MINES.

DIRECTION & GROWTH: TIER I: INFORMATION GATHERING

1.* WHAT ARE THE COMPETENCIES OF THE FIRM—THINGS YOU ARE REALLY GOOD AT DOING (OR COULD BE) WHICH WOULD: POSITIVELY IMPACT YOUR CUSTOMER, GIVE YOU ACCESS TO BUSINESS YOU DO NOT HAVE OR HAVE NOT FULLY LEVERAGED, AND BE HARD FOR OTHERS TO COPY?

(continued)

TEMPLATE 2-1: INTENSIVE BUSINESS REVIEW *(continued)*

2.* WHAT COULD YOU DO WHICH WOULD CHANGE THE WHOLE WAY IN WHICH BUSINESS IN YOUR INDUSTRY IS DONE (E.G., VOICE INPUT REPLACING KEY BOARDS FOR PCS)?

3.* WHAT COULD YOU DO TO OBTAIN PREFERENTIAL ACCESS TO A BROAD RANGE OF NEW OPPORTUNITY (E.G., ELECTRONICS WHICH FORM THE FOUNDATION TO A PLATFORM OF SEVERAL ELECTRONIC APPLICATIONS)?

4.* WHAT CRITICAL SKILLS DO YOU HAVE THAT PUT YOU IN A POSITION OF INFLUENCING YOUR COMPETITORS (E.G., AND AIRLINE OWNING RESERVATION SYSTEMS SERVICING OTHER CARRIERS)?

5.* WHAT KNOWLEDGE DO YOU USE TO OPERATE THAT COULD BE SOLD TO OTHERS, IN PARTICULAR TO THOSE COUNTRIES REPLICATING YOUR TECHNOLOGY (E.G., INTERACTIVE MULTIMEDIA LEARNING IN SAFETY TRAINING)?

* Questions 1–5 are derived from Lecture Notes of Gary Hamel, London Business School, Senior Executive Program, Society of International Business Fellows, 1991.

DIRECTION & GROWTH: TIER II: PATTERN ANALYSIS

1. ASSESS CURRENT AND DEVELOPABLE COMPETENCIES AND CONTRAST WITH MARKET DEMAND. RANK-ORDER BUSINESS STRATEGIES (SECURE BUSINESS, EXPANDING BUSINESS, NEW BUSINESS) BY CAPITAL REQUIREMENTS, CASH FORECAST, PAYBACK, RATE OF RETURN OR OTHER BENEFIT.

2. IDENTIFY ENTRY ALTERNATIVES FOR PROBABLE SECURE AND GROW STRATEGIES: GROWTH OF EXISTING BUSINESS, ALLIANCES/JOINT VENTURES/PARTNERSHIPS, ACQUISITIONS.

3. WHAT STRATEGIES WILL EFFECT A PATTERN OF INCREASING RETURNS FOR YOUR DOMINANCE IN THE MARKETPLACE? FOR EXAMPLE, ARE YOU ABLE TO:

   A. ESTABLISH STRATEGIC BUSINESS RELATIONS WHICH CREATE A PIPELINE THROUGH WHICH OTHER DEALS MAY BE DONE?

   B. CO-BRAND WITHIN A FACILITY OR LOCATION?

   C. DEVELOP A NEW TECHNOLOGY BY PLACING OLD AND NEW TECHNOLOGIES TOGETHER ON A PLATFORM?

   D. BUNDLE A NEW TECHNOLOGY WITH AN OLD TECHNOLOGY AS AN EXTENSION TO AN OLD TECHNOLOGY BY OFFERING IMPROVED PERFORMANCE OR ADDITIONAL FEATURES?

   E. ESTABLISH A GATEWAY TECHNOLOGY THROUGH WHICH OTHER TECHNOLOGIES MUST PASS TO BE UTILIZED?

LEARNING & ORCHESTRATION: TIER I: INFORMATION GATHERING

1. ASSESS CURRENT WORK CULTURE FOR MISSION ORIENTATION AND LIFE WORTH LIVING AT WORK.

2. ASSESS OPPORTUNITY FOR SHARED DUTIES AND BACK-UP TO OTHER ROLES.

3. ASSESS THE CAPABILITY OF THE PLANNING AND MONITORING SYSTEM.

   A. DOES THE PLANNING AND MONITORING SYSTEM PROVIDE REAL-TIME OR NEAR REAL-TIME FEEDBACK TO ALL LEVELS?

   B. DOES IT PROMOTE AN OUTWARD FOCUS ON CUSTOMERS, COMPETITORS, COMMUNITY, CONTRACTORS, SUPPLIERS AND REGULATORS? IS CONTRIBUTION BENCHMARKED?

   C. DOES THE PLANNING SYSTEM EXPLAIN AND EDUCATE, FACILITATE FOCUS THROUGH COMMUNICATION OF PLANS AND PRIORITIES, INVITE INPUTS OR PROVIDE MEANINGFUL INVOLVEMENT ABOUT HOW WORK GETS DONE BY THOSE CLOSEST TO IT?

   D. HOW CAN THE PLANNING AND MONITORING SYSTEM CAN BE ENHANCED TO ADDRESS THE ABOVE?

4. ASSESS THE CAPABILITY OF THE PERFORMANCE MANAGEMENT SYSTEM.

   A. ARE EXPECTATIONS FOR PERFORMANCE CLEAR AND UNDERSTOOD? DO PEOPLE KNOW HOW TO LEVERAGE THEIR CONTRIBUTIONS TO SUPPORT THE MISSION AND APPRECIATE WHAT IS A PRIORITY?

   B. ARE REWARDS AND RECOGNITION ALIGNED TO SUPPORT FULFILLING EXPECTATIONS AND PURSUING THE MISSION? DO ALTERNATE REWARDS EXIST AT ALL LEVELS TO INVITE OWNERSHIP, MOTIVATE CONTRIBUTION AND MOVE COMPENSATION FROM ENTITLEMENT TO A MARKET-BASED MECHANISM WHERE REWARDS ARE BASED ON SVA PERFORMANCE?

   C. IS THERE A MEANS FOR MANAGING PERFORMANCE THAT INCLUDES CONTINUOUS EDUCATION, TRAINING AND COACHING BUT ULTIMATELY ADDRESSES TERMINATION FOR THOSE WHO DO NOT PERFORM, LEARN, OR ADAPT?

   D. ARE THE METRICS REPRESENTATIVE OF EFFORT AND ALIGNED TO BOTTOM-LINE RESULTS VERSUS ACTIVITIES WHICH MAKE PEOPLE LOOK GOOD? ARE THE METRICS UNDERSTOOD BY ALL AND LEVERAGE POINTS CLEAR? ARE THE METRICS EXAMINED TO DETERMINE CONTINUOUS IMPROVEMENTS AND INNOVATIONS?

TEMPLATE 2-1: INTENSIVE BUSINESS REVIEW *(continued)*

5. IS HIERARCHY VALUE-ADDING BY INTEGRATING BUSINESS ANALYSIS, INTERACTING IN THE BUSINESS ENVIRONMENT, DETERMINING DIRECTION, COACHING, AND CHALLENGING THE ORGANIZATION TO STRETCH?
6. BASED ON A REVIEW OF THE INFRASTRUCTURE REQUIREMENTS AND CURRENT CAPABILITIES, HOW SHOULD THE INFRASTRUCTURE BE CONFIGURED?
   A. HIERARCHY: STRUCTURE, DUTIES, AUTHORITIES
   B. WORK UNITS/TEAMS CONFIGURATION
   C. INDIVIDUAL RESPONSIBILITIES
7. WHICH STAKEHOLDERS NEED TO BE INFORMED ABOUT CHANGES?
   A. INVESTORS
   B. DEBT HOLDERS
   C. EMPLOYEES
   D. PARTNERS
   E. CUSTOMERS
   F. COMMUNITY
   G. SUPPLIER
   H. REGULAR
   I. OTHER (IDENTIFY)

LEARNING & ORCHESTRATION: TIER II: PATTERN ANALYSIS
1. WHAT ARE THE OPTIMAL MEANS FOR COMMUNICATING, EDUCATING AND SOLICITING FEEDBACK ABOUT CHANGE WITH STAKEHOLDERS?
2. WHAT STRUCTURES, POLICY OF GOVERNANCE AND RELATIONSHIP BUILDING ARE SUPPORTIVE OF A FLEXIBLE AND RESPONSIVE ORGANIZATION?
3. WHAT CAN BE DONE TO IMPROVE ADAPTATION AND STRENGTHEN CAPABILITIES FOR EMERGING WITH NEW PATTERNS?

PARTNERING: TIER I: INFORMATION GATHERING
1. REPORT ALL EXISTING PARTNERING RELATIONSHIPS: R&D CONSORTIA, JVS, ALLIANCES, LLCS/LLPS MERGERS AND ACQUISITIONS.
2. DESCRIBE YOUR PARTNERING EXPERIENCES.
3. RANK-ORDER CURRENT RELATIONSHIPS BY:
   A. POTENTIAL TO CONTINUE RELATIONSHIP
   B. POTENTIAL TO SUPPORT GROWTH
   C. CULTURAL COMPATIBILITY
4. LIST ALL PARTNERING NEEDS AND IDENTIFY PROSPECTIVE PARTNERS.
5. ASSESS THIRD PARTY RELATIONSHIPS AND DETERMINE PARTNERING POTENTIAL.
   A. VENDORS/SUPPLIERS
   B. CONTRACTORS
   C. REGULATORS
   D. DISTRIBUTORS
   E. PARTNERSHIPS/ALLIANCES
6. LIST KEY ATTRIBUTES FOR EACH PARTNER AND PROSPECTIVE PARTNER.

PARTNERING: TIER II: PATTERN ANALYSIS
1. IS THERE A PATTERN TO YOUR PARTNERING? PLEASE EXPLAIN THE CURRENT CIRCUMSTANCE AND ITS ADVANTAGES/DISADVANTAGES.
2. WHAT SHOULD BE YOUR PHILOSOPHY AND NORMS FOR PARTNERING?
3. HOW CAN YOUR CURRENT PRACTICES OF PARTNERING BE OPTIMIZED?
4. HOW CAN YOUR CURRENT PRACTICES OF PARTNERING BE LEVERAGED FOR FUTURE PARTNERSHIPS?
5. LIST CONTINUING PARTNERS AND THEIR KEY ATTRIBUTES.
6. LIST PROSPECTIVE PARTNERS WITH WHOM YOU CAN BETTER ESTABLISH PATTERNS OF INCREASING RETURNS FOR DOMINANCE IN THE MARKETPLACE.

TECHNOLOGY: TIER I: INFORMATION GATHERING
1. FORECAST INDUSTRY TECHNOLOGY IMPROVEMENTS AND INNOVATIONS.
2. EXAMINE CURRENT USE OF INFORMATION TECHNOLOGY (IT).

(continued)

TEMPLATE 2-1: INTENSIVE BUSINESS REVIEW *(continued)*

    A. PC/NETWORKS: CAPABILITY OF PERSONNEL TO USE CURRENT TECHNOLOGY
    B. ELECTRONIC COMMUNICATION: E-MAIL, ELECTRONIC BULLETIN BOARDS TO SUPPORT STATUS
       REPORTS ON MULTIPLE INITIATIVES/PROJECTS, ETC.
    C. EXPERT SYSTEMS TO GUIDE WORK
    D. ORDER MANAGEMENT PROCESSING
    E. OPERATIONAL STEWARDSHIP
    F. INTEGRATED FINANCIAL SYSTEMS
    G. LOGISTICAL CONTROL/TRACKING
    H. SALES DATABASES TO SUPPORT PITCHES
    I. RESEARCH AND TECHNOLOGY DATABASES
    J. THIRD-PARTY PARTNERING DATABASES FOR STEWARDSHIP, DESIGN, AND INVENTORY CONTROL
    K. CUSTOMER INTERFACING AND DATA BASING FOR CANDIDATE PROFILE AND HR DEVELOPMENT PLANS
    L. REGULATOR INTERFACES TO MINIMIZE DISRUPTION
    M. INTERACTIVE LEARNING TO REDUCE EXPENSE OF EDUCATION AND DEVELOPMENT
    N. TELE- AND VIDEO CONFERENCING
    O. DATABASE MANAGEMENT TOOLS
  3. REVIEW IT TRENDS IMPACTING BUSINESS.
  4. PLOT ALTERNATIVES AND IDENTIFY EDUCATION REQUIREMENTS/COST/SCHEDULE/MILESTONES.

TECHNOLOGY: TIER II: PATTERN ANALYSIS
  1. WHAT TECHNOLOGIES ARE EMERGING FROM YOUR INDUSTRY OR OTHER INDUSTRIES WHICH COULD
    DISRUPT THE FLOW OF GOODS OR ITS ADMINISTRATION?
  2. WHAT CAN YOU DO TO CAPTURE THE OPPORTUNITY IN THE DISRUPTION AT LEAST AS WELL AS
    OTHERS WILL DO, IF NOT BETTER?
  3. WHAT TECHNOLOGIES CAN YOU ENVISION AS EXPLOITABLE IN SETTING PATTERNS FOR DOMINANCE?
  4. ARE THERE ANY TECHNOLOGIES WHICH WILL BE PARTICULARLY INVITING TO THE INVESTMENT
    COMMUNITY?
  5. CAN YOU ENVISION FINANCIAL ENGINEERING WHICH WILL ACCELERATE CAPITAL DEPLOYMENT FOR
    TECHNOLOGIES WITH THE POTENTIAL TO SET PATTERNS FOR DOMINANCE?
  6. CAN YOU ORCHESTRATE THE APPLICATION OF TECHNOLOGY ON AN ACCELERATED BASIS AHEAD OF
    YOUR COMPETITOR, AND THEREBY ACHIEVE DOMINANCE?

TIER II
  1. ANALYZE THE AFOREMENTIONED AND DETERMINE WHAT COMPETITORS ARE LIKELY TO DO WHICH
    WOULD DISRUPT THE MARKET AND/OR IMPACT YOUR BUSINESS.
  2. IDENTIFY SUBSTITUTION THREATS OR TRENDS SUGGESTING LESS USE OF YOUR FIRM.
  3. DEFINE ACTIONS YOU COULD TAKE IN THE MARKETPLACE TO PUT YOUR COMPETITORS AT A
    DISADVANTAGE (FOCUS ON NO MORE THAN FIVE).
  4. ASSESS YOUR VULNERABILITIES AND DETERMINE LEVERAGE POINTS TO COUNTER VULNERABILITIES.

(text continued from page 20)

Some feel the business plan would be sufficient. Here is what is normally missing. The business plan is most often written to launch a new
business or significantly expand another. The plan might be sound but
might miss out on an accurate view of the context for the sponsor.
Many new ventures are defeated before they start because the sponsor
unwound the support or overburdened the venture with unnecessary
overheads. In other cases, the wrong ventures were backed because a
thorough examination of what is possible has gone undone. These are

the things a business plan focused only on the venture will miss. To avoid such omissions, an intensive business review is appropriate. The intensive business review (IBR) is the groundwork for effective business plan development, orchestration, and stewardship.

When we were first introduced to the concept of intensive business reviews, it was at Shell in the mid-1980s. Then it was a strategy tool, supplanted by a like process called the Strategy Evaluation Session (SES). Both processes had as their objectives to develop business strategies based on a careful review of the current business and a thorough understanding of the marketplace.

Over the years, we have enhanced the processes we learned with greater sensitivity to include a global view of marketplaces, current partnering practices, and an understanding of investment vulnerabilities. This investment risk assessment tool came from Exxon Research and Engineering which taught us a few years earlier on a South American megaproject to thoroughly assess a business landscape. Further improvements came from Gary Hamel and C. K. Prahalad's writings from the early '90s to now. This introduced the notion of core competencies and strategic intent.[2]

Michael Porter's work in competitive analytics broadened the IBR review of what a competitor could do to influence your outcomes.[3] Valuation models were updated from Net Present Value (NPV) models to give primary attention to Stern Stewart & Co.'s Economic Value Added (EVA™—a Stern Stewart trademark) and like Shareholder Value Add (SVA) models.[4]

Footnoted is the excellent treatment of the valuation process by G. Bennett Stewart, III. McKinsey & Company consultants Tom Copeland, Tim Koller and Jack Murrin wrote a comprehensive book on valuation methods, if alternatives to EVA are preferred.[5] A sound introduction to valuation methods can be found in Timothy Luehrman's articles "What's It Worth? A General Manager's Guide to Valuation"[6] and "Using APV: A Better Tool for Valuing Operation."[7] An assessment of information technology, organizational norms and infrastructure also expands the original version of an IBR. Another enhancement to the IBR came from complexity challenges that invite analysis of patterns impacting value.

There is another distinction introduced to the IBR. An intensive business review builds best from complete customer intimacy. Customer intimacy reveals what customers want and what they know. This is the inchoate stage for value. All value accrues from a customer expectation. This is true, too, when you must nurture the expectation.

Finding out what customers know ultimately unravels what they do not know. The latter is important for understanding how to engender acceptance for products and services you want to lead your customer to in the future.

At the same time, the questions must be asked in the IBR for customers that might be earned in the future. This promotes reaching out to new regions and different segments of the market, along with challenges for innovations and bundling to capture the attention of prospects. The latter promotes growth and offers a firm a meaningful reason for revitalization.

The IBR scans the competitive field and adaptive forces from all quarters—regulatory, global pressures, technology advances, and more. As the successive assessments of existing business performance and infrastructure, growth and venture development, information technology, organization, and competencies unfold, the complexity is beyond the comprehension of any one person.

What is created is a business landscape. The task of the IBR today involves more than deductive risk management and market projections. It is to determine action in chaos by examining the interactions of the array of information. This examination will reveal where to adapt, when to ride a wave of adaptation, and how to emerge with patterns to dominate a market opportunity.

A decade ago, the insights would not be as creative nor would they be needing constant attention. Today, the key elements of the IBR should be maintained and frequently screened. Two competitive tools are needed: a competitive database and business analytics that capture the most critical determinants of value.

The competitive database has three pivotal and interactive elements: a customer intimacy profile, a competitor assessment, and a customer interaction report—Templates 2-2, 2-3, and 2-4, respectively These maintain a vital understanding of the marketplace and narrow the view of the customer to optimize for immediate requirements. The competitive database produces a comprehension of the future and how best to establish patterns within customer acceptance—current and future.

Distilling the landscape to the critical determinants of value is the job of the trellis and the business model. Our illustration is based on a channel partnership for a major energy concern (see Template 2-6). The most important influences to value were selected for their correlation with changes in SVA, materiality (market share and net income performance), and growth. From these, critical interdependencies were mapped. The interdependencies, in turn, helped to determine the action items for the business model. The model expresses in plain language what happens to impact value. This guides action planning and stewardship of progress at all levels.

TEMPLATE 2-2: CUSTOMER INTIMACY PROFILE

- CUSTOMER IDENTIFICATION NUMBER
- STRATEGIC INTENT STATEMENT
- CUSTOMER REQUIREMENTS
- ISSUES, TRENDS, OPPORTUNITIES FOR CUSTOMERS
- FINANCIALS (E.G., NET OPERATING PROFIT AFTER TAX [NOPAT], COST OF CAPITAL, ECONOMIC CAPITAL, EVA, SALES, FLOW OF FUNDS STATEMENT)
- RISK MANAGEMENT ASSUMPTIONS AND PRACTICES
- TECHNOLOGY VISION
- TRANSITIONS (IN PEOPLE, ORGANIZATION OR OWNERSHIP)
- THREATS
- RESOURCES
- WORK CULTURE
- CORPORATE-TO-CORPORATE RELATIONS
- FIELD OFFICE-TO-FIELD OFFICE RELATIONS
- CUSTOMER'S VIEW OF HOW FIRM VALUE-ADDS
- CUSTOMER'S PERCEPTION OF FIRM
- CUSTOMER'S PERCEPTION OF FIRM'S NEEDS
- CUSTOMER'S PERCEPTION OF FIRM'S BEST OPPORTUNITY WITH THE CUSTOMER
- STRATEGIC SPONSORS FOR FIRM IN CUSTOMER
- OPERATIONAL ALLIES IN CUSTOMER
- GAPS BETWEEN STRATEGIC AND OPERATIONAL LEVELS FOR FIRM
- SUPPLIER SELECTION CRITERIA
- HOW DECISIONS GET MADE
- TRENDS IN SELECTION
- TRENDS IN CHANNEL
- VIEW OF COMPETITION
- THREAT OF COMPETITION TO YOU AND YOUR RELATIONSHIP
- BUSINESS TO BE CAPTURED
- CURRENT BUSINESS PARTNERS

TEMPLATE 2-3: CUSTOMER INTERACTION REPORT

- CUSTOMER ID
- COMPANY NAME
- FIRM CONTACT
- CONTACT FIRST NAME
- CONTACT LAST NAME
- TITLE
- CORPORATE/FIELD
- ADDRESS
- PHONE NUMBER
- FAX NUMBER
- LAST MEETING DATE
- CRITICAL CHANGE TO CUSTOMER'S INTENT/RELATIONSHIP WITH FIRM
- NEW INTERESTS
- NOTES
- CUSTOMER SUGGESTIONS
- FOLLOW-UP ACTION ITEMS
- COMMITMENTS AND AGREEMENTS TO DATE

TEMPLATE 2-4: COMPETITOR ASSESSMENT

- COMPETITOR ID
- STRATEGIC INTENT STATEMENT
- ISSUES, TRENDS, OPPORTUNITIES FOR COMPETITION
- TECHNOLOGY DEPLOYMENT, VISION, COSTS AND SCHEDULE
- FINANCIAL CAPACITY AND ITS DEPLOYMENT (FINANCIALS, E.G., NOPAT, COST OF CAPITAL, ECONOMIC CAPITAL, EVA, SALES, FLOW OF FUNDS STATEMENT)
- RISK MANAGEMENT ASSUMPTIONS AND PRACTICES
- TRANSITIONS (IN PEOPLE, ORGANIZATION OR OWNERSHIP)
- THREATS TO FIRM (LIST COMPETENCIES AND ACTION PLANS)
- VULNERABILITIES TO FIRM'S STRATEGIC INTENT
- RESOURCES
- WORK CULTURE
- COMPETITOR'S PERCEPTION OF FIRM'S BEST OPPORTUNITY WITH CUSTOMERS
- VIEW OF FIRM
- CURRENT BUSINESS PARTNERS/PROFESSIONAL SERVICE PROVIDERS/INFRASTRUCTURE SUPPORT PROVIDERS
- PRODUCT BUNDLING
- SERVICES PROVIDED (NOTE IF BUNDLED TO A PRODUCT)
- PRICING (RANGE)
- CHANNEL INCENTIVES (TYPE, RANGE FOR EACH)
- EPC PRACTICES, COSTS AND SCHEDULE
- G&A COSTS

The partner selection process requires profiling similar to those found in customer profiles and competitor assessments (see Template 2-5). Often customers and competitors are prospective partners. For them and others who may work with your firm, it is prudent to know their business capabilities and intent. The following case illustration is one approach to bring forth an intensive business review and an analysis of business databases on prospective partners. It addresses financial; commercial; and work cultural, organizational and technological characteristics. We recommend the following steps in preparing partner profiling templates, as shown in the case illustration:

- Determine if the prospective partner is economically viable—if not, then for each feature justifying association, establish an SVA value. Scrutinize what you will get for what you must pay. For example, if you want access to China's market, what value do you place on the channel opportunity created by the partnership? If the price of the partnership exceeds the value, challenge the partnership.
- Test for business fit—does the partnership align to your strategy and will the partner be compatible with your culture.
- Examine closely the partner's infrastructure and operational capability.
- Assess reputation as business partner and industry player.

The profiling templates in the case illustration were created by brainstorming requirements for the partnership, and then integrating characteristics of current partners. Brainstorming was inspired by the future vision for the joint venture. The characteristics based on current experience reflected on what made a good partner, and traits among poor performers that should be avoided. The development of templates can be facilitated by reviewing the high performance organization characteristics presented in Chapter 10.

(text continued on page 40)

TEMPLATE 2-5: PARTNER PROFILING TEMPLATE

AFTER COMPLETING TEMPLATE, ASSIGN AN OVERALL RATING FOR PARTNER DESIRABILITY.

OVERALL RATING:	1	2	3	4	5
	LOW				HIGH

DESCRIBE PARTNER'S:
☐ ASPIRATIONS: _____   ☐ EXPECTED OUTCOMES: _____

☐ ALIGNMENT WITH THE FIRM
    ○ DISTRIBUTOR
    ○ NONE

ALIGNMENT GRID

DON'T KNOW

YEARS OF THE FIRM AFFILIATION	3 5 7 10 15 20 25	☐
COOPERATION WITH THE FIRM AGENDA	Low — Medium — High	☐
INFRASTRUCTURE FIT TO THE FIRM AGENDA	Poor — Fair — Good	☐
INFRASTRUCTURE POTENTIAL FOR THE FIRM AGENDA	Poor — Fair — Good	☐
AGREEMENT ON GROWTH STRATEGY	Low — Medium — High	☐
AGREEMENT ON VALUES & BELIEFS FOR OPERATIONS	Low — Medium — High	☐
WILLINGNESS TO PURSUE CONTINUOUS INNOVATION IN BUSINESS A AND BUSINESS B RETAIL SALES	None — Some Extent — Great Extent	☐
TRUST IN PARTNER	Missing — Moderate — Strong	☐

(continued)

PARTNER PROFILING TEMPLATE *(continued)*

POTENTIAL FOR COMPLEMENTARY VALUE-ADD TO THE FIRM

	LOW		MEDIUM		HIGH	DON'T KNOW
OVERALL OPERATIONAL EFFICIENCIES	O	O	O	O	O	☐
BUSINESS A OPERATIONAL EFFICIENCIES	O	O	O	O	O	☐
BUSINESS B OPERATIONAL EFFICIENCIES	O	O	O	O	O	☐
OPERATIONS MANAGEMENT STAFF	O	O	O	O	O	☐
PARTNER SELECTION	O	O	O	O	O	☐
DEVELOPMENT	O	O	O	O	O	☐
PROJECT MANAGEMENT	O	O	O	O	O	☐
NEW BUSINESS START-UP						
• A	O	O	O	O	O	☐
• B	O	O	O	O	O	☐
• OTHER	O	O	O	O	O	☐
OTHER ASSETS TO CONTRIBUTE	O	O	O	O	O	☐

CONCERNS VOICED ABOUT AFFILIATION WITH THE FIRM

	NO CONCERN	LOW		MEDIUM		HIGH	DON'T KNOW
LACK OF FOCAL POINT . . . MULTIPLE POINTS OF CONTACT/CONTRADICTIONS AMONG THE FIRM PARTIES	☐	O	O	O	O	O	☐
TAKE OVER BY THE FIRM . . . THE FIRM DICTATES POLICY	☐	O	O	O	O	O	☐
THE FIRM PURSUES SALES TO DETRIMENT OF MARGIN	☐	O	O	O	O	O	☐
DELAY IN DECISIONS IMPACTING GROWTH EFFICIENCY	☐	O	O	O	O	O	☐
CAPITAL AVAILABILITY WHEN NEEDED	☐	O	O	O	O	O	☐
OBLIGATIONS TO USE THE FIRM TECHNOLOGIES/PRACTICES	☐	O	O	O	O	O	☐
DISTRIBUTIONS RESTRICTED TO THE FIRM PREFERENCES	☐	O	O	O	O	O	☐
IMPOSITION OF THE FIRM AUDIT REQUIREMENTS	☐	O	O	O	O	O	☐
IMPOSITION OF THE FIRM RISK MANAGEMENT POLICIES (ENVIRONMENTAL, OTHER LIABILITY)	☐	O	O	O	O	O	☐
OTHER (PLEASE EXPLAIN)	☐	O	O	O	O	O	☐

_____

_____

PARTNER PROFILING TEMPLATE *(continued)*

PARTNER NET WORTH & FINANCIAL CONDITION
☐ **KEY PARTIES PERSONAL WORTH**

_____ $ _____
(PARTY)   (NET WORTH)

SOURCE OF FUNDS (BUSINESS ACTIVITY, INHERITANCE, ETC.)
_____

(INFORMATION SOURCE)   (DATE)

_____ $ _____
(PARTY)   (NET WORTH)

SOURCE OF FUNDS (BUSINESS ACTIVITY, INHERITANCE, ETC.)
_____

(INFORMATION SOURCE)   (DATE)

_____ $ _____
(PARTY)   (NET WORTH)

SOURCE OF FUNDS (BUSINESS ACTIVITY, INHERITANCE, ETC.)
_____

(INFORMATION SOURCE)   (DATE)

_____ $ _____
(PARTY)   (NET WORTH)

SOURCE OF FUNDS (BUSINESS ACTIVITY, INHERITANCE, ETC.)
_____

(INFORMATION SOURCE)   (DATE)

_____ $ _____
(PARTY)   (NET WORTH)

SOURCE OF FUNDS (BUSINESS ACTIVITY, INHERITANCE, ETC.)
_____

(INFORMATION SOURCE)   (DATE)

☐ **TYPE OF ENTITY:**

○ SOLE PROPRIETORSHIP
○ PARTNERSHIP
○ LLC
○ CORPORATION

DON'T KNOW

☐ **VENTURE WORTH:** _____ ☐
                   (INFORMATION SOURCE)
☐ **CREDIT RATING:** _____ ☐
☐ **TOTAL ASSETS:** _____ ☐
☐ **TOTAL LIABILITIES:** _____ ☐
☐ **AVERAGE MONTHLY**
  CASH FLOW _____ ☐

☐ **LITIGATION IN PROGRESS**

○ YES (LIST BELOW)
_____
_____
_____
_____

○ NO
○ DON'T KNOW

☐ **REGULATORY REVIEW, NOTICE OF VIOLATION OR SANCTION**

○ YES (DESCRIBE BELOW: AGENCY, RISK)
_____
_____
_____
_____

○ NO
○ DON'T KNOW

(continued)

PARTNER PROFILING TEMPLATE *(continued)*

COMPETENCIES

- ☐ DIRECT OPERATIONS
- ☐ OTHER OPERATIONS
  - ○ LEASE
  - ○ MAINTENANCE SERVICE
  - ○ OTHER (PLEASE SPECIFY)

  _____
  _____
  _____
  _____

- ☐ BUSINESS DEVELOPMENT
  - ○ BUSINESS A
  - ○ BUSINESS B
  - ○ NEW BUSINESS GROWTH
    - ☐ EXPORT
    - ☐ OEM
    - ☐ INFRASTRUCTURE SERVICES
    - ☐ OTHER (PLEASE SPECIFY)

    _____
    _____
    _____
    _____

  - ○ ACQUISITIONS/MERGERS
- ☐ SITE PROJECT MANAGEMENT
  - ○ IMPROVEMENTS < $ _____
  - ○ IMPROVEMENTS > $ _____
  - ○ NEW LOCATIONS
- ☐ FINANCE
  - ○ ACCOUNTS & CONTROLS
  - ○ BANKER RELATIONS
  - ○ FINANCE
- ☐ VALUE CHAIN OPTIMIZATION
  - ○ MERCHANDISING
  - ○ INTERACTIVE MARKETING
  - ○ OUTSOURCING
  - ○ CUSTOMER INTIMACY/OPTIMAL EXCHANGE TO CONSUMER
  - ○ TRANSACTION MANAGEMENT (ORDER MANAGEMENT/ISIT)
  - ○ INVENTORY/RESOURCE PLANNING
  - ○ PRODUCT/SERVICE R&D

CURRENT BUSINESS RELATIONS

- ☐ OTHER MAJOR FIRM:

  _____
  (WITH WHOM)   (FOR WHAT)
- ☐ INDEPENDENT:

  _____
  (WITH WHOM)   (FOR WHAT)
- ☐ OTHER ALLIANCES:

  _____
  (WITH WHOM)   (FOR WHAT)
- ☐ NON-COMPETE AGREEMENTS:

  _____
  (WITH WHOM)   (FOR WHAT)

GOVERNANCE & CAPITAL STRUCTURE

- ☐ ACCOUNTS & CONTROL REVIEW

  METHOD
  - ○ CASH
  - ○ ACCRUAL

  INFRASTRUCTURE
  - ○ UTILIZES PROFESSIONAL ACCOUNTING FIRM FOR ANNUAL REVIEW AUDIT ONLY (NAME & LOCATION)

    _____
    _____
  - ○ UTILIZES PROFESSIONAL ACCOUNTING FIRM FOR ALL ACCOUNTING AND RECORDKEEPING (NAME & LOCATION)

    _____
    _____
  - ○ IN-HOUSE PROFESSIONAL ACCOUNTING STAFF

  STAFFING
  - ☐ UNABLE TO HANDLE CURRENT BUSINESS
  - ☐ ABLE TO HANDLE CURRENT BUSINESS ONLY
  - ☐ ABLE TO HANDLE SUPPORT TO JV
  - ☐ CAPABLE OF GROWTH TO SUPPORT JV

PARTNER PROFILING TEMPLATE *(continued)*

GOVERNANCE & CAPITAL STRUCTURE *(continued)*

<u>PROFESSIONALISM</u> (CHECK ALL WHICH APPLY.)

☐ CPA ON STAFF
  CHECK IF A PRINCIPAL IN THE VENTURE? ○

☐ CFP ON STAFF
  CHECK IF A PRINCIPAL IN THE VENTURE? ○

☐ ACCOUNTING MANAGER ON STAFF
  CHECK IF A PRINCIPAL IN THE VENTURE? ○

☐ DEGREE ACCOUNTANT
  CHECK IF A PRINCIPAL IN THE VENTURE? ○

  ○ IN-HOUSE BOOKKEEPING STAFF ONLY

  ○ ENTREPRENEURIAL PREPARATION

  ○ OTHER (PLEASE EXPLAIN)
  _____

☐ STEWARDSHIP

  ○ TOTAL REVENUES

  ○ GROSS PROFIT

  ○ TOTAL SALES—INSIDE

  ○ TOTAL COST—INSIDE

  ○ GROSS PROFIT—INSIDE

  ○ GROSS PROFIT—ALL SALES

  ○ OTHER INCOME

    ☐ RENT INCOME

    ☐ LICENSES INCOME

    ☐ ROYALTY REVENUE

    ☐ BUSINESS D REVENUE

    ☐ BUSINESS E REVENUE

    ☐ OUTSOURCING SERVICES

    ☐ ALLOWANCES FROM CHANNEL

    ☐ MONEY ORDER FEES

    ☐ BUSINESS F REVENUE

    ☐ INTEREST INCOME

    ☐ TAX COLLECTION ALLOWANCE

    ☐ REBATES AND DISCOUNTS

    ☐ BUSINESS G REVENUE

    ☐ BUSINESS H REVENUE

    ☐ PAY PHONE REVENUE

    ☐ EQUIPMENT RENTAL INCOME

    ☐ MAINTENANCE FEES

    ☐ TOTAL OTHER INCOME

○ EXPENSES

  ☐ SALARIES & WAGES

  ☐ PAYROLL TAXES

  ☐ PAYROLL TAXES—UNEMPLOYMENT

  ☐ EMPLOYEE BENEFITS—W/C

  ☐ EMPLOYEE BENEFITS—INB

  ☐ UNIFORMS

  ☐ ELECTRICITY

  ☐ OTHER UTILITIES

  ☐ REPAIRS & MAINTENANCE

  ☐ REPAIRS & MAINT.—MAJOR PROJECTS

  ☐ SUPPLIES

  ☐ CHEMICALS

  ☐ PROFESSIONAL SERVICES

  ☐ BANK SERVICE CHARGES

  ☐ CASH OVER/SHORT

  ☐ COMPUTER SERVICES

  ☐ FREIGHT EXPENSE

  ☐ INSURANCE

  ☐ EQUIPMENT RENTALS

  ☐ MO MACHINE RENTAL

  ☐ ADVERTISING & PROMOTIONS

  ☐ AUTO MILEAGE

  ☐ CUSTOMER SERVICE

  ☐ CREDIT CARD SERVICE FEES

  ☐ CREDIT CARD CHARGEBACK—NET

  ☐ LICENSES & PERMITS

  ☐ MANAGEMENT FEES

  ☐ PROPERTY TAXES

  ☐ RENT

  ☐ VOLUME REBATES

  ☐ TOTAL LOCATION EXPENSES

○ EBITDA BEFORE MANAGEMENT FEE

(continued)

PARTNER PROFILING TEMPLATE *(continued)*

COMMUNICATION

BUSINESS COMMUNICATION SOPHISTICATION

	NEVER	RARELY	SOMETIMES	OFTEN	ALWAYS	DON'T KNOW
USES AGENDA IN MEETING	O	O	O	O	O	☐
CAPABLE OF CONFLICT RESOLUTION	O	O	O	O	O	☐
BRAINSTORMS	O	O	O	O	O	☐
PROBLEM-SOLVES	O	O	O	O	O	☐
SHARES INFORMATION	O	O	O	O	O	☐
LISTENS	O	O	O	O	O	☐
REPORTS SUCCINCTLY & CLEARLY	O	O	O	O	O	☐
SUCCESSFULLY USES TELECONFERENCING	O	O	O	O	O	☐
SUCCESSFULLY USES VIDEO-CONFERENCING	O	O	O	O	O	☐
HANDLES ISSUES WITHIN OWN AUTHORITY	O	O	O	O	O	☐
MANAGES TIME WELL	O	O	O	O	O	☐
COMMUNICATES ISSUES & PROBLEMS FOR TIMELY RESOLUTION	O	O	O	O	O	☐
KEEPS AN OPEN MIND ABOUT NEW IDEAS AND RUMORS	O	O	O	O	O	☐
COMMUNICATES EFFECTIVELY ACROSS CULTURES WITH EMPLOYEES, CUSTOMERS & OTHERS	O	O	O	O	O	☐
CHALLENGES COUNTERPARTS TO PERFORM AT THEIR BEST... "PUSHES BACK" IN A PRODUCTIVE MANNER	O	O	O	O	O	☐

COMMUNICATION INFRASTRUCTURE

	YES	NO	DON'T KNOW
ACCESS TO TELECONFERENCING	O	O	☐
ACCESS TO VIDEO-CONFERENCING	O	O	☐
E-MAIL CAPABILITIES	O	O	☐
FINANCIAL SOFTWARE	O	O	☐
COMPATIBLE WITH FIRM	O	O	☐
INTEGRATED FINANCIAL SYSTEM	O	O	☐

PARTNER PROFILING TEMPLATE *(continued)*

COMMUNITY PROFILE

REPUTATION

	YES	NO	DON'T KNOW
HONESTY & INTEGRITY	○	○	☐
RESPONSIBLE	○	○	☐
RESPECTS CUSTOMERS	○	○	☐
RESPECTS BUSINESS RELATIONSHIPS	○	○	☐
STRONG BUSINESS ACUMEN	○	○	☐
FINANCIAL STRENGTH	○	○	☐

NETWORKS (DESCRIBE THE PARTNER'S BUSINESS NETWORKS)

	YES	NO	DON'T KNOW
BANKERS & OTHER FINANCIAL INSTITUTIONS	○	○	☐
EPC FIRMS	○	○	☐
LOCAL GOVERNMENT	○	○	☐
COMMUNITY AUTHORITIES	○	○	☐
BUSINESS BROKERS	○	○	☐
SPECIALTY INVESTORS	○	○	☐
MAJOR PLAYERS PLANNERS	○	○	☐
KEY INVESTORS IN COMMUNITY	○	○	☐
PERMITTING AUTHORITIES	○	○	☐
REGULATORS	○	○	☐
SUBCONTRACTORS	○	○	☐
VENDORS	○	○	☐
COMMUNITY AFFAIRS	○	○	☐
OTHER DISTRIBUTORS	○	○	☐
OTHER CHANNELS	○	○	☐
HEAD OFFICE	○	○	☐

(continued)

PARTNER PROFILING TEMPLATE *(continued)*

THE FIRM BUSINESS MODEL: FINANCIAL REVIEW FORM

PARTNER CANDIDATE

PARTNER: (Attach Previous 3 Years Consolidated
                                                    Financial Statements)

HEADQUARTERS ADDRESS:

KEY CONTACT: NAME: OWNERSHIP: ☐ SOLE PROPRIETOR
                TEL (O):   ☐ PARTNERSHIP/CORP.
                TEL (H):

                E-MAIL:
                BEST TIME TO CONTACT:

BUSINESS INCOME STREAMS:

   CURRENT   ○ YES ○ NO   IF YES, THE FIRM AFFILIATION (TYPE) _____ (YEARS)

   CURRENT BUSINESS: _____

   BUSINESS (LIST ALL): _____
   _____

EMPLOYEES:

FINANCIAL SUMMARY[1]:

	PREVIOUS 3 YEARS	CURRENT	FORECAST 5 YEARS
	— — —	—	— — — — —

REVENUES

(IDENTIFY BY BUSINESS
INCOME STREAMS):

EBIT:

INTEREST:

PRE-TAX INCOME:

PRE-TAX CASH FLOW:

CAPITAL:
  EQUIPMENT/IMPROVEMENTS
  INTELLECTUAL PROPERTY
  LAND
  FACILITIES
  ACQUISITIONS
  OTHER

FREE CASH FLOW:

[1]SOURCE OF INFO: ☐ AUDITED FINANCIALS ☐ OTHER (EXPLAIN) _____

PARTNER PROFILING TEMPLATE *(continued)*

THE FIRM BUSINESS MODEL: FINANCIAL REVIEW FORM

PARTNER CANDIDATE

CALCULATE ECONOMIC VALUE-ADD FOR 10 YEARS, USE ___% AS AVERAGE COST OF CAPITAL FOR EACH BUSINESS ___% FOR THE TOTAL OF ALL BUSINESSES.

NOPAT—COST OF CAPITAL = _____

TOTAL VALUE =
SYNERGIES ___ + PURCHASE VALUE ___ = NET VALUE-ADD ___ + PREMIUM ___ + EQUITY ___
+ LIABILITIES ___

TOTAL VALUE ENHANCEMENTS   COMPARABLE VALUE ASSESSMENT
                 NET VALUE-ADD   COMPARABLE VALUE $ _____
- NETWORK SERVICES CREDIT + _____   COMMON FEATURES TO CANDIDATE:
                                    ○ VOLUME _____ GAL
- LOYALTY INCENTIVE   + _____   ○ NET INCOME $ _____
                                      ○ FACILITY CONDITION _____ YRS
TOTAL EXPECTED NET VALUE-ADD   ○ EQUIPMENT MODERNIZATION _____

VALUE DIFFERENCE   TOTAL EXPECTED VALUE – COMPARABLE VALUE = $ _____

CONTRIBUTION METRICS

PREVIOUS YEAR STATION CONTRIBUTION	STATION #									
	1	2	3	4	5	6	7	8	9	10
% REVENUE										
% REVENUE INCOME										
% FEE										
% O&M CONTRACT										
% ROYALTY										
% MANAGEMENT FEE										
% CAPITAL										
% FREE CASH FLOW										

PREVIOUS YEAR
CONTRIBUTION

% REVENUE
% CAPITAL
% FREE CASH FLOW

Templates 2-6 and 2-7 describe the inputs required for a trellis and business model. What is most important is determining: 1) the forces requiring adaptation, and 2) the emerging opportunities for the landscape.

Determining "where next" in growth is a special topic for examining patterns. One important pattern is the knowledge base among players on the landscape. The IBR questions posit useful ways to detect patterns. When all is said and done, there will likely be numerous ways to pursue growth. The choice of what to do will be a function of the knowledge gleaned from the IBR.

To sort out the patterns of knowledge among players, we concocted the "Ralls Window." It simply examines where you have the best opportunity vis-à-vis competition to capture growth opportunity. The basis for choosing among opportunities is to determine the relative position of knowledge for the opportunity among you, your cus-

---

TEMPLATE 2-6: THE BUSINESS LANDSCAPE: A TRELLIS OF VALUE INTERDEPENDENCIES

CATEGORY	LEVER(S)	IMPACT TO SVA	IMPACT TO GROWTH	MATERIALITY	LEVEL(S) IMPACTED
BUSINESS MODEL					
	BUSINESS PLANNING	0	0	0	MEGA
	VENTURE HUNTING	0	0	0	MEGA-MACRO
	FINANCING	0	0	0	MEGA
	BUSINESS MIX	0	0	0	MICRO-NANO
	COMPETITIVE RESPONSE	0	0	0	MICRO-NANO
	DISTRIBUTION	0	0	0	MEGA-MACRO
INVESTOR RELATIONS					
	"PARTNER" FIT	0	0	0	MEGA-NANO
	STEWARDSHIP AND GUIDANCE	0	0	0	MEGA
	TRANSFORMATION	0	0	0	MEGA-NANO
	PARTICIPATION	0	0	0	MEGA
	ALIGNMENT TO FIRM	0	0	0	MEGA
	FIRM CAPABILITY INFUSION	0	0	0	MEGA-NANO
GOVERNANCE					
	FINANCIAL STRUCTURE	0	0	0	MEGA-MACRO
	ORGANIZATION DESIGN	0	0	0	MEGA-NANO
	LEGAL AGREEMENTS	0	0	0	MEGA-MACRO
	AUTHORITIES AND RESPONSIBILITIES	0	0	0	MACRO-NANO
	ACCOUNTS AND CONTROLS	0	0	0	MACRO-MICRO
PORTFOLIO MANAGEMENT					
	STRATEGY IMPLEMENTATION	0	0	0	MICRO-NANO
	BUSINESS COMMUNICATION	0	0	0	MICRO
	TALENT, COMPETENCIES AND MOTIVATION	0	0	0	MEGA-MICRO
	TECHNOLOGY TRANSFER: BEST PRACTICES	0	0	0	MEGA-MICRO
	ENTREPRENEURSHIP	0	0	0	MEGA-NANO
	INFRASTRUCTURE DEVELOPMENT	0	0	0	MICRO
	OPTIMIZATION	0	0	0	MICRO-NANO

© J. GARRETT RALLS, 1997, 1998

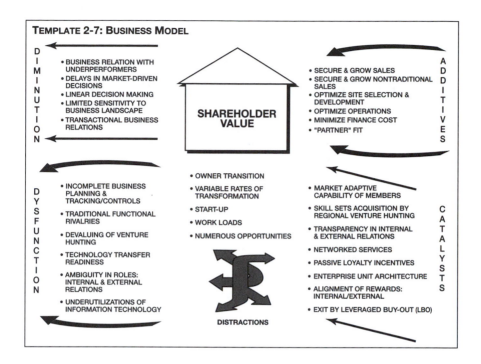

TEMPLATE 2-7: BUSINESS MODEL

DIMINUTION
- BUSINESS RELATION WITH UNDERPERFORMERS
- DELAYS IN MARKET-DRIVEN DECISIONS
- LINEAR DECISION MAKING
- LIMITED SENSITIVITY TO BUSINESS LANDSCAPE
- TRANSACTIONAL BUSINESS RELATIONS

SHAREHOLDER VALUE

ADDITIVES
- SECURE & GROW SALES
- SECURE & GROW NONTRADITIONAL SALES
- OPTIMIZE SITE SELECTION & DEVELOPMENT
- OPTIMIZE OPERATIONS
- MINIMIZE FINANCE COST
- "PARTNER" FIT

DYSFUNCTION
- INCOMPLETE BUSINESS PLANNING & TRACKING/CONTROLS
- TRADITIONAL FUNCTIONAL RIVALRIES
- DEVALUING OF VENTURE HUNTING
- TECHNOLOGY TRANSFER READINESS
- AMBIGUITY IN ROLES: INTERNAL & EXTERNAL RELATIONS
- UNDERUTILIZATIONS OF INFORMATION TECHNOLOGY

- OWNER TRANSITION
- VARIABLE RATES OF TRANSFORMATION
- START-UP
- WORK LOADS
- NUMEROUS OPPORTUNITIES

DISTRACTIONS

CATALYSTS
- MARKET ADAPTIVE CAPABILITY OF MEMBERS
- SKILL SETS ACQUISITION BY REGIONAL VENTURE HUNTING
- TRANSPARENCY IN INTERNAL & EXTERNAL RELATIONS
- NETWORKED SERVICES
- PASSIVE LOYALTY INCENTIVES
- ENTERPRISE UNIT ARCHITECTURE
- ALIGNMENT OF REWARDS: INTERNAL/EXTERNAL
- EXIT BY LEVERAGED BUY-OUT (LBO)

tomers, and competitors. Following the window are general principles for what do in each panel of the window.

Categorizing Adaptive Forces

There are many ways to classify forces with potential to change the landscape. One is to categorize by the function to value. This is illustrated in the business model described in Template 2-7. Value can be created by riding a wave created by others or by events in the marketplace. In Template 2-7, these are identified as either additives to value, or catalysts for value development. Value can also be lost.

"Seismic" forces are the numerous forces which may disrupt value, distract attention from value, dilute value, or destroy it altogether. In Template 2-7, the loss of value is labeled as distraction, diminution, or dysfunction. Diminution captures the destruction or dilution of value. These require new learnings, policies, or actions to resolve. Dysfunction describes practices which are not working as they should, or events not managed well. These are easily addressed by resolving conflicts and getting on with business by fulfilling existing expectations for performance.

Table 2-1. Ralls Window

	KNOWN TO CUSTOMER	UNKNOWN TO CUSTOMER	
KNOWN TO FIRM	Bidding Contest 1	Competitive Access Play * 2	KNOWN TO COMPETITOR
KNOWN TO FIRM	Proprietary Partnership Opportunity * 3	Opportunity to Lead Customer to Business Growth * 4	UNKNOWN TO COMPETITOR
UNKNOWN TO FIRM	Risk of Long Term Exclusion 5	Blind Side to Possible Market Erosion 6	KNOWN TO COMPETITOR
UNKNOWN TO FIRM	Opening for Exploitation 7	Discovery Opportunity * 8	UNKNOWN TO COMPETITOR

* 2-3-4-8 Growth Solutions

Panel #   Action

1. **Avoid-Absorbs Time & Energy**—Commodity-like play
2. **Pursue & Sustain Relationships**—Get to a decision maker first with an exclusive contract by leveraging relationships
3. **Pursue & Sustain Relationships**—Establish long-term strategic alliance
4. **Pursue & Sustain Relationships**—Be persuasive: Present a strong case to decision makers . . . build to a proprietary partnership
5. **Conduct Competitor Analysis**—Seek information from customer relationships
6. **Conduct Competitor Analysis**—Invest in R&D, continuous improvement monitoring in related fields & business systems
7. **Seek Information from Customer Relationships**—Study customer; track competitors closer—make inquiries of those with relations to competitor
8. **Invest in R&D, Continuous Improvement Monitoring in Related Fields and Business Systems**—Play in the game . . . invent and lead customer to your solution for their need; create industry consortia

---

Another scheme for categorizing adaptation is to calibrate the potential impact in some manner. We like to use four categories: Never Experienced, Previously Experienced-Mild, Previously Experienced-Moderate, and Previously Experienced-Severe. Never-before-experienced trends lack credibility. They are the runaway comets about to smash earth. No one believes the danger exists until they are too close to avoid some effect from an impact. In these cases, we coach with others' experiences, as well as simulate and encourage experimentation with the experience—if possible.

Where there has been experience, there can be difficulty when the level of past experience does not match up to what the anticipated impact might be. The greater challenge is getting people to believe the impact will be more severe. Few people have to be convinced not to worry. The challenge plays out much like earth tremors in California. No one wants to talk about the "big one," and people are quick to dismiss the initial rattle and roll as a tremor. Again, the experiences of other industries, along with simulation and experimentation facilitate understanding.

Yet another categorization is to judge adaptive influences by their origins. For example, what is the source of the wave? Could it be from another industry as was the case when Saskatchewan Wheat Pool adapted global positioning systems to precision farming? Or does the wave come from competitors, regulators, community action, trade agreement, natural forces in the environment, war or crime, or somewhere else?

Creating categories is an art unique to each landscape. Mixing the aforementioned categories is common. The tasks at the end of the day are to be complete, and bring forth reality. It is better to acquaint people with the categories before giving a read on their status. The orientation improves understanding and use. The orientation will surface differences of opinion with the scheme used and open discussion for new categories.

Pattern Detectives

Regardless of how categories are chosen, the work to be done is knowing what is coming and discovering patterns which will offer increasing returns, leading to dominance in the market. This begs the question, how do I decode patterns? The first assistance we offer are the pattern analysis inquiries in the IBR. These deal with the various subjects in the IBR self-reflection, offering guidance about specific kinds of patterns.

Generally, good guidelines to follow in searching for patterns are provided as follows:

Searching for Patterns

- Do not rule anything out in the beginning.
- Invite people with experience with the landscape to think back across time to determine trends, cycles or patterns.
- Look at all interactions.

(continued)

Searching for Patterns *(continued)*

- Examine across subjects for interdependencies, e.g., understand how organizational variables like structure, communication or control influence decisions about technology, marketing or financial engineering.
- Give more attention to patterns appearing across time—ones which endure or build with repetition.
- Watch for mutations—situations which evolve unexpectedly.
- Notice events or processes which enable other events or processes.
- Note events and processes which share space, time or intensity.
- Understand cause-effect dynamics—look for clusters rather than for single effects.
- Notice relationships among people; identify networks and understand how they behave—what they do together, influence, or seem to be impacted by.
- For all kinds of relationships, notice frequency, importance or impact, and, in the case of humans, affect (liking or disliking).
- Look for catalysts which make things happen.

When patterns are identified, list the patterns and understand how they may interact. Relate patterns to important outcomes. End-result outcomes in firms will be performance indicators such as shareholder value-add, materiality (share held and net income), and growth. Intervening influences to these outcomes may need to be reviewed to appreciate what is happening. In this case, human communication, transformation, satisfaction, learning, governance, investor interactions, and other factors may need to be studied for patterns and interdependencies leading to an impact on business outcomes.

Examine the level of involvement in an organization for a pattern. See how levels change behavior as a result of the pattern. Look for similar dynamics among partners.

The final listings should be those most important to the outcomes. Group them as they make sense to you or as they help in understanding, explaining, or predicting patterns.

Another hint is to avoid depending too much on empiricism. The past does not always repeat. We do build language and knowledge on the basis of prior experience. These can lead us to see again only what is familiar, or to avoid the discomfort of uncertainty. We can also get into a perceptual rut whereby we see things according to our own view or paradigm. This is why it is important to constantly challenge empirical conclusions. If they withstand the challenge, their utility will be clear.

On the whole, the above is coaching for taking a systems view of the world and of the landscape under consideration. This means you search for how anything affects anything else. You see the world as a place where a movement in one field can influence another.

The Patterns We Know

This is coaching for "naked," general observation—that is, taking into account the world as it is observed without assumptions or biases. While this coaching is good, things have been learned about the nature of patterns in value found in partnering. What follows are insights from learnings narrowed to our discussion. They have value if you understand that these are in themselves hints as to where to look, or as propositions about how interactions form patterns. They are not absolute truths just because they were experienced by others.

General Partnering Patterns

- A partner's past experiences in partnering may constitute a pattern, or evidence an evolving pattern of events within partnering—know your prospective partners and their histories.
- Relationships are impacted by financial status—bad times create tension, and good times cause bad habits to be overlooked.
- The insertion of another party by one partner without getting everyone's okay will disturb the other(s). Even when the addition of another makes sense, there is a good chance tensions will surface.
- Behavior in the negotiation to create a partnership will often carry over into the operation and negotiation for future growth.
- Dysfunction among partners which gets swept aside through avoidance or denial; this will resurface at inopportune times in the partnership.
- Choices in organization—command and control, hierarchy, function, learning, transparency, communication—will impact commercial and technological decisions.
- Without special consideration in agreements, sponsors will over-involve themselves in the partnership; it will be difficult for members of the partnership to confront such behavior.
- Without special consideration in agreements, joint business planning and stewardship will not take place.

(continued)

General Partnering Patterns (*continued*)

- Use of sponsors' resources and services is a frequent cause of friction in partnerships.
- Sponsors can ensure planning and growth.
- Sponsors in trouble in their own business will disrupt partnerships.
- Partnerships permitted to function as independent enterprises will progress further than ones precluded from growth.
- In emerging economies, dynastic families may play an important role in securing a level political, labor or crime-free playing field.
- In emerging economies, large partnerships have such vast impact that a broad range of members in a community become influential stakeholders and act accordingly.
- Without a business education, exits from partnerships are treated as emotional separations and devolve into disharmony.
- Disharmony in exits leads to the destruction of value for all concerned.
- While the sequence for invitations to partner make good business sense, there is an opportunity cost to pay when later marriage partners become aware of earlier preferences.
- Career expectations of employees to the partnership influence outcomes, at times without regard to the good performance available to the partnership.

There are numerous permutations of interactions among partners and no one book can capture them all. The above list encourages you to think through the data generated.

Sources for Information to Complete a Landscape

Archives reviews, literature searches, and networking are the primary means for gathering information used to compose a landscape for a firm. Archives reviews are the searches of one's own databases. Most organizations, however, do not actively involve all employees in inputting their knowledge of the marketplace. Surprisingly, employees at the lower levels often have knowledge of competition through friends, relatives, contact with vendors in common with competitors, and other shared business relations. In our electronic age, it is ridiculous not to avail ourselves of these valuable insights.

Literature searches today employ the powerful search engines of the Internet. Networks, web sites for firms, public filings such as the EDGAR database of the U.S. Securities Exchange Commission (SEC),

TEMPLATE 2-8: HOW TO DO A LITERATURE SEARCH

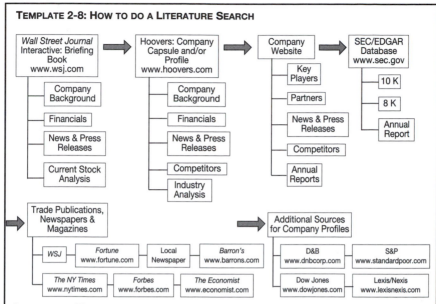

ADDITIONAL RESOURCES ON THE INTERNET

CIA's International Economy Statistics
- http://www.odci.gov/cia/publicaitons/hies97/toc.htm

Cleveland Federal Reserve Bank's World Economy Surveys
- http://www.clev.frb.org/research/index.htm

Canadian Business Information
- http://www.strategies.ic.gc.ca

Financial Information
- http://www.moneypages.com/syndicate
- http://www.moneypages.com/syndicate/finance/foreign.html
- US Companies
  http://www.reportgallery.com/
- UK-Based Companies
  http://www.hemscott.co.uk/hemscott/
- European Company Annual Reports
  http://www.carol.co.uk/

Legal Web Sites
- Eslamboly & Barlavi
  http://www.lawguru.com/
- Lawyers Weekly
  http://www.lawyersweekly.com/

Internet Business Webliography
  (Library of Internet Sites)
- http://www.lib.isu.edu/weblio.html
- US and International Marketing Page
  http://www.lib.isu.edu/bus/marketin.html
- Japan Economic Trends
  http://www.jetro.go.jp/japan/index.html

Patent Research
- US '71
  http://www.patents.ibm.com/ibm.html
- Ex-US
  http://www.patscan.ubc.ca/free.html

Price's List of List
- http://www.gwis2.circ.gwu.edu/~
  gprice/listof.htm
- http://www.gwis2.circ.gwu.edu/~
  gprice/directhtm

ADDITIONAL SOURCES OF INFORMATION

Directories

Johnson Survey
John S. Herold, Inc.
35 Mason Street
Greenwich, CT 06830
Dun & Bradstreet
Moody's
Standard & Poor's
Value Line
Arnold Bernhard & Company, Inc.
711 Third Avenue
New York, NY 10017
Cambridge Corporation (Yearbook on
  Corporate Mergers)
P.O. Box 64
Ipswich, MA 01938

Newsletters

The Acquisition/Divestiture Weekly Report
Quality Services, Inc. (Publisher)
3887 State Street
Santa Barbara, CA 93105
(805) 682-2097
National Review of Mergers & Acquisitions
Tweed Publishing Company
23 Main Street
Tiburon, CA 94920
Computerized Services
(Selects targets against requester's financial criteria)
Acquisition Clearinghouse—(305) 491-5211
Dun & Bradstreet's Mergers—(212) 285-7803
Standard & Poor's—(212) 208-8417

and news releases can reveal detailed information about firms—
yours and others. Proprietary newsletters, analysts' reports, and
financial histories reports can extend this knowledge base in important ways.

Carefully examine news releases for information regarding
alliances. Template 2-8 outlines sources for conducting a literature
search. This template is easily outdated as the Internet provides
broader access and new services become available. There are ways to
short-circuit the process. For example, when your human resources
group establishes partnerships with executive search firms, enroll the
research departments of these firms for your benefit in assessing partners. These firms have capable groups available with an understanding of your firm's needs and what is happening among your competitors and prospective partners.

Other possibilities are to hire firms which gather competitive intelligence (a growing industry), use the research services of a university
library, or purchase detailed profiles from commercial database
firms. Use Template 2-8 to order requests prepared by others.

Network News

What is missing gets done by networking. Networking is a confused art for three reasons. Most impacting of the three reasons is
how networking was strained by repeated use during a decade and a
half of downsizing. Outplacement firms posted names indiscrimi-
nately on bulletin boards; decision makers were inundated with calls.
Downsizing and the resulting overlapping responsibilities narrow the
time available to network.

The second reason for the confusion is the amount of information
about networking published and taught in employment and marketing seminars. Oftentimes conflicting, some information suggests
manipulation and other questionable practices. This created resistance on the part of those at the end of the daisy chain.

The third reason is new barriers to direct conversation. These
include caller ID and voice mail displacing the human screening by
assistants. Now we will risk making things more complicated with
advice about how to manage networks.

Managing Networks

- Do not harvest networks too soon—unless you pay for the service or really must harvest now to succeed.
- Prepare for networking; map out who you have access to with what you need to know.
  ⇒ Request input from own staff.
  ⇒ Conduct literature searches to surface names of individuals, firms, regions of interest.
  ⇒ For public companies, scrutinize SEC required documents for key names and issues, e.g., annual reports, 10Ks, 8Ks.
- Utilize corporate resources to reach professional service providers (M&A Dept., Senior Finance, Senior Executive Board, Legal, Audit/Accounting Functions, Senior Technical Talent, Procurement/Customer Sales & Services, Regulatory, Human Resources).
  ⇒ Investment Bankers/Merchant Bankers
  ⇒ Market Analysts (Research Dept.)
  ⇒ Public Affairs/Relations
  ⇒ Law (Partner)
  ⇒ Accounting (Partner)
  ⇒ Marketing Research
  ⇒ Management Consultants
  ⇒ Executive Search
  ⇒ Commercial Bankers
- Contact business colleagues: faculty, college classmates, professional associations, recruiting contacts, vendors, contractors and anyone else in a position to observe.
- Include relatives.
- Be iterative—revisit ideas, observations, and names with keen observers.

People provide better information at different points in the evolution of a strategic business relation. In the following table, key sources are contrasted to the information they typically provide.

Table 2-2.
Who is Useful When?

Relationships	Kind of Information Provided: Deal		
	Discovery	Closings	Operations
Your Customers	✓		✓
Their Customers	✓	✓	✓
Your Contractors, Vendors	✓		✓
Their Contractors, Vendors	✓	✓	✓
Law Firms	✓	✓	✓
Accounting Firms	✓	✓	✓
Executive Search Firms	✓		✓
Market Analysts	✓	✓	✓
Investment Bankers/Merchant Bankers	✓	✓	✓
Commercial Bankers	✓		✓
Funds	✓	✓	
Consulting Companies	✓		
Market Research Firms	✓		
Government Agencies—Non-Regulatory	✓	✓	✓
Regulators	✓		✓
Technical Subject Matter Experts	✓	✓	✓
R&D Centers	✓		
Trade Associations/Lobbyists	✓		
Friends/Relatives	✓	✓	✓
Databases	✓	✓	✓
Legal Records/Government Archives	✓	✓	✓
Direct Contact	✓	✓	✓
Labor Union Leadership	✓	✓	✓
Government Owner Representatives	✓	✓	✓

Networking is particularly important where privately held firms, foreign firms, or enterprise units smaller than the level reported in annual reports or SEC documents are the target of your inquiry.

Some foreign firms may be of sufficient size and presence in the U.S. market that SEC documentation is mandated. Always pursue the EDGAR database. Foreign stock exchanges will require some reporting. Two caveats: they rarely match the rigor of the SEC and documents may require translation. Sometimes MITI, the Japanese trade agency, offers good reports in their database in multiple languages.

With the noted exception of foreign firms appearing in SEC archives or similar foreign databases, the missing information is formidable. In this case, there is value in advancing the investment in networking.

Here are the most useful sources: the target's suppliers, customers, bankers, and employees. We advocate transparency in all transactions. That is, tell the parties you are considering partnering and want to understand their corporate culture, business practices, and the character of key personalities in ownership or leadership. Template 2-9 is the draft of a letter to prospective partners explaining your intent to learn more about them.

Some like to invite the other party to do the same, and still others feel the inquiry should include the involvement of a professional investigator. Due diligence gives the opportunity to get at the details if things get serious. Doing your own homework as a business person or professional in someone's employ is very different than an inquiry by investigators. In emerging economies fraught with criminality, investigation is justified.

TEMPLATE 2-9: CONTACT/FOCUS LETTER

(ALLIANCE DEVELOPMENT CASE ILLUSTRATION)

PERSONAL & CONFIDENTIAL

Dear Potential Partner,

I am writing to present for your consideration an idea with the promise for substantial mutual benefit. I have thought very carefully about this for some time, and believe now is the appropriate time to get in touch with you.

Here at our company we have invested extensively in plastics as a logical extension of our products' future performance. As you know, we have a strong, loyal following to our plastics products and are always looking for means to strengthen our market presence. Plastics is one of the most important ways for us to add value to consumers. This philosophy of providing consumers with superior performance has been rewarding for all of us.

I assumed the responsibility of Regional Account Manager last year and was charged to secure our plastics business and grow. As you know, our company is a team-based organization. While I am your key contact, what I have learned from you along with my own ideas are integrated into this team process. We see you as having high potential to be a partner in bringing additional value-added products and services to the consumer. We are fully in accord on this view with our National Accounts Management Team and with the Board of Directors.

A significant challenge for enhancing our current collaboration to become strategic partners is Project Plastic. We have considered two paths for introducing Project Plastic: leveraging our own resources or integrating our resources with strategic partners. Our conclusion is that getting together with strategic partners might be potentially more effective, along with introducing the appropriate intellectual property agreements which could be a step-out position for our industry.

I am an admirer of your company and have made an effort to learn about your strategic interests. Our recent partnership conference helped us to understand your expectations and preferences. To learn more about how we might mutually support one another, I invite you to dinner some time next week.

I plan to telephone your office early next week.

Sincerely yours,

Template 2-10 guides you through the network interviewing process. It addresses how to start the conversation, how to phrase and sequence questions, and provides general tips on getting exacting information, along with suggestions about handling challenges to the conversation.

TEMPLATE 2-10: AN INTERVIEW FORMAT FOR NETWORKING INQUIRY

STEP 1: ESTABLISH RAPPORT AND EXPRESS INTENT
  A. **NEW CONTACT:** BRIEFLY EXPLAIN WHO YOU ARE. IF LINKED BY SOMEONE—EXPLAIN THE RELATIONSHIP. BE CLEAR AS TO YOUR INTENT. (E.G., "I AM CONSIDERING BUILDING A PARTNERING RELATIONSHIP WITH XYZ. TO CONVINCE OTHERS ON MY TEAM THIS IS A GOOD IDEA, I AM LEARNING ABOUT THEM FROM PEOPLE WHO ARE IN POSITIONS TO OBSERVE XYZ. THAT IS WHY I WANT TO TAKE A FEW MOMENTS OF YOUR TIME TO UNDERSTAND YOUR VIEW OF XYZ.")
  B. **ESTABLISHED CONTACT:** GO OVER A NON-SENSITIVE TOPIC—A BRIEF REMINISCENCE OR, BETTER YET, SHARE SOME NEWS OF INTEREST TO THE PERSON. AGAIN, BE CLEAR ON YOUR INTENT. (E.G., "I AM CONSIDERING A PARTNERING RELATIONSHIP. TO SELL THE IDEA HERE, I NEED TO BE ABLE TO DEMONSTRATE I HAVE DONE MY HOMEWORK ON XYZ. YOU'RE IN A GOOD POSITION TO OBSERVE XYZ; I AM CALLING TO GET YOUR VIEWS.")

STEP 2: ASK BROAD QUESTIONS
THIS IS DONE FOR AT LEAST TWO REASONS:
  • TO CAST A LINE AND SEE WHAT YOU CATCH WITHOUT PREJUDICING A RESPONSE WITH A MORE DIRECTED QUESTION.
  • TO STRENGTHEN RAPPORT AND BUILD TO MORE SENSITIVE QUESTIONS WHICH MAY FOLLOW.

POSSIBLE QUESTIONS:
  • IN GENERAL, WHAT IS YOUR OPINION OF XYZ?
  • HOW WOULD YOU DESCRIBE XYZ TO AN INVESTMENT ANALYST (OR TO YOUR STOCKBROKER)?
  • IF YOU WERE ASKED TO BUY STOCK IN XYZ, WHAT WOULD YOU THINK ABOUT FIRST?

STEP 3: PROBE FOR MORE INFORMATION WITH GENERAL PROMPTS
  • TELL ME MORE.
  • ANYTHING ELSE?
  • DESCRIBE THAT, PLEASE.
  • HOW DO YOU MEAN?
  • GIVE EXAMPLES.

STEP 4: ASK DIRECTIVE QUESTIONS
  • WHAT IS THEIR STRATEGIC DIRECTION?
  • ARE THEY DOING ANYTHING SPECIAL IN HOW THEY APPROACH CUSTOMERS?
  • ARE THEY HAVING ANY PARTICULAR PROBLEM? LITIGATION? FINANCIAL PROBLEMS? INTERNAL TURMOIL? ABOUT TO BE SOLD? ENVIRONMENTAL ISSUES? CUSTOMER PROBLEMS?
  • WHERE ARE THEY HEADED IN TECHNOLOGY?
  • WHO ARE THEY PARTNERING WITH NOW? HOW IS IT WORKING?
  • WHERE IN THE WORLD ARE THEY DOING BUSINESS? WHICH MARKETS ARE ESTABLISHED, HAVING PROBLEMS, OR JUST GETTING STARTED?
  • DESCRIBE XYZ'S THREE GREATEST CHALLENGES.
  • WHO ARE THEIR KEY PLAYERS? WHAT ARE THEIR BACKGROUNDS?
  • HOW DO DECISIONS GET MADE?
  • DO THEY HAVE RESOURCES TO GROW?
  • WHAT ARE THEY CHARGING FOR ABC PRODUCT/SERVICE?
  • WHAT INCENTIVES DO THEY OFFER THEIR CHANNEL?

TEMPLATE 2-10: AN INTERVIEW FORMAT FOR NETWORKING INQUIRY *(CONTINUED)*

STEP 5: PROBE QUESTIONS WITH GENERAL PROMPTS

STEP 6: DO NOT "OVERSTAY" YOUR WELCOME. EXPRESS APPRECIATION.
LEAVE THE DOOR OPEN FOR FUTURE COMMUNICATION. ASK FOR A GOOD CONTACT WHO COULD HELP AS MUCH OR MORE.

GENERAL TIPS:
- OUTLINE QUESTIONS BEFOREHAND. CHOOSE 3 AS A MINIMUM INQUIRY. BE PREPARED TO ASK MORE IF OTHER PERSON FEELS COMFORTABLE TO CONTINUE TALKING.
- TAKE COPIOUS NOTES.
- DO NOT HESITATE TO ASK FOR NAMES, TELEPHONE NUMBERS—GET CORRECT SPELLINGS.
- LET PEOPLE ABOVE YOU KNOW WHAT YOU ARE DOING JUST IN CASE A PLAY IS WORKING WITHOUT YOUR KNOWLEDGE OR A SENSITIVITY EXISTS WHICH PRECLUDES YOUR EFFORT.

TYPICAL CHALLENGES:
1. WHAT'S IN IT FOR ME TO TELL YOU?
   "I AM NOT SURE. I CAN OFFER TO SHARE A SYNOPSIS OF WHAT I LEARN. WHAT IS YOUR E-MAIL OR FAX NUMBER? I'D APPRECIATE ANY THOUGHTS ON THE SYNOPSIS."
   "I WILL OWE YOU ONE."
2. CAN I TELL XYZ YOU CALLED?
   "I HAVE NOT TALKED TO THEM AS YET, AND I WOULD PREFER THEY HEAR IT FROM ME FIRST. BUT, IF NOT TELLING THEM CAUSES DISCOMFORT, THEN HERE IS WHAT I FEEL IS APPROPRIATE: I AM DOING SOME BRAINSTORMING AT THIS POINT IN TIME. IF IT EVOLVES INTO ANYTHING, OTHERS ON MY TEAM WILL HAVE TO CONSIDER THIS ALONG WITH MANY OTHER POSSIBILITIES. AT THIS POINT, I RESPECT THEIR POTENTIAL AND VALUE WHAT CAN BE LEARNED TO ACCURATELY DESCRIBE XYZ TO MY COLLEAGUES. IF THEY WANT TO CONTACT ME, FEEL FREE TO GIVE MY NAME AND NUMBER."

REFERENCES

1. Sahlman, William A., "How to Write a Great Business Plan," *Harvard Business Review,* July-August, 1997, p 99.

2. Hamel, Gary, and C. K. Prahalad, *Competing for the Future,* Harvard Business School Press, Boston, 1994.

3. Porter, Michael E., *Competitive Advantage: Creating and Sustaining Superior Performance*, Free Press, New York, 1985.

4. Stewart, G. Bennett, III, *The Quest for Value: The EVA™ Management Guide,* Harper Press, 1991.

5. Copeland, Tom, Tim Koller, and Jack Murrin, *Valuation,* Second Edition, John Wiley and Sons, 1996.

6. Luehrman, Timothy A., "What's It Worth? A General Manager's Guide to Valuation," *Harvard Business Review,* May–June, 1997, p 132+.

7. Luehrman, Timothy A., "Using APV: A Better Tool for Valuing Operations," *Harvard Business Review,* May–June, 1997, p 145+.

CHAPTER 3

Refining Business Intent

The day we can ignore complexity is gone, but does this mean we must swim in the details, to risk drowning in the minutia? No, refinement is appropriate. Surprisingly, the process normally takes less time than the meeting time typically invested in planning. Why is this so?

Time gets wasted in planning business intent and growth for three reasons. One is that poor group dynamics are used. People feel manipulated by agendas that restrain and by advisers who attempt by spin or coercion to narrow discourse to their view. In the meetings, everyone applauds the "new openness" and the opportunity to speak out. In the halls, the discussion heads south.

More pedestrian than hallway coups, but equally impacting is not having a forum to sift through the facts. In the absence of a forum and the chance to explore alternatives, people develop a position and advocate across their networks. The debate is done without a means to confront, to build on others' ideas, and to interweave differing interpretations—which in juxtaposition reveal new ways of interpreting. The dominant politics will win out over the careful consideration of the facts and insights that shareholders have already paid for.

The other barrier to effectiveness in planning is duplication of effort. Work is duplicated among factions, between levels, and across functions. Failing to have an effective and thorough forum compounds problems by generating confusion that absorbs energy and time unnecessarily.

To address this situation, we offer a process for managing complexity and forthrightly refining information into a business intent. The process is outlined in Figure 3-1:

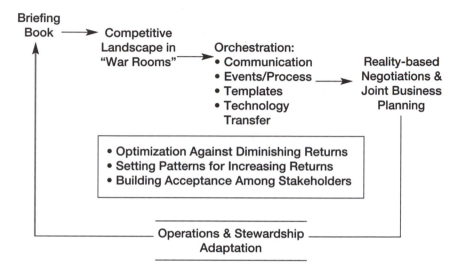

Figure 3-1. Complexity facilitation process.

The process is initiated with the careful compilation of information in a briefing book. Often in the decision-making phase, the briefing book is updated or reissued as war rooms are repeated. The briefing book helps get everyone on the same page. In the first war room, less than half the participants will have given the briefing book full attention. After that session, the book will get close attention by all.

The briefing book reports the landscape information. As presented in Figure 3-2, preliminary analysis and identification of patterns is completed. Expect these to be debated. The key is not to defend the briefing book contents but to offer it as a point of departure for discussion.

Note that select items are underscored in the illustration of the briefing book topics. They warrant additional attention. The first is *partner profile*. A profile of partners and prospective partners is taken from the competitor database to provide a report on what is currently known about them. War room reviews demonstrate the potential of broad involvement in commercial intelligence. Inviting war room participants to add what they know will enhance profiles.

The partner profile influences a war room in a way that is important to customer intimacy. At the core of any human communication or learning is a simple principle: Start where they are—not where you want them to be. You begin with what a person knows and wants. Then you can build an agenda for persuasion to your view or idea. The partner profile is the intelligence to know how to listen, where to begin, and what to say first.

Third party interviewing is often completed in preparation for war rooms. Consultants are able to learn perceptions of you held by prospective partners. Insight to the other party's expectations, or what relationships need improvement, is likely.

A review of the *cultural due diligence* should address two issues: First, how compatible are you and the prospective partner? Give particular attention to this if an ally to acquire or conventional acquisition strategy is planned. Second, taking into account the first point, how is it best to integrate the different cultures? Too often, regardless of the compatibility, the financial terms or other benefits are considered more important and the deal gets done. "Working things out" then becomes the challenge.

The war rooms may do little more than raise the issue of cultural compatibility, as good information may not be available at this juncture. What is accomplished is awareness as to the importance of cultural integration and its impact to extracting value from operation.

A major contribution for war rooms is the juxtaposition of *capital deployment* options. In planning—in particular, growth discussions—a review of capital requirements for all projects may overlook ongoing business. On the other hand, new business may be sidelined. Or, new business gets treated as though it were a special case, permitting general expense and operational budgets for other businesses to "carry" the initial investments.

These choices can easily sidetrack value. For this reason, we recommend that each project should be measured on its true merits, and the Shareholder Value Added (SVA) reported for every project. After all, SVA reports the life revenue of the project. It is explicit about the front-end investment needed and its impact on cash flow. What is expected for a project warranting support is that the latter years' revenues more than offset the initial investment. Such transparency defeats the need to play the game of "hide the initial cost."

In the pursuit of a global agenda, there is another important reason to address capital deployment comparisons. Comparing domestic and international opportunities sparks the debate about emphasis—at home or abroad. Again, one side or the other might otherwise dominate and avoid economic realities—short-term or long-term.

Going abroad is more often a narcotic which tempts and rushes capital without careful consideration. But, in some organizations, international projects are ignored. Emerging economies in particular may be avoided. In place of finding out where these economies may be important to strategy, they are passed over in decision making about capital.

The contrasting of SVAs among domestic and international projects permits international projects to stand on their own, on the terms of their local conditions. The value extracted is what is compared. This prompts home offices to leave international projects alone and not try to draw them into cultural conformity, or align them to financial reporting practices inconsistent with regulatory or business practices of the country in which the business is conducted. Further, currency variations are not used as excuses but are factored as a risk management issue—for domestic as well as for international projects.

Investment vulnerability is as much an education as it is a risk-management exercise. Inclusion in the briefing book prevents risks from being set aside. Inclusion promotes education and understanding of unlikely risks.

Rigorous Business Analytics & Patterns	**Partner Profile**
Third-Party Interviews	**Business Intelligence on Existing Business Relationships**
Learning Issues & Articles	**Current Performance Summary**
Economic Models for Growth	**Opportunities/Risk Landscape**
Cultural Due Diligence	**Capital Deployment Comparisons**
Investment Vulnerability	**Technology Summary**
Shareholder Value-Add	**Strategic Intent**

Figure 3-2. Briefing document.

The war room is depicted in Figure 3-3a–e. War rooms are a swirl of facts covering technology, commercial information, financial engineering, organization, and orchestration. The dynamic in the room is interactive, complex, and turbulent. In the beginning, it appears to be a well-orchestrated briefing, with almost a seminar-like pace for learning. Then the volume of information facilitates comprehension and creative insight (see Figure 3-4).

In Chapter 4, we will explain that our capacity to comprehend is determined both by what we absorb and what is around us. Our mind functions by what is in our memory and consciousness, as well as by what our senses are simultaneously inputting to our mind. If our environment is an efficient processor of information, as is a war room, we are less dependent on memory and our own speed of comprehension. The richness of thought in the display of information, the tête-à-tête blistering in sidebar debates, or group interactions among participants are catalysts to a higher plane of thought. In this manner, we "build" on the ideas of others in nanoseconds, and leap to still newer ideas as the world outside and inside mix in the complexity of our mind. The concept is called adaptive cognition.

Additional benefits are accrued from the war room. One is ownership for results. War rooms leave people with a sense of meaningful involvement, and their personal responsibility to make things happen is reinforced or expanded. The other advantage is yet one more enhancement to creativity. That is, non-linear solutions are easier to be seen in a war room setting.

Not only do illustrations and posting of ideas and multimedia make non-linear insights possible, the war rooms mix participants having different levels, functions, and backgrounds. The mix prompts challenges and introduces ideas which might otherwise be ignored. A review of Chapter 4 is appropriate in preparation for facilitating or participating in a war room. Chapter 4 covers complexity dynamics and the substance to a business landscape.

Using PC networks and multimedia, a focus is maintained. Ideas are managed within and across topics in a war room. Interactions and complex subjects are tracked. Select participants may come and go according to their unique contribution. Technical experts may attend more frequently for technology discussions. This is not to exclude them from other subjects. They can be very impacting to business discussions. Their intervention, however, may be more appropriate or poignant at critical intersections in the session rather than throughout.

(text continued on page 64)

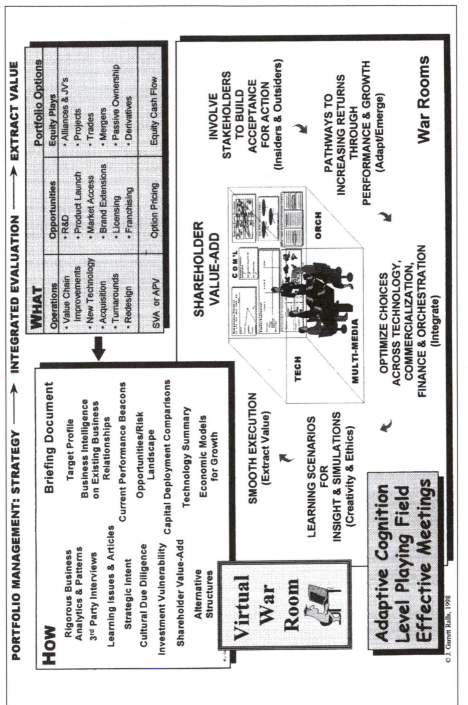

Figure 3-3a. The war room.

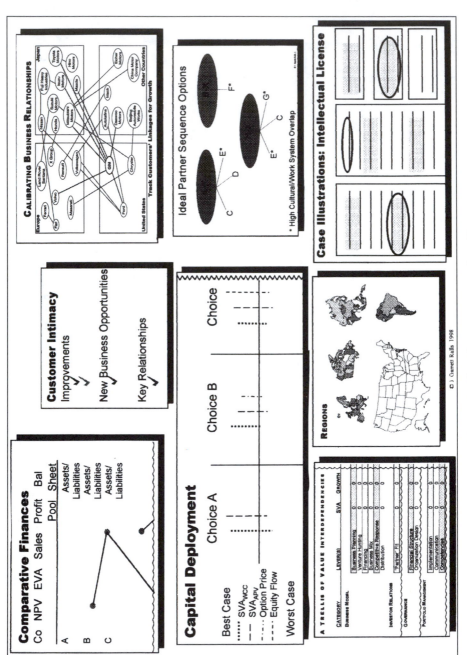

Figure 3-3b. The commercial wall.

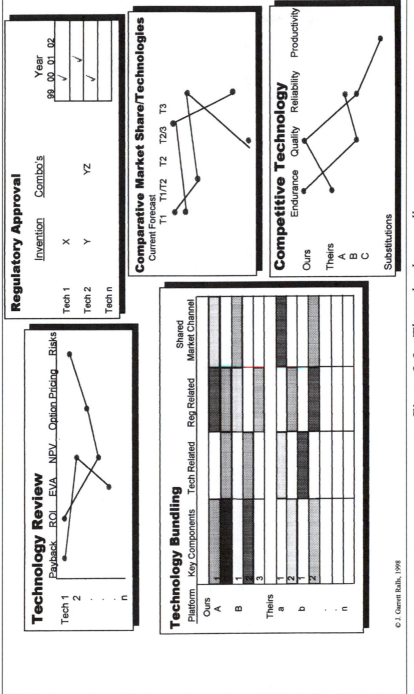

Figure 3-3c. The technology wall.

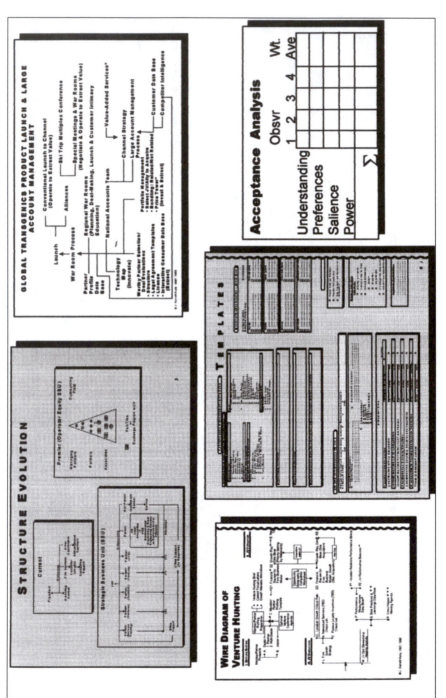

Figure 3-3d. The orchestration wall.

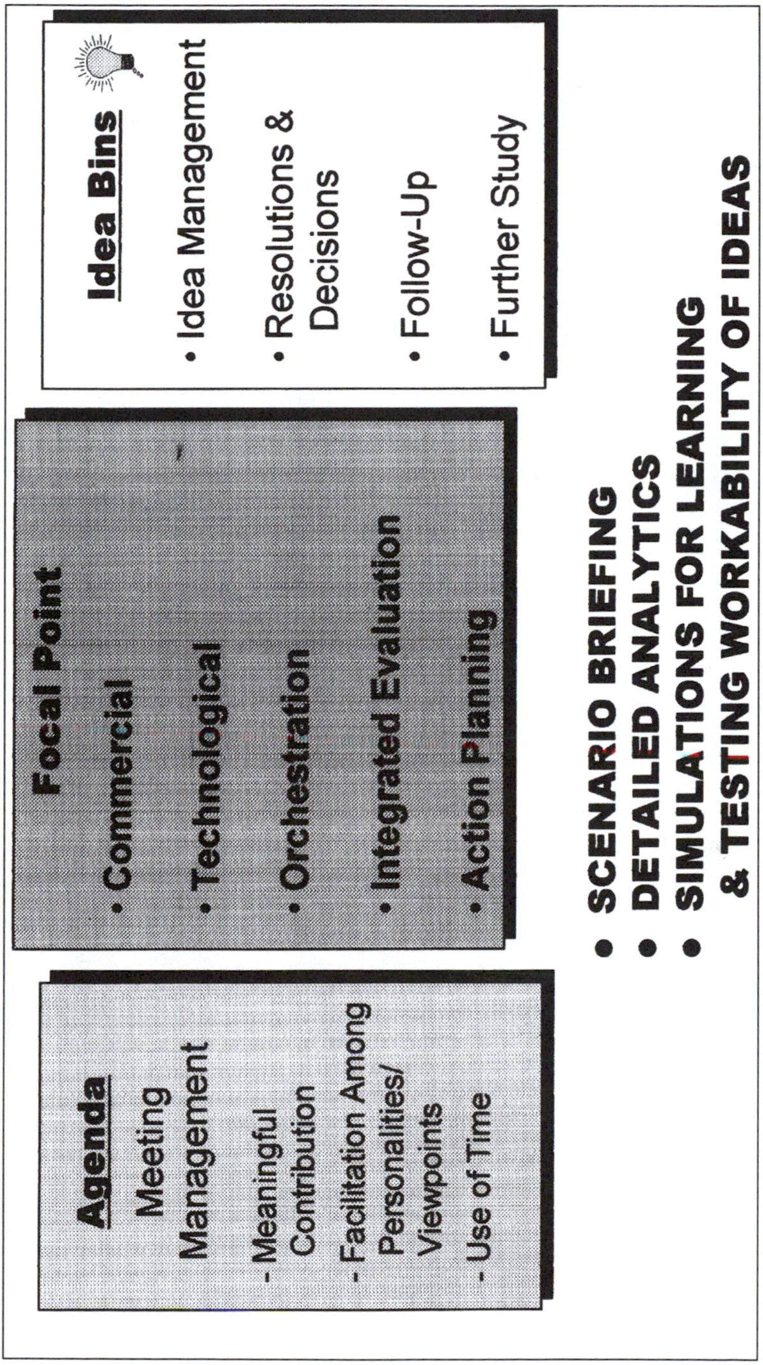

Figure 3-3e. The multi-media wall.

(text continued from page 58)

The decision to involve or have selective involvement is not subject to any formula. It is a matter of judgment. Consideration must be given to the use of the person's time, talent, and the timing for maximum impact. Regardless of who or what expertise, there are usually strong personalities to be facilitated. Superior and advanced facilitation is required to sustain a level playing field among participants for discovery and discussion.

War room sessions are typically a day or two in length. Longer than this and participants fatigue, producing diminishing results. The best setting is off-site, and the best schedule is an open-ended day. Start early and go until the group decides to end. Most experienced war room participants will continue for 10 hours but will not reconvene in the evening. The opportunity to subgroup or have personal reflective time in the evening can be important to the second day's performance. Many firms find two to four war rooms may be needed to reach decisions about growth and partnering, and then to plan the orchestration of the strategies.

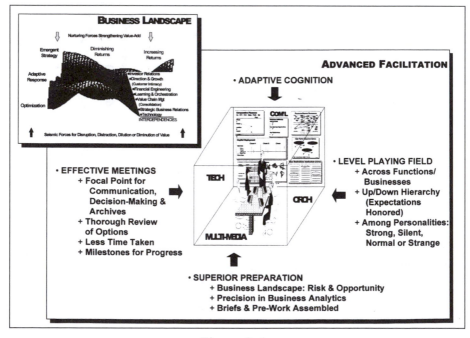

Figure 3-4.

Some organizations elect to structure a virtual war room. There are two aspects to such an effort. One is involving people in diverse locations without making them travel. Their input can be focused or, with media tools, as active as a direct participant's. The second aspect of the virtual war room is participation between meetings across an organization, again without regard to location or time of day. The war room is enhanced and inputs are provided to better the basis for decisions in later sessions.

War rooms are effective executive development experiences. People from cross functions can learn from one another. The group dynamics and the display of information does not put the uninformed at risk. They can learn at their own pace and participate when they feel comfortable.

War rooms can be used for simulations to instruct those responsible for implementation of action plans. Negotiating teams, operators, and others benefit from scenario testing and exposure to the complexity of all pertinent information. Participants in war rooms quickly learn the basis for decision-making and the sensitivities for managing value. One-day or shorter war room sessions can be very effective means for communicating to stakeholders, investors, and employees. Again, the participants comprehend strategies quickly and enjoy the experience in a way that promotes ownership for decisions.

Some people think that the term "war room" brings the wrong connotation to mind for the 21st century. We don't argue with this and invite clients to call the sessions whatever they choose. Though there is a war of sorts, it is not among humankind. The conflict is knowledge's quest to conquer chaos.

Figure 3-5 represents the array of business, group dynamic, and learning processes that are important to capturing chaos and managing complexity through war rooms.

We participated in war rooms during games sponsored by the Department of Defense to understand the transformation that defense industries faced with the end of the Cold War. This experience led to involvement in war rooms for defense planning and intelligence simulations. We were impressed with how diverse, detailed information was managed. The linear process, however, defeated creativity, and the command-and-control atmosphere stymied involvement.

We experimented with substituting business analytics and introducing creative problem-solving techniques. We further refined the process

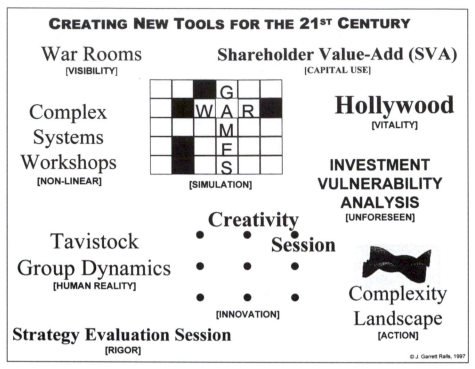

Figure 3-5.

by introducing learning approaches from what we called "complex systems" workshops in which decision-making was interspersed with briefings and learning simulations, as means for improving the quality of decisions.

No Sleeping in War Rooms

Were this not enough, we visited Emmy-nominated director Keiren Kasun-Fisher on the set of Nickelodeon's *Roundhouse,* a variety show for children. Though the attention span of thirteen-year-olds should not be equated to adults, the differences are not great. What we found by observing transitions between comedy, dance, and dramatic skits is that movement among subjects and activities can be done in a way that a common theme is supported and attention maintained. For war rooms, we found that changing the pace, facilitating movement between briefings and discussions, and sometimes using small groups and visualizations facilitated communication, understanding, and the quality of discussion. We also found that our participants remained awake and enthusiastic.

The next four visualizations are representative of tools often used to gain attention, summarize complex issues with diagrams and icons, and foster interactions with information. We have learned a lot by studying the works of Dave Sibbet of Grove Consultants in San Francisco[1] and Edward Tufte of Yale University.[2] Both offer insight on how to portray information visually, save time, make complexity easier to understand, and invite group participation through the manner in which information is displayed.

It is important to recognize that adults are very visual in learning and absorbing information. Consult Sibbet and Tufte for methods of display. We coach people to visualize their own illustration and then use Sibbet's techniques to bring the illustration into being. Tufte offers technique, and much about how icons with the display of information can tell a story better than words. We find Tufte more useful in understanding what is happening in the eye of the beholder. Here are a few hints about visualization in war rooms that we put forth based on our experience:

Making the Walls Speak for You

- If you are interactive with a group with icons and illustrations, develop icons and sketches ahead of time—this way you are ready for ideas as you hear them.
- In interactive settings, make certain you or your machines do not slow down the momentum within the group.
- Illustrations prepared ahead of time should be given more attention for showing relationships. Networks, sequences, and other relationships should be well thought out: Does the picture make the complexity easier to grasp? Are relationships accurately displayed or is the drawing more conveniently drawn or printed in this manner? Do relationships or matters of importance that are introduced by the drawing really exist? (Do not stymie creativity but also do not introduce fallacies.)
- Avoid being too cute or too fancy—keep things simple, legible, and easy to comprehend
- Portray complicated ideas in a mural or with a storyboard in which ideas develop across panels. This should be done in a manner to show how things unfold, why patterns are developing, and what outcomes can be expected.

(continued)

Making the Walls Speak for You *(continued)*

- Provide a means for editing—do not make things so fancy they cannot be enhanced.
- Provide "lap" copies for the briefing book and as handouts during sessions. Catalog the illustrations and maintain earlier versions.
- Allocate subject matter by "zones" within the room. As illustrated above, have one wall for Technology Issues, another for Financial Engineering Issues, and so on. Police each area.
- Manage ideas carefully. Have "idea bins" in which thoughts are captured on the walls, in an interactive format. Segment by zones and have a general idea bin. Collate after each session. Within an idea bin, list separately: ideas, follow-up actions, and needs for further information.
- Maintain a central focus. If there is one illustration which is capturing attention, bring it forward to the central focus.
- Pace the review of illustrations to the group's inclination. Go faster or slower according to their expectations. Be careful in presentation— yours or others—that not too much detail is explored and the review stifles progress or depletes energy from the group.
- Have fun—include whimsy value-adds by eliciting humor and inspiring creativity.

Figure 3-6 illustrates how a U.S. client used multiple relationships with Japanese dynastic families to access a waste management technology. Shown are how families link on different interests and how effective linkages can be made by moving among interests.

In Figure 3-7, the network of a client's customer is used to sort through prospective overseas partners. This technique was introduced to us by Dr. Kathleen Robertson of The Robertson Group. The importance of relationships can be discerned and sequencing in the courtship for partners can be mapped. The diagram indicates what other firms may share or have by way of access. These displays are dynamic. All relationships are in movement and this complication needs stewardship.

COMPETING INVESTMENTS: MOVIES, WATER RIGHTS, OIL EXPLORATION

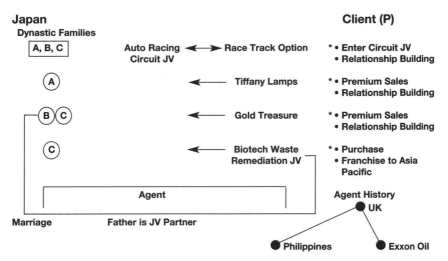

Figure 3-6. *Dynastic family global venturing.*

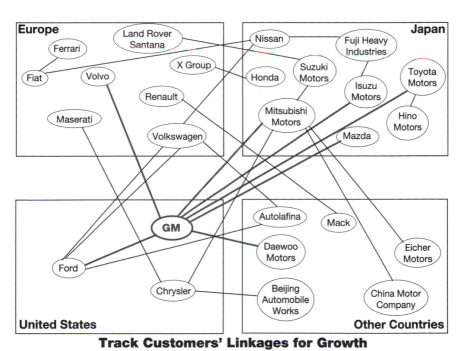

Track Customers' Linkages for Growth

Figure 3-7. *Calibrating business relationships.*

In the next two figures, we see templates for examining the influence of dynastic families in funding decisions within emerging economies. These templates prove useful as components in tracking the current relationships within a joint venture as illustrated in the second figure. One of the challenges for the firm was to find out how to contain criminal influences impacting their JV with a foreign government. In a broader way, this illustrates how complex relationships across firms, customers, governments, and communities impact value. Whether domestic or international, knowing who will influence progress and how they will do so is important knowledge. Sorting it all out is complex.

Figure 3-8. Emerging economies: funding influences.

All of these visualizations and others come together in the visual representation of the landscape as seen below. S-Plus is the software available for creating a topographical representation of forces and impacts on any subject, including a business. This software is available from Mathsoft, Inc. The software does not automatically create a business landscape. It does permit coding in numerous variables you see on your landscape. Careful judgment of these variables then projects a three-dimensional representation of emerging opportunities, the impending influences to value, or waves that the firm may ride to extract value.

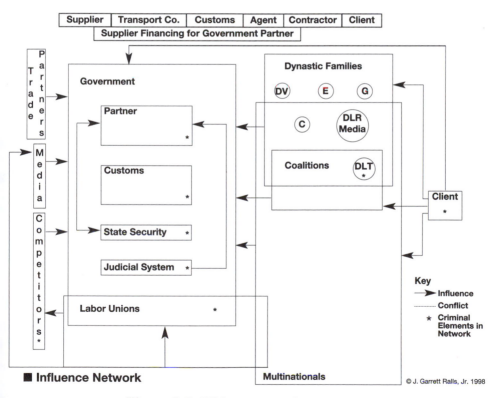

Figure 3-9. JV in an emerging economy.

The good work of the briefing documents and the war room sessions is to provide a business direction. Specifically, the operation of the business and the consideration of new business must be determined.

REFERENCES

1. Sibbet, David, "I See What You Mean," *A Workbook/Guide to Group Graphics,* Sibbet & Associates, 1981.

2. Tufte, Edward R., *Visual Explanations,* Graphics Press, 1997.

CHAPTER 4

War Room Strategies

WAR ROOMS

The sift of information and collection of interactions leads to tangible outcomes for creating value. As previously mentioned, the involvement itself can be motivating. Substantial knowledge is gained. But where does this lead?

First is the self-reflection derived from the intensive business review. What is headed our way? How may we adapt or ride the wave to exploit its inherent opportunity? What can we do to make a difference that is material and important? Does it make sense to continue in existing businesses? If not, how best to exit and extract remaining value? If so, what do we need to secure or grow business? Are there new businesses we need to consider? If so, what do we need—money, talent, knowledge? How do we access these and make things happen?

These questions force you to contrast capital projects, and lead to your articulation of strategies. In turn, these strategies enable a firm to position itself to set the best patterns in the marketplace. Among these strategies, or in an aggregate of strategies, will probably be a plan for growth. Taken together, the strategies sketch a route through the landscape.

What surfaces from these strategies is another tangible outcome from war rooms: a map to the future based on an interpretation of the landscape. Progress across the route respects the contours of the landscape, along with trends ebbing and eroding the landscape, and emerging forces from your firm.

Timing for approaching certain parties is revealed in war rooms, and this sets the speed along the route through the landscape. The best observers for various players, forces in the marketplace, places across the business landscape, and key subjects are identified. Processes are defined for integrating knowledge as it is needed, or forces relevant points to our attention. Observer inputs will calibrate the speed of progress and cause detours.

The best sequence for approaching prospective partners when there are multiple possibilities is outlined. In this pursuit of partners, there is a very lively process: If refusal is experienced, where best to try next? The landscape can be in constant movement. Others may already be there ahead of you on the subject of interest, or they may have involvement on other agendas, blocking you from access. Or, you may simply decide to pass on an opportunity because it could entangle you with a competitor, or with an undesirable party or circumstance. The route may need to be reset many times in the journey to eventually link with the right partners.

Another tangible outcome for war rooms is to define your own decision making. First, parameters for investment and risk are set in the war room sessions. Then decision-making paths are outlined. As things change, or as opportunities approach the final moves, who makes the last decision? Along the way, who needs to be kept informed, and what audiences for decisions need to be orchestrated?

The war room results in an action plan with clear responsibilities defined. Scenarios with positions are agreed upon and simulated. Knowledge of how to conduct negotiations, initiate cultural integration, successfully start up operations smoothly, and promote continuous value-added growth is developed and nourished (see Figure 4-1).

Above all, war rooms promote insight. Insight is a tangible when it results in new ways of sustaining or enhancing value. War room settings bring forward, in an accelerated format, understanding of what truly diminishes or advances value.

Although war rooms are not essential to different thinking, they are more likely to make it happen. The war room is an event in the life of the firm. In this event, the rigidity inborn to established practice and habit meets the chaos of the marketplace. The chaos is almost overwhelming. The discourse in a war room flails at the inadequacies of

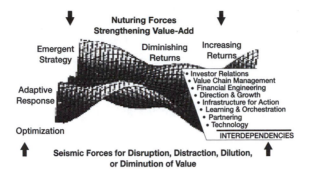

Figure 4-1. Complexity landscape model for business.

old policies and methods. The rush from broadened awareness adds to the feeling of being overwhelmed. Yet, this is reality and avoiding reality serves no purpose.

There is a drama in war rooms. It is the confrontation to the chaos. Choices are made. A focus results. The choices are made by those who are well informed. The choices are made by those who see the breadth, depth, seismic movement, and purposeful launches of energy, effort, and time throughout the business landscape. The participants perceive more choice. They understand better how choices play out, and what contingencies are available. They use focus as a tool to test the need to adapt and to guide adaptation, as well as to guide emerging action.

Focus sets a momentum as well as a direction. The focus contributes to a pattern for dominance. In this way, rigidity melts away into flexibility and enables the transformation of the turbulence into value. This is the business acumen of the 21st century and the beauty in a commerce we have yet to experience.

Defining Growth

Getting to the tangibles surrounding growth strategies can be involved in war room discussions. In the briefing book in support of war rooms and within the war room, we recommend first defining growth interests. Outlined in the following text are questions found to be useful in fleshing out growth possibilities. Primarily, they focus on the intensive business review inputs to the business landscape.

Growth Interests

Customer expectations:
[Learnings from customer feedback or analytics]

Competencies to be extended:
[Linear extensions to current capabilities]

Competencies to be developed:
[Derive from Intensive Business Review]

Competencies to be acquired:
[Derive from "Competencies to be Developed." Select those which must be obtained quickly to take advantage in the marketplace or are less costly to purchase than develop.]

Competitive leverage opportunities:
[Assess advantages from competitors' assessments]

These inquiries prompt strategy discussions, with emphasis on what needs to be developed in terms of competencies and capabilities. This discussion determines how best to obtain such resources. In our global world, more often than not, the answer is partnering.

To illustrate what growth might look like, we posited current competencies and transformational competencies for a client owning 16 global businesses. The transformational competencies speak to growth issues. The following table presents our thoughts that elicited "different thinking." Including preliminary briefs of this nature helps learning and introduces new ideas.

Determining how to move forward means translating growth interests into growth pursuits. Again, below are key questions for defining growth strategies. These questions focus on the means for making growth happen: consolidation within an industry or sector, extending market share for an existing business, or entry into new business. As noted below, there are several means for achieving entry.

With answers to the above, a firm can then articulate its "growth mandates." Following are what might have been growth mandates for one of the 16 businesses from our earlier illustration of product competencies.

First, our business decides to take advantage of global consolidation. It sets this mandate:

Grow the Business by Absorbing Domestic and International Firms

---

Growth Pursuits

Rationalization Opportunities:
Share Expansion:
Entry:

- Technology
- Services
- Financial Engineering
- Channel Access
- Globalization Opportunities
- Acquisitions
- Privatization Opportunities (National Assets)

Table 4-1.
Product Competencies

Current Competency	Transformation Competency
• Products Marketing-Sales Transactions (Conception to Execution)	• ASEAN/Asia Growth Participation
• Channel Access	• Global Distribution
• Logistics Management	• Matrix for Cross-Sell Among Product Lines (Internal Interconnect Agreement)
• Research & Development	• Licensing
• Product Technology Commercialization	• Technology Transfer to Developing Markets
• Engineering/Manufacturing	• Project Management for Developing Markets
• Procurement	
• Strategic Planning	• Financial Engineering Services
• Corporate Finance	• Fund Management
• Competitor Benchmarking	• Business Brokering
• Market Research	• Alliance Management

Then they decide there is an important opportunity to license technology in three Pacific Rim countries and set this mandate:

Grow the Business by Licensing Technology in Countries X, Y, and Z

Finally, they see their special access to favorable credit terms and to their own wealth as cause to enter into brokering deals in their industry, in allied industries, and among their value chain. Given the volume of deal-making ahead for global consolidation, they develop a tactic and a mandate:

Tactic: Acquire a Boutique International Investment Banking Firm

**Grow the Business Through Financial Engineering
of Our Value Chain**

This mandate could involve several activities: the acquisition of the investment banking capability, the consolidation, the incorporation of licensing to the new entity, or the introduction of new credit and derivative plays into the channel.

Mandates require strategies and tactics to support them. We recommend that these projects forecast specific outcomes which are measurable. Primarily, we recommend that all capital projects be compared on the basis of SVA. The aggregation of strategies to a mandate should also be reported with SVA. Additional measurements for evaluating a project or its progress are noted in Figure 4-2.

In the war room, the strategies, tactics, and metrics for stewardship of performance and progress are developed for mandates. Then the prospective partners are identified with the timing and sequence for approaching partners. In conjunction, a means for keeping such information in real time to track changes in the landscape are concocted and responsibilities assigned.

All of this is done and orchestrated in the context of the entire business landscape. Strategies to achieve secured business, growth, and exits are planned and implemented in concert. Their stewardship is likewise examined for interdependence and mutual support.

Business Plans

Business plans are the next logical step to bringing forth strategy to reality. Where a new business is started, or where a joint venture/alliance

---

Metrics for Strategic Business Relationships

- Budget Variances
- Cost and Schedule
- Economic Value Added or Shareholder Value Added
- Cash Flow
- Net Income
- Market Share
- Rate of Return
- Innovations
- Product Performance
- Rework
- Guarantee Requests/Expenses
- Product Quality at Delivery
- Materials Usage/Expense
- Packaging Quality/Expense
- Transport Time Performance/Charges
- Technical Consults (Quality, Frequency, Duration)
- Complaints/Compliments

Issues/Opportunities for SBR Metrics

- Well-Developed Metrics are Essential to SBR Synergy and Conflict Resolution
- Draw Upon Dispute Resolution Accounting for Formula of Worth for Points in Time
- Need to be Comprehensive and Sensitive to All Possible SBR Outcomes

---

Figure 4-2.

is substantial, a business plan is appropriate (a good rule of thumb is a venture equal to the value of one of your business units, or with a value over $5 million). The war room can be used to outline and review a business plan. We recommend that the detail work be done outside a war room by a specialist team, much like the preparation of a briefing book.

Template 4-1 outlines how to develop a comprehensive business plan. This outline is especially useful in joint business planning among partners. Though the outline does not follow exactly the format recommended by William Sahlman earlier in this chapter, it does address his four key points of people, opportunity, and context, along with risk and reward.

TEMPLATE 4-1: BUSINESS PLAN GUIDE

EXECUTIVE SUMMARY
- CONCEPT
- MARKET OPPORTUNITY (INCLUDES RELATIVE POSITION TO OTHER OPPORTUNITIES)
- INVESTMENT, PAYBACK, PAY OUT, SVA
- CAPACITY TO MAKE HAPPEN
- BENEFITS AND RISKS TO ALL PARTIES

OPPORTUNITY OVERVIEW
- MARKET SITUATION ASSESSMENT (PRICE RANGE, VOLUME, COGS, ETC.)
- OPPORTUNITY: MATERIALITY (NET INCOME + SHARE)
- COMPETITOR/ SUBSTITUTION THREAT
- RISK ANALYSIS: FINANCIAL ENGINEERING ALTERNATIVES
- FINANCIAL FORECASTS (BOOTSTRAP/THRESHOLD/ AGGRESSIVE)

OPPORTUNITY SHARING
- INVESTMENT (CASH OR EQUIVALENT)
- PROFITS
- INFRASTRUCTURE
- TALENT
- FACILITIES
- BUSINESS PRACTICES: BUSINESS PLAN, MARKET LAUNCHES, ETC.
- EXIT STRATEGIES

MANAGEMENT & ORGANIZATION
- STRATEGY DEVELOPMENT AND STEWARDSHIP CYCLE/CONTENT (METRICS)
- DECISION-MAKING: DAILY-CASH MANAGEMENT-INVESTMENT
- KEY PLAYER-APPOINTMENT/ REMOVAL/ REPLACEMENT
- CONFLICT RESOLUTION-DISPUTE RESOLUTION PRACTICES
- TIMELINE: OPPORTUNITY COMMERCIALIZATION

The compilation of briefing books and participation in war rooms combine to complete nearly all the major work of preparing a business plan. The refinement of the information to a document takes little time and is more exacting in comparison to conventional planning. War rooms educate major players and decision makers. War rooms avoid the rush, and prevent cutting corners and political pressure to make plans artificially "fit" expectations of decision makers. Projections tend to be more realistic and well thought out. Businesses endorsed by war rooms generally have high potential.

Doing Joint Business Planning in a War Room

There are special settings of war rooms and applications of the complexity facilitation process related to business planning. One is preparation for negotiation and joint business planning. The war room follows an agenda much like it would for developing a business plan for a start-up, a major expansion, or an extension of a business. The business opportunity is defined against the landscape and an implementation plan is orchestrated. This work includes simulations and contingencies for negotiation.

In some settings, sessions will be conducted for financial backers to elicit their understanding and support. Other key stakeholders may have sessions planned for them or join in with the backers. This process is very impressive to bankers, in particular. Efforts of this nature can lead to the second special setting: a joint-planning war room where the goal is to develop a joint business plan.

War rooms for joint business planning can come before an agreement is reached. Negotiations may reach a point where a task force among partners is formed to create a business plan. The plan better defines value extraction and investment responsibilities. The business plan then becomes a sound basis for completing terms and conditions. The task force probably would never get launched were there not a very serious intent to complete the deal. The process of the task force is rare, and not because it does not make sense. There are few organizations that are secure in who they are and what they are about. When a task force has been used, however, there is a greater chance for the organization to survive and thrive.

In the future, we can anticipate more joint discussions prior to finalizing the deal—not from new joint ventures but from the logical extension of current ventures. As these ventures take on their own destiny and pursue growth, participants will file joint business plans with owners to revitalize their charter or embark on a new one. The force of numbers will make the practice of joint planning happen. This is something we consider to be a good thing.

What is more likely to be the case, though, is that the deal is done and a joint business plan is pursued. Our counsel to clients is to make joint business planning and its stewardship to be a term and condition in the agreement. It is sad that sound business practice should need to be made a legal requirement. Given recent history, however, this legal parameter is needed. Too many alliances and joint ventures fail, and do so because planning was poor or nonexistent.

Before exploring the nature of a joint business plan war room, consider what the business plan normally means to an entrepreneur. First, it makes the entrepreneur focus. The entrepreneur gathers all the information and boils it down to communicate to and persuade investors. Most often, the entrepreneur faces sophisticated and wily investors.

These investors play with their own money. Sophisticated is a word of special meaning. It translates in the common person's experience to mean that this investor is very wealthy and so well informed that the government agency charged with watching for fraudulent deals and the courts deem the person able to take the risk. These investors are a tough audience. They are practiced at it. They live by the deal and for the deal. By and large, bankers, including deal-making investment bankers, do not have the same level of involvement with transactions. Their risk is with other people's money, and time at work includes taking care of the institution as well as doing the deals. The investors are more focused.

Why express this here? The entrepreneur has a tough audience to face with the business plan. They are looking for the deal which will yield on the average a 35% compounded return. The corporate world is raising its hurdle but is still not in this league of difficulty.

Making the case to this audience is difficult and demands a systems view of what is at play. Questions may come on any subject. Experienced business people, the investors will foresee important interdependencies and test the entrepreneur's ability to grasp the complexities of the marketplace. Keep in mind, the high level of expectation is due in part to the rate of failure venture investors experience. The really good ones with impressive records are still as demanding about expected return.

The war room process to build a business plan approximates the entrepreneurial experience. The entrepreneur must build a team. The planning process must persuade key players to join in. This is a team-building effort achieving an order of magnitude greater than the best retreats. The debate, the shared work effort and, eventually, the common risks build ownership. Here, too, the joint business plan development is analogous.

Working the detail together builds ownership for the new, shared direction. The process permits a small group to work so closely that there is a good opportunity to appreciate cultural differences and work with them, past them, or through them. The common purpose of the business plan task permits little chance to avoid and provides powerful reasons for getting down to business. The bonds established yield returns beyond the business plan to where the work is done to extract value—not just eloquently describe it.

The point is what is available in business planning to the entrepreneur is accessible to partners in joint business planning. Business acumen will be better. Scrutiny to test the acumen will be more precise. The team completing the plan will learn about collaborating. They will communicate important information to others about how to work together as partners.

Joint business planning should be fully transparent for the overlap of interests. In other words, you reveal everything about yourselves that you are going to have in common. If there is concern that the deal may not be done, then construct the appropriate confidentiality agreements and contingent remedies. Transparency in the common area of work does not mean you share things which are not a part of the overlap.

Joint business planning should begin with an exploration of who the players are, what is expected of them back home, what they think the opportunity is, and how they normally go about doing planning. With candor, the group tasked with the business planning can then define what needs to be done, how to satisfy the expectations of all significant parties, and how they can work together. In some cases, their method of operation may take advantage of the skill of one party. At times, it may be best to do work in a new way. There may even be a need to do things two or more ways.

For example, valuation models may be different among partners. The best method could be more than one method. Clarify differences in interpretation and in outlooks of what can be the same data. Multiple models may eventually satisfy everyone and clarify why differences in interpretation exist. For example, a European, privately-held firm may use very different assumptions about accounting than those used by U.S. multinationals. By sharing models, the differences in use of terms or data eventually emerge.

Failure to reconcile makes the relationship fragile. Fragile does not mean defeat. It means special handling. Multiple valuation models and being transparent among partners about differences in approach require special care.

Joint planning sessions must be realistic. Building and sustaining teamwork, however, should never be used as an excuse for denying reality. Keeping everyone happy with false information or impressions about value will catch up with you.

There will be times when a caucus is needed. They will happen, so it is best to factor them in. Make requesting them okay and using them acceptable. Throughout the operation, they will be needed from time to time. In the early times together, such as in planning, it is best to get used to them and not be offended.

War rooms for joint business planning must be prepared differently from other war room sessions. Extraordinary effort needs to be made to make information credible. This includes getting information from all parties and ensuring that displays of information do not cause any bias. If bias is perceived, it must be addressed without defensiveness and handled in a timely manner. In these sessions, more attention must be given to ensure that everyone is on the same page.

Further, more effort must be made to foster a level playing field—among interactions and within databases. If the process must slow or stop to accommodate the demands of one side for data validation, so be it. Protect the credibility of the process. Reestablishing credibility comes at a higher cost than doing it right from the onset.

The marvel of joint business planning is that once all parties believe the intent to work together is genuine and that data are not cleverly manipulated—that they are as much in control as others in the process—the cooperation is extraordinary. Not only does the group tend to produce better results than like groups within any of the partners, participants report best-of-career team experiences and an unbeatable group harmony.

Three ingredients will sponsor success in joint business planning. We mentioned the importance of using complexity facilitation in a war room setting. The complication in the joint discussion is even greater than within a firm. The complexity warrants a similar investment.

Another key ingredient is pre-work on a collaborative philosophy which should be a part of the war room planning within the firm. The discussion leading to a statement of collaborative philosophy should be complete and should address topics outlined in Template 4-2. This is a mechanical tool for what must be a heart-and-soul conversation about values, business priorities, risk management, work culture norms, and expectations—both personal and corporate.

The statements will be important in educating players and expressing intent to partners. Their greatest value is in the awareness created by the experience of coining the statements. This is why it is important for some of those involved in drafting the statement to be active in the joint business planning and within the operating team.

TEMPLATE 4-2: COLLABORATIVE PHILOSOPHY GUIDE
- COMMERCIAL PURSUIT (PAYBACK, RETURN, LOSS)
- ETHICS
- TREATMENT OF SELVES
- TREATMENT OF OTHERS
  - COMPETITORS   + REGULATORS   + CONTRACTORS
  - CUSTOMERS   + VENDORS   + SISTER UNITS
- EXIT STRATEGY (METHOD, TRIGGER EVENT)
- SPONSORSHIP
- INFORMATION SHARING
- CONFLICT RESOLUTION
- OWNER STEWARDSHIP
- DECISION MAKING BY OWNERS
- OPERATIONAL DECISION MAKING
- LEVERAGE OF INFORMATION TECHNOLOGY (E-MAIL, TELECOM, GROUPWARE, ETC.)
- MIXING CORPORATE OR NATIONAL CULTURES
- CAPITAL FUNDS MANAGEMENT
- FINANCIAL ENGINEERING

The third key ingredient is to have a third-party facilitator. There should be someone in the room who hears all parties—not just their own school song. The facilitator's success is determined by progress in the joint venture. This should be a highly skilled individual, experienced in complexity facilitation and conflict resolution among strong personalities. Conventional meeting facilitation is not enough. Knowing how to group with different beginnings and possibly different expectations is critical to success.

Template 4-3 is a criteria for selecting advisors which also applies to third-party facilitators. Facilitators must also possess knowledge of advanced group dynamics as described above. Capable internal consultants may be competent to do the work. The risk is how this is seen by the other parties. Later in the process, internal consultants can be effective. At the onset and on the most sensitive issues, they will be suspect. Do not even consider teaming internal consultants from each party. This group would end up needing its own facilitator.

Table 4-2 lists the comparative benefits of third-party involvement in building strategic business relations.

Table 4-2.
Comparative Benefits of Third-Party Involvement in SBRs

- Technology transfer for self-reliance
- Bias for shared success objectives
- Willingness of potential partners to *share critical information* to third party for confidential analysis of partnering opportunity
- Facilitation, conflict resolution, and focus to shared vision
- Catalyst and facilitator for merging cultures and creating optimum SBR entity
- Access to in-depth background information on potential partners
- Use of third-party's network for financing in SBR development
- Sponsorship to industry analysts to promote SBR value to marketplace
- Technology forecasting and network to technology resources
- Life cycle management experience in inviting partners to SBR

Often, the facilitation is impaired by advisors from other professions, essential to the deal making or operation. Template 4-3 lists advisors you encounter in business relations, their success characteristics, and criteria for selection.

TEMPLATE 4-3: SELECTING ADVISORS

TYPICAL ADVISORS ROLES
- LAWYERS (CONTRACT, TAX, REAL ESTATE, INTELLECTUAL PROPERTY)
- ACCOUNTANTS (AUDIT, DISPUTE RESOLUTION, TAX)
- CONSULTANTS (TECHNICAL, IT, WORK CULTURE, HR, BENEFITS, PENSION FUND)

SUCCESS CHARACTERISTICS
- PRIOR EXPERIENCE IN SUCCESSFUL VENTURES
- RAISES ISSUES WITH OPTIONS TO ADDRESS THEM
- JOINS WITH OTHERS EASILY
- UNDERSTANDS THE ALLIANCE AND ARTICULATES LEVERAGE POINTS
- DEMONSTRATES RESPECT FOR OTHER DISCIPLINES
- DOES NOT NEED TO BE SEEN AND HEARD ALL THE TIME
- OFFERS A VALUE-ADDING NETWORK
- NETWORKS FOR THE ALLIANCE

SELECTION TIPS
- SEEK REFERRALS
- INVESTIGATE PERFORMANCE: PRIOR CLIENTS, BANKERS, COMPETITORS
- INTERVIEW BY ALL TEAM MEMBERS
- DESCRIBE SUCCESS/DISAPPOINTMENTS
- TELL HOW SERVICE WILL VALUE-ADD
- CLARIFY REWARD EXPECTATIONS
- EXPLORE NON-CASH COMPENSATION

Figures 4-3 and 4-4 are two case illustrations from an energy firm engaged in joint ventures. First is a meeting agenda to launch joint business planning, followed by a critical path for joint planning.

JOINT BUSINESS PLANNING MEETING AGENDA

• PRELIMINARY: AFFIRM OR SIGN CONFIDENTIALITY AGREEMENT
• OVERVIEW OF JV CONCEPT (YOUR FIRM'S VIEW OF WHAT SHOULD BE DONE)
• MEMBER/PARTNER'S VIEW OF WHAT'S POSSIBLE WITH JV
   ⇒ DESCRIBES POTENTIAL VALUE-ADD
   ⇒ EXPRESSES GROWTH ASPIRATIONS
   ⇒ STATES EXPECTATIONS FOR YOUR FIRM'S PARTICIPATION
• GROUP BRAINSTORMS JV GROWTH SCENARIOS
   ⇒ ACQUISITIONS
   ⇒ IMPROVEMENTS
   ⇒ ESTIMATES OF CAPITAL REQUIREMENTS
• JV SCOPING
   ⇒ REVIEW JOINT BUSINESS PLANNING TEMPLATE
   ⇒ DEVELOP CRITICAL PATH FOR COMPLETING JOINT BUSINESS PLANNING (USE TEMPLATE AS
     POINT OF DEPARTURE)
   ⇒ ASSIGN JOINT TEAM FOR COLLATING INFORMATION AND PREPARING PLAN
•AFFIRM ASSIGNMENTS AND SET DATE/LOCATION FOR NEXT MEETING

Figure 4-3.

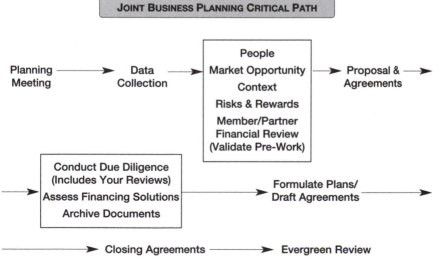

JOINT BUSINESS PLANNING CRITICAL PATH

Planning Meeting → Data Collection →

People
Market Opportunity
Context
Risks & Rewards
Member/Partner
Financial Review
(Validate Pre-Work)

→ Proposal & Agreements →

Conduct Due Diligence
(Includes Your Reviews)
Assess Financing Solutions
Archive Documents

→ Formulate Plans/ Draft Agreements →

→ Closing Agreements → Evergreen Review

Figure 4-4.

WHEN ALL IS SAID AND DONE IN A WAR ROOM

Regardless of the setting, war rooms and the complexity facilitation process exist to address chaos and the dysfunctional rigidity in our traditions of doing business. They are about a new precision in picking the right business pursuit, and fueling it with the best talent, resources, partners, and support needed to succeed.

In a firm today, the firm does not know what is most important until it has grasped the complication in its business landscape, and availed itself of the full potential of the firm's collective mind. The days when those highest in the firm possessed the vantage point are over. Everyone, those closest to the work as well as those most responsible to owners, must participate in setting the patterns if dominance in the marketplace is to happen. By dominance, we do not mean unfair market exploitation. We mean doing what it takes to extract value in a turbulent, global market. This means holding a meaningful market position capable of earning a competitive return on capital. Be prepared.

PART TWO

Entering Negotiations

CHAPTER 5

Contours in
Negotiation

Negotiation unfolds in the latter moments of preparation. Negotiation arrives on the scene when a thorough self-reflection proves where to go next in terms of knowledge, position, and resources. The targeting narrows to the best prospective partners or ventures and, ultimately, the party or parties to be engaged are closely scrutinized. Whether presenting an invitation to negotiate, or answering one, preparation journeys into a series of events which begins with a dance between prospective partners, involves a romance, but must close to access value-add.

Our discussion of negotiation is organized into four areas: 1) what negotiations should be about in the 21st century, 2) grounding in reality the exploration of business interests between parties, 3) the negotiation process for strategic business relations, and 4) a review of a recommended template. The introduction concludes with a reflection on negotiation prescriptions for the last 25 years of this century.

We Are a Product of Our Past

In the last half of the 20th century, negotiations made frequent headlines. In this historical context, the term brings to mind major news events beginning in the post-World War II era and leading up to the Vietnam period: controversial labor disputes, protracted international peace negotiations, or cold-war gamesmanship in United Nations quorums.

In general business, retail was as lively as ever in this era with respect to transactions between buyers and sellers, or retailers and consumers. Only in the quietest corridors of corporations where purchasing agents walked, did large-scale commercial or value-chain negotiation engender much attention. Companies were bought and sold but not at the fevered pitch that was to come later. Negotiations were the province of diplomats, labor leaders, senior executives, buyers, car salesmen, real estate agents, and consumers.

The energy crisis would be catalytic to a new emphasis on negotiation aimed at large deals. The momentum in negotiation accelerated as the fuel crisis-driven consolidations gave way to the deal-making in the go-go years of the eighties. Then giant concerns tumbled across industries and sectors. Stockholder advocacy and takeover specialists sped the process along. By the time the nineties began, Hollywood brought attention to Wall Street and the deal makers. In the mid-nineties, jargon and acronyms like OPM ("other people's money"—a deal maker's credo) were as widely known as the day's political slogans or catchy advertising clichés.

In this time frame of the late '80s and '90s, negotiation of alliances and joint ventures surfaced as a major force on the business landscape for three reasons. One was to share the cost of research and development. Multinationals, not wishing to bear all the cost of research, formed consortia among themselves. In areas like high technology, biotechnology, and other businesses with entrepreneurial cottage-industry roots, the marrying of resource-rich multinationals or venture capitalists with idea-rich, garage-based inventors took place in research consortia, alliances, or joint ventures.

Another reason for partnering-styled negotiation was to respond across industries to mega economic opportunity such as: 1) projects for the civilian aerospace industry, Department of Defense contracts involving hundreds (even thousands) of vendors, and other government-based initiatives for infrastructure and services, or 2) value-chain optimization in consumer goods led by Walmart and other wholesalers. In the latter case, margins began to tilt in the direction of the consumer, and value-chain optimization was promoted.

The third reason for partnering negotiation is that the automobile industry began to collaborate among manufacturers to optimize procurement, market access, and allay nationalistic concerns with cross-border manufacturing. In the end, negotiation practice for partnering became as featured in business as deal making in mergers and acquisitions. The emphasis here was on shared responsibility in the value chain.

In corporate seminars on negotiation, a philosophy of win-win was popularized in contrast to the film industry portrayal of ruthless deal makers. The value chain-based negotiation was recognized by seminar leaders as a terrific opportunity to resell their wares. Reality in the norms of negotiation was a mixture of both win-win and gamesmanship. There was usually a great deal of posturing about seeking a win-win solution. This was more rhetoric than genuinely exploring mutual needs.

What did not happen in these learning sessions was an adjustment to evolving business realities. The uniqueness of value-chain partnering, research consortia, alliances, or joint ventures was not given much, if any, attention in seminars. Missing, too, was an understanding of the growing importance of transparency and interdependence. Little or no emphasis was given to concepts and constructs for strategic business relations. In the last few years, journal articles and other writings have begun to address these issues at length. Most seminars, however, continue to ignore or treat lightly these important determinants of value.

Had greater emphasis been given to the realities unfolding in business for the next century, more value would probably be perceived in pursuing win-win strategies. The genuineness inherent to win-win was further diluted by the unwinding of value-chain partnering in the auto sector. The quality movement in the eighties had found a following in auto manufacturing operations. Innovative product managers and plant managers began to build effective bridges for optimizing across the value chain.

The importance of the auto sector elicited a pattern other industries followed, most notably, other giants like aerospace, defense, and petrochemicals. Unfortunately, a centralized optimization effort in auto procurement disrupted the model process. The shift in emphasis was effective at accumulating short-term price concessions across the supply side. A new pattern was set.

Joint optimization ended as price reductions were forced. Optimization was restricted to internal controls of the value chain, and attitudes to optimize for self in negotiations returned in place of collaborative views. This forebearance of major customers has not been forgotten. Another downside is that it has been contagious as other industries followed the trend to pursue the short term in procurement.

The effect to date on practice is again a mixed bag. A few seminar providers, in particular those associated with information technology aimed at value-chain optimization, do promote win-win. This, however, is rudimentary teamwork we have seen before from the quality movement in supplier-customer action teams (SCATs). SCATs have been potent, but are not always based on the fullest application of win-win. SCATs are also limited to only one dimension of partnering, i.e., value-chain optimization.

What Win-Win Really Means

Our mentor, Herb Shepard, introduced the win-win view of the world with a simple matrix:

The Shepard Window

	Good for Others	Bad for Others
Good for You	WIN/WIN	WIN/LOSE
Bad for You	LOSE/WIN	LOSE/LOSE

Herb taught us to bring more meaning to the matrix with emotionally loaded terms. Key words are placed in each panel of the matrix. The word represents the meaning of the phrase in its application to any negotiation.

The Shepard Window

	Good for Others	Bad for Others
Good for You	WIN/WIN Life	WIN/LOSE Homicide
Bad for You	LOSE/WIN Suicide	LOSE/LOSE Genocide

The most powerful word on the matrix is "life." Vitality is more than winning today. It is creating a realistic future, with new revenues and resources to sustain business and make it grow. Continuity into the future is realized in strategic business relations when both parties do more than just win in the first deal. Continuity is derived from growth.

Vitality for a firm is both constant renewal, and the opening of doors to multiple future opportunities. Achieved is a position for continuous value-add. The position is earned by carefully selecting partners, working hard at making relations work, and putting forth effort to see the world differently and make growth happen.

Most seminars in the last 25 years voice win-win. They examine defensive strategies for recognizing manipulations and coping with emotional outbursts. Many courses offer offensive tactics involving intimidation, staging clever ploys, concocting legal tricks, and otherwise exploiting prospective partners.

The 21st century will be more about working with partners with a genuine intent to do what is right for the marketplace. This is in contrast to focusing primarily on optimizing for your needs. The shared focus across value chains will be the primary customer, or end user. The distribution channel will only exist for two reasons: 1) the most basic tasks such as delivery or order management, or 2) value-added services. The channel will become more and more a service provider, e.g., technical assistance, application service, or convenience.

Multimedia coupled with rapid delivery services will supplant most other aspects of the channel, e.g., inventory, display, promotion, and sales. Through multimedia and rapid delivery services, direct access to end users is provided to manufacturers. Small manufacturers, in particular, benefit from the process by sharply reducing entry costs associated with channel development, or minimizing the levy for channel services. Multimedia will offer access for end users to virtually all the providers of products or services.

The emphasis on competing by delivering value to the end user prompts better behavior in value chains. No one wants to be known for excessive margins or poor conduct. In a world which is more transparent and compelling, economic reasons sustain relations across time. Any exploitation of partners will be known quickly and will remain on your name tag. The detriment of being a lousy partner will more severely diminish value; on the other hand, a reputation for sound strategic relations will access more opportunity and accelerate value creation.

This thumbnail sketch of negotiation practices in recent business history provides a platform for the next discussion about what could be in business negotiation. It is based on the premise that the evolving events in globalization and technology advancements will necessitate that "could be's" be transformed into "will be's."

As the discussion moves to the future, use this thumbnail sketch to remind you where people may be today in their negotiation practice and appreciate the history behind these norms. To get to where you want to be in negotiation, you must begin where the other party is.

What It Should Be About Anyway

This book has been all about negotiation. A very special form of negotiation is required for building strategic business relations. What is special is building a deal based upon the effort and value put forth by each party. The objective is to secure an association genuinely based on mutual benefit and shared contribution. Contribution need not be equal, but benefit should be aligned to the economic value of the effort put forth. A dollar of effort should receive the return on the value of a dollar. The sense of fair play will gain credibility for future business. The association is to be so sound in its foundation that continuity across time and access to other opportunity is highly probable.

In this, there is harmony. Harmony among partners: relationships work and build to new ties. Harmony in nature: resources are optimized and the pattern of increasing returns is growth. Whether environmental or economic, resources are conserved and deployed for growth. In the pursuit of growth, nature's resources are at least sustained and ideally revitalized. Economic endeavors emerge to create value and open the door to still more opportunity.

In the 21st century, we know more and there is greater opportunity. We can establish patterns which create good. We can subordinate ourselves to evil. We can engage in destructive competition and consume one another. We can do nothing and chance what patterns will evolve of their own accord to set a new order. To act or not, and how to act, are our choices. The use of knowledge and the resulting good fortune are thus ours to earn through the patterns we set.

In complexity, there is both precision and a broad, sticky kind of goo that holds things together. In business, the exactness appears in choosing partners, talents, and niches. In business, the goo is harmony that can be found in relationships, in a willingness to be flexible and do what needs to be done regardless of rules and roles, and in an inclusiveness in attitude and legal commitment for smart risk. As we know, capable risk management leads to more of whatever is sought as value.

In the 21st century, negotiation is about declaring and justifying value positions. This is a departure from today's popular model of exploitation where potential is partially milked and no side fully wins. The negotiation available to us now and into the future is analogous to cracking the combination unlocking potential.

To arrive at an accurate assessment, there must be a candid, transparent conversation to discover credible information, and the information should evidence positions and interpretations of value. The conversation must be grounded in reality.

CHAPTER 6

Grounding Negotiations in Reality

We coach negotiators to ground their discussion in reality. Business is about making money and this is a topic where most people demand precision. The validation process in deals, called due diligence, usually does the job of getting to the facts. The term is used to describe a variety of circumstances, but most often follows an agreement on terms and conditions, and serves to prove that what is said is for real. Due diligence is the process of validating claims that may restrict final closing or that may trigger contingencies for compensation should inaccuracies of significance or misrepresentation be discerned.

Environmental risk, other legal liabilities, and financials are addressed with vigor in a due diligence. Nonetheless, these elements of a due diligence may have controversy imbedded within as the interpretations and assumptions are explored. The due diligence process can be delayed or may fail should major discrepancies or omissions be uncovered.

What is less likely to gain careful scrutiny in a due diligence, but have high impact on extracting value from the venture, are: marketing, sales, and price information; interpretations in accounting information, e.g., the worth of a facility or piece of equipment; and technology forecasts. These are typically presented as assumptions which are based, in whole or in part, upon some empirical database or survey.

Advice from negotiation experts can be as strong about not using databases in a negotiation as they are about the pursuing "win-win" concepts. We part company with them on both counts as we view the 21st century. Negotiation experts claim that negotiations can become too emotional or controversial over the accuracy of databases. In either case, the database does not get used. As a result, the true value is not confronted but is avoided, disguised, or denied. These are not smart business choices. They are not psychologically healthy.

Our experience with negotiation runs a broad spectrum. Like most people, we have negotiated personal purchases. Gary, for instance, began early as the go-between to his English-only-speaking parents in the bazaars of Turkey. In more conventional settings, we have bought cars and homes. In business, we conducted or coached: both sides in labor and management collective bargaining in domestic and foreign settings; small deals for start-ups, to mega joint ventures between governments and multinationals; and procurement contracts valued from those in the thousands to those in the billions for commodities and one-of-a-kind products. Our business experience spans the world. We have also been advisors to and in—on rare occasions, in the thick of things—negotiations with kidnappers and terrorists.

In the extreme circumstances with more than economic exchange at issue, we can understand zero-sum tactics. To our dismay, however, it is much more prevalent than these circumstances. So for a moment we will address extreme circumstances and zero-sum tactics; not in advocacy but to both contrast zero-sum approaches with what we think should be done in dealing directly with reality, and to describe what could be irrational behavior on the other side of the table.

Here is what zero-sum looks like. From a position of perceived power—and this often is a misperception—you may receive unrealistic or extreme demands. Even when power is real, in time, things may change. Power-based moves can easily lead to a later time where the tables are turned. Of course, those who use this ploy are myopic, and this logic flies over their heads.

Another zero-sum position is to claim no authority. You hear the claim after sensitive information is shared or a commitment is in motion. "No authority" puts the decision with a party or parties elsewhere. It is a power play to empower the folks sending the negotiator. The negotiation is in effect over until the principals arrive for the other side.

Akin to the claim of no authority is ignoring deadlines. The dodge is an avoidance of reality. The hope is for a change in circumstances to gain an advantage. Zero-sum tactics include tactics to gain advantage by working on your emotions. Parties may try to inflict you with guilt, impose for a special need, or claim a right—one to be litigated if not respected. At the end of the day, these are attempts to twist fate by twisting arms.

Zero-sum can surface in concessions. There are two cases: stinginess in concessions or treating your concessions as weaknesses to be exploited. Stinginess either belies good faith for the moment and the future, or slows the process. Jumping on another person's concession erodes trust and does not invite further consideration of the concession or of other concessions. Yet, for the one-trick ponies, these choices are made. The reality herein denied is a strategic relation.

Does zero-sum ever make sense? You may become involved in a "life and death" situation—with no move left except a bluff. We have been told to consider zero-sum in business when working with the naïve or in a one-shot situation. Those offering the advice may be willing to do this. We aren't. We want more than a one-trick pony.

Searching for how to bring the focus to reality in building strategic relations, we turned to the '60s writings of Dr. William Glasser. In his books, *Schools Without Failure* and *Reality Therapy,* Glasser introduced to the therapy world a simple premise: Do not explain away a person's irrational behavior. Instead, help them to confront it and to learn to better cope with life.

Glasser and his colleagues earned recognition for exceptional results in treating delinquent adolescents. We have used his approach throughout our careers. We only became purposeful about teaching people Glasser's view in negotiation a few years ago. Traditional negotiating courses were not serving our clients' needs.

In our consultations or seminars, it seemed redundant to teach negotiation. Then we encountered clients claiming they were taught to use dysfunctional tactics for strategic relations. This is when we returned to Dr. Glasser's original work and adapted key points to strategic business relations negotiation.

Outlined on the following page are application tips for the basic steps in coping with irresponsible behavior you may encounter with strategic relations: involvement, admission, and relearning.[1]

Steps for Coping with Irresponsible Behavior

Involvement
- Be so involved with your partner that you can help the partner share views of reality, face reality, and see how unrealistic irresponsible positions might be
  - ⇒ Share strategic intents and discuss core competencies
  - ⇒ Have vision discussions
  - ⇒ Create multiple scenarios and discuss alternatives' pros & cons

Admission
- Help the partner admit to the unrealistic position taken
  - ⇒ Invite the partner to state the impact of the irresponsible choice on them, you, competitors, and customers . . . now and in the future
  - ⇒ Ask the partner what they would do if placed under similar circumstances
  - ⇒ Jointly articulate a criteria of success; pose options and jointly evaluate options

Relearning
- Teach partners how to be successful in a responsible manner, i.e., fulfill their needs in a way without depriving others of the ability to fulfill their needs
  - ⇒ Offer alternatives
  - ⇒ Assist in bringing alternatives to life . . . in planning together or working inside their system
  - ⇒ Help fulfill their needs

Outlined next are about a dozen different scenarios we find likely in contemporary negotiations. What to do about the situation is noted below each circumstance. In all, it is common sense combined with the integrity to hold yourself and other parties in the negotiation to a responsible course.

Irresponsible Behavior: Typical Scenarios
- In their unsuccessful effort to satisfy needs, irresponsible negotiators have a common flaw: they all deny reality to some degree
  - ⇒ Help them see reality through data and logic
  - ⇒ Help them realize they must fulfill their needs within the framework of market reality
- No matter how irresponsible or inadequate the behavior may seem to you, it has meaning and validity to the other person
  - ⇒ Start where they are—not where you want them to be
  - ⇒ Learn how they see the world by listening
- Target changing behaviors—once changed, they bring along attitudes
  - ⇒ Ask what is being done, not why
  - ⇒ Move to action planning
  - ⇒ Encourage experiments
- Introduce "Win-Win" as an objective to share
  - ⇒ Realize, however, that saying it is not enough
  - ⇒ Lead partners to win-win experiences

IRRESPONSIBLE BEHAVIOR: TYPICAL SCENARIOS (continued)
- PARTNERS MAY SAY "NO" TO INVOLVEMENT BECAUSE THEY TRIED IT BEFORE AND GOT HURT
  - ⇒ BE PERSISTENT
  - ⇒ PLAN EARLY SUCCESSES; WORK ON OBVIOUS-OUGHT-TO-BE'S FIRST TO DEMONSTRATE SUCCESS (STAY AWAY FROM ONE-SIDED CONCESSIONS)
- PARTNERS MAY SAY "NO" IN AN ATTEMPT TO BE INDEPENDENT BUT REALLY MEAN "YES"
  - ⇒ OFFER YOUR PROPOSAL AS AN INVITATION . . . DO NOT PRESS TOO EARLY FOR AN ANSWER
  - ⇒ RECOGNIZE THEIR POWER BUT BE PERSISTENT
  - ⇒ REINFORCE THAT THEY HAVE CHOICES
  - ⇒ HAVE THEM DESCRIBE MERITS OF EACH CHOICE—DO NOT HESITATE TO ASSIST AFTER YOU HAVE FIRST LISTENED CAREFULLY
- REJECT UNREALISTIC BEHAVIOR (OR STATEMENTS) BUT STILL ACCEPT THE PARTNER AS A PERSON WHILE MAINTAINING INVOLVEMENT
  - ⇒ ESTABLISH RAPPORT BEFORE TOUGHING OUT DIFFICULT ISSUES
  - ⇒ OFFER "APPRECIATES BEFORE WISHES" — TELL THEM WHAT YOU ADMIRE, RESPECT, OR FIND BENEFICIAL ABOUT THEM BEFORE OFFERING IMPROVEMENT SUGGESTIONS
  - ⇒ EXPRESS THOUGHTS IN A CALM MANNER WITHOUT EMOTION
  - ⇒ BE DIRECT AND SUCCINCT
- TEACH PARTNERS BETTER WAYS TO FULFILL NEEDS WITHIN THE CONFINES OF REALITY
  - ⇒ DESCRIBE REALITY
  - ⇒ DRAW A MENTAL PICTURE OF WHAT SUCCESS COULD BE FROM THEIR VANTAGE POINT
  - ⇒ POINT OUT ALTERNATIVES AVAILABLE TO THEM AND THE COMPARATIVE BENEFITS
- BE HUMAN AND PERMIT PARTNER TO PARRY WITH YOU ON YOUR VALUES AND INTENT
  - ⇒ BE A GOOD ROLE MODEL FOR A RESPONSIBLE NEGOTIATOR
  - ⇒ BE OPEN TO IMPROVEMENT SUGGESTIONS
- BE RESPONSIBLE: TOUGH, INTELLIGENT, SENSITIVE
  - ⇒ BUT NOT: ALOOF, SUPERIOR, SACROSANCT
  - ⇒ GET TO THE POINT
  - ⇒ BE PERSISTENT
- KEEP IN MIND: YOUR TASK IS A RESPONSIBLE NEGOTIATION LEADING TO A SUCCESSFUL OPERATION
  - ⇒ YOUR TASK IS NOT TO MAKE THE PARTNER HAPPY BUT TO LEAD THEM TO A RESPONSIBLE SOLUTION—ONE THAT WORKS BECAUSE IT PAYS OFF FOR BOTH SIDES
  - ⇒ HOLD THE PARTNER TO A RESPONSIBLE COURSE; YOU MAY SUFFER ANGER BUT MAY BE REWARDED BY RESPONSIBLE BEHAVIOR; TAKING THE RESPONSIBLE COURSE WILL NEVER PERMANENTLY ALIENATE (IF "DISCIPLINE" IS TEMPERED WITH CARING)

Much of what appears in bold in the "Steps for Coping with Irresponsible Behavior" and an even greater portion of the "Typical Scenarios" is taken directly from Glasser's writings as previously noted.

Altering statements to fit partnering and commerce leaves an impression that this has been our original thought. Two comments must accompany this accrediting. One is that Glasser's work functions to help people adjust to life better in any circumstance. We advocate the learning of these principles by everyone. The second point evolves from a comment about society, in general. We set a pattern of permissiveness and another pattern of avoiding confronting irresponsible behavior over the past three or four decades. The effect is that civility is in decline, social responsibility has eroded, and violence and criminality have grown. A pattern based on reality is needed to offset and reverse the trend.

At the end of the day, there is a simple rule of thumb. In a negotiation for a strategic relation and when the other side begins to fight with you, or engages in flight, then your job is to return them to work. In Table 6-1, an array of behaviors categorized into fight, work, and flight will help you recognize the patterns within negotiations. It is much easier to recognize an evolving pattern and address it early. This is our spin on a tool Herb Shepard gave us.

Table 6-1.
Fight/Work/Flight

Fight	Work	Flight
• Argues	• Seeks others' viewpoints	• Avoids differences
• Makes differences bigger	• Identifies common ground	• Smoothes over differences without a solution
• Takes a win/lose attitude	• Takes a win/win attitude	• Willing to lose to get discussion over
• Uses questions to pin you down	• Seeks information with questions	• Asks irrelevant questions
• Uses leading questions	• Invites others to be involved with questions	• Uses questions to distract
• Ignores others, doesn't listen	• Active listener	• Spaces out—doesn't pay attention or listen
• Interrupts	• Is patient	• Shows no interest
• Twists what is said to fit own needs	• Paraphrases to check communication	• Says nothing or changes subject
• Tries to steal others' ideas	• Credits others	• Questions why idea needs to be considered—wants to do something else
• Dominates discussion	• Encourages everyone to participate	• Does not participate
• Repeats	• Uses time effectively, helps keep group on track	• Takes side trips too often
• Puts people down with humor	• Uses humor to add perspective and reduce tension	• Clowns to avoid keeping at task
• Criticizes	• Tells it like it is	• Lets others speak for him
• Blames others	• Takes responsibility	• Makes excuses
• Takes a firm position	• Considers pro-con	• Agrees with everything
• Resists experiments	• Experiments	• Uses only proven ideas
• Takes resources	• Uses resources	• Wastes resources

The objective is to begin the relationship you want to last, and to grow into additional value opportunities, with the same goodwill you want for operations. Sharp tricks and gamesmanship do not foment trust. Your choices in behavior are only half the story.

Encountering irresponsible behavior in others signals the need for decisions. The first is, do you want a long-term relationship with someone who does not show you respect, or plays games? Will you be able to turn around the behavior and establish a foundation for responsible conduct? Is it worth the effort? Is there someone else in the other party's firm who can encourage responsible behavior along with you? How best to enroll that person in your cause?

Before leaving the subject of reality, there is a special circumstance to address. In the case where your firm, regardless of your personal reputation, has a reputation for exploiting partners, the past may count more than the value of the deal. This is a higher risk if the personality across the table was a career victim.

Bad past partnering behavior often elicits irresponsible behavior. This is when experiments to test the relationship before making riskier commitments, demonstrations of good intent (such as sharing your treasure chest of future opportunities), and extra effort to be a good citizen in negotiation are important.

Extraordinary effort may be appropriate to reestablish reputation. Meetings at multiple levels, retreats to provide formal and informal discussions, or invitations to participate in sessions to formulate your strategic plan build bridges for credibility.

REFERENCES

1. Glasser, William, M.D., *Reality Therapy: A New Approach to Psychiatry,* Harper and Row, 1965, p. 3–41.

CHAPTER 7

The Negotiation Process for Strategic Relations

The work flow diagram in Figure 7-1 maps the steps in negotiation. In any given situation, some steps may be sequenced differently or omitted. In our presentation, the process begins with a contact letter.

The contact letter is illustrated in Template 7-1. It is used to explain your interest, make an invitation for exploratory discussion, and convey the seriousness of intent. The letter at once should convey professionalism and an air of informality. Too casual or too rigid can be turn-offs. Behaviors advertised must be exhibited in the meeting. The other party will size you up against the words in the letter.

Critical Path for Negotiating Process

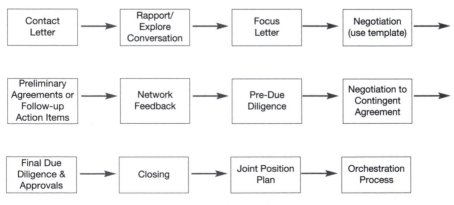

Figure 7-1. The early steps.

TEMPLATE 7-1. CONTACT/FOCUS LETTER

(PRE-ACQUISITION)

Personal & Confidential

Dear Mr. Target:

I am writing this letter to you to present for your consideration an idea which might well prove of substantial mutual benefit. I have thought very carefully about this matter for some months, and believe that it is now the appropriate time for me to get in touch with you.

Two of my closest friends and I started this company about X years ago, after being in the same industry for over Y years. Our company consists of two related businesses: manufacture of plastic coatings and production of high quality plastic parts for autos. We employ a total of about 375 people.

Our customers have been very loyal to us and have given us business year-in-year-out—and probably well over half of our production is repeat business. Moreover, I would like to think that this excellent, long-standing relationship we have with our customers is because we are always ready to "break our backs" to make sure that our customers are completely happy—even if sometimes their demands seem unreasonable. A sincere adherence to this simple policy has brought us an ever-growing amount of business from an increasingly larger number of departments within the same company—and this clearly shows up in our financial performance.

I took over the presidency of this company in [year]. After a bad year in [year], fiscal 'YZ showed a profit and for fiscal 'LL (ended June 30th) the results are very satisfactory indeed. The balance sheet, too, is in good shape: we have no liquidity problems, our borrowing capacity is good, and we maintain a very satisfactory relationship with our bank. All in all, despite the current sluggish economy, availability of cash is certainly not a problem.

In summary, then, we have a well-run, tight ship, staffed by competent and very loyal people at all levels, with a good record, and in solid financial position. Thus, it seems to me, and my people are fully in accord with this view, that now is the appropriate time to undertake well-thought-out, prudent steps to expand the scope of our operations.

After discussing these ideas among ourselves, and exploring the matter with some of our closest customers, we have come to the conclusion that one of the avenues of expansion which would seem to offer a really attractive potential is the business of recycling plastic. The reason, I am sure, is obvious to you: practically all our customers are presently purchasing this service from others, and there is good reason to think that our sales people should be able to obtain a substantial piece of this business from the customers they have been serving so well for years.

Thus, we have considered two strategies: entering this business "from scratch" and joining hands with an existing company. Our conclusion is that getting together with another company might be potentially far more effective in view of the fact that we could then also market our other plastic business to the customers of the other company. In other words, *both* businesses should be enhanced materially. In addition, of course, if our merger partner should require additional financing, we would be in a position to offer such assistance.

I have known of your company for some time, but not until recently have I made an effort to find out something about it. My "homework" indicated that it might be advantageous for both of us to at least explore possible areas of mutual interest. My thought is that if this letter elicits your further interest, you might accept my invitation for dinner sometime next week.

I plan to telephone your office early next week.

Sincerely yours,
Paul Plastic
President

(continued)

TEMPLATE 7-1. CONTACT/FOCUS LETTER *(continued)*

(ALLIANCE DEVELOPMENT CASE ILLUSTRATION)

Personal & Confidential

Dear Potential Partner,

I am writing to present for your consideration an idea with the promise for substantial mutual benefit. I have thought very carefully about this for some time, and believe now is the appropriate time to get in touch with you.

Here at our company we have invested extensively in plastics as a logical extension of our products' future performance. As you know, we have a strong, loyal following to our plastics products and are always looking for means to strengthen our market presence. Plastics is one of the most important ways for us to add value to consumers. This philosophy of providing consumers with superior performance has been rewarding for all of us.

I assumed the responsibility of regional account manager last year and was charged to secure our plastics business and grow. As you know, our company is a team-based organization. While I am your key contact, what I have learned from you along with my own ideas are integrated into this team process. We see you as having high potential to be a partner in bringing additional value-added products and services to the consumer. We are fully in accord with this view in our national accounts management team and the board of directors.

A significant challenge for enhancing our current collaboration to become strategic partners is Project Plastic. We have considered two paths for introducing Project Plastic: leveraging our own resources or integrating our resources with strategic partners. Our conclusion is that getting together with strategic partners might be potentially more effective, along with introducing and administering the appropriate intellectual property agreements—a step-out position inevitable for our industry.

I am an admirer of your company and have made an effort to learn about your strategic interests. Our recent partnership conference helped us to understand your expectations and preferences. To learn more about how we might mutually support one another, I invite you to dinner some time next week.

I plan to telephone your office early next week.

Sincerely yours,

In the meeting, the task of building rapport is as important as expressing your case for the deal. This is a time to explore interests and intents. The key is to sit on your hands long enough to listen and not impose a position. Declare your intent to get down to business, and for you this means getting to know a prospective partner's needs and how they see themselves.

Being clear on this gets the process rolling and builds the image of a "get down to business" kind of player. Even where there are cultural needs not to appear too business-like, too quickly, this asserts an interest in who others are—a palatable subject in many settings.

From the very beginning and throughout the negotiation process there are fundamental outlooks for success. These are outlined on the following page.

FUNDAMENTAL OUTLOOKS FOR SUCCESSFUL NEGOTIATION

- **Listening**—Beginning where the prospective partner is, not where you are nor where you want them to be
- **Cultural differences**—Leveraging them for creativity rather than using differences to divide
- **Systems thinking**—See all the parts, understand how each aspect of the deal impacts another: customers, owners, employees, community, competitors, etc.
- **Dualism**—Valuing competing interests as equally important in the same moment
- **Focus**—Discerning the few, critical priorities and orchestrating resources and energy to make them happen—before moving on to the next opportunity

---

Valuing competing interests at the same time begins with the first interaction with the other party. There are four dichotomies typical to negotiating in business relations. First, there are your interests and theirs. Even if the venture under discussion will be based on overlapping interests, there will still be some difference. You cannot sacrifice your own position, and you will need to show respect for theirs. Second is the emphasis on the deal today, in contrast to the future, whether that means effective operation or growth. Value functions from both ends.

The third cause for dualism is individuals in comparison to institutions. There are, in all negotiations, the firms and the representatives of the firm. The distinction is less when there is only one owner and the owner participates in the negotiation—though there remains a difference. The firm is an entity. It can sustain the death or other loss of principals. It is where the value is. As for representatives, they are known to work their own agendas from time to time.

You must track both agendas: firm and representative. You will need to listen to and value both messages. It is important to note when they are at odds. In addition, commitments made without power will not survive for long. Personal agendas may need to be brought to the attention of the firm. If someone turns on their firm or subordinates their agenda to your benefit, this is irresponsible behavior. The advantage such a move gains will not sustain itself in value extraction.

It is important to step aside for a moment and comment about value extraction and acquisitions. Even in the cases where the previous owner goes fishing after the deal is closed, a relationship in the future may spring up. Liability issues for products or regulator compliance may prompt the need to re-negotiate as an alternative to litigation. More pedestrian issues may benefit from an occasional phone call or an invitation for the former owner to visit. Keep in mind, then, value extraction goes beyond the day of closing. Collusion with the unethical conduct by a representative can end a rapport you will need someday.

The contrast of irresponsible behavior to responsible behavior is tough to manage. We are coaching you to confront irresponsible behavior. There are limits. At times, it will just happen. Ego will surge, humor will roll, or feelings will get hurt. Like harmony, where we expect conflict and know we will have to be responsible for periodically restoring harmony, responsible behavior must be restored in the process. At times, however, the process will be irrational. You may need to value the craziness as well as the good use of databases, maturity, and mutual respect.

In the first meeting, look to share only the concept of the deal. Provide what you would feel comfortable giving in a briefing to an industry analyst. You must assume what is shared will soon be known to others. If there is some compelling reason to reveal more, get the appropriate confidentiality agreement signed. It is difficult for us to perceive a meeting where this would be required, or make sense in terms of building a relationship. Being too intimate too soon scares people, and makes them doubt what you are about.

Nasty Negotiations

There is good reason for caution. Negotiations are used as a guise for deception. Disinformation is a tool in competitive intelligence that unscrupulous people use. We label players as such from an ethics point of view. It does not make sense in terms of value. Once disinformation is known to come from you, all statements about your product and business will be held in doubt until validated. Your associates in the value chain who are duped or implicated with you will want to settle the score. Stakeholders will lose faith. Putting your word at risk is foolish. Outplacement is the appropriate response to staff advocating disinformation more than once.

There are several ploys you may encounter and these influence the kind of information you want as background in the early conversations. Some people pursue talks about partnering so they may use the announcement of talks to avoid attention to other matters, e.g., litigation, financial troubles, labor disputes, etc. Strong players should be wary of weaker players, or troubled players who seek them out for alliances. Ask about such matters in the conversation. More importantly, research them before you meet.

Another purpose for feigning interest in partnering is to gain competitive intelligence. No one is likely to confess this, but you can be sensitive to the detail and level of inquiry. Should the other side push, wanting specific information, this is the time to reconsider talks, or bring forward an onerous confidentiality agreement. Keep in mind that the other side may not be a competitor at the moment. The business intent of the other side may be to glean competitive information as part of a decision to compete in the future.

The most sensitive ploy is an attempt to access information about trade secrets. If there are early tours of your facilities or meetings involving your sales and technical staffs before confidentiality agreements are signed, give your staff direct instructions not to reveal anything about trade secrets. They should also be told two things about inquirers. One is that they are trained to pick up bits and pieces from different conversations, some of those being with different people. They will then put it all together, often developing seemingly innocent questions to ask over dinner or in the next visit or meeting. These questions permit them to fill in the cracks. The other thing to tell your people is not to assume that non-technical people cannot understand or absorb technical information.

Deception includes engaging with you to preclude others from dealing with you. Tight schedules for early commitments will smoke out this irresponsible behavior. Anyone wanting exclusive talks should be prepared to move quickly and offer demonstrations of intent. Otherwise, hold parallel discussions. This is a particularly important concern when you hold access to opportunity, such as a technology that will redefine the way business is done.

A less hurtful act, but still an intent to deceive, is pursuing partnering talks to gain status. Sometimes this can lead to something good for you. Be cautious, however, of requests for early announcements or unilateral announcements without your approval or prior notice. It can be grandstanding to benefit from your reputation and this can cause problems.

To illustrate, we were with a major concern's CEO to discuss growth through partnering. His complaint was that a minor agreement with a Japanese firm in a supplier-customer relationship with one of his subsidiaries was being taunted as a major partnership for the whole corporation by the Japanese supplier. The CEO moved to quell the association for fear his real major Japanese partner would be offended.

The early conversation sets the atmosphere and pace. Share control over the process at a minimum. Do your homework and take every opportunity to explore who the prospective partner is. Be transparent as it is warranted. Be clear at the onset of your intent. Your expression of the intent may be more sophisticated as time passes. In a similar vein, intent may change to adapt to what becomes known or available for consideration.

Influence irresponsible behavior to a responsible course. Failing to do so, consider dropping the relationship. Irresponsible deals do not last. Finally, see irresponsibility in the early discussion as a task for work. By the way, expect irresponsible behavior somewhere in the process and learn to cope. It is still a big part of norms in negotiation.

The next step in the negotiation process is the "Focus Letter." We advise clients, in the first and subsequent meetings, to offer to prepare a summary of the discussion. Jot down the key points and invite the other party to provide their suggested edits. In the letter, capture what you see as the shared interest and identify what you believe are the individual objectives of all parties to be involved. Lay out the next steps and keep the momentum going to move forward or to bring the discussion to its logical end, whichever is appropriate.

For substantial deals to your firm, make certain you are not inviting unnecessary risk. Have your attorney examine the letter. Keep the tone informal yet businesslike. This is not the time to introduce complex, legalistic statements.

A positive response to a focus letter will soon lead to actual negotiation. In 1991, we attended a lecture by Ashook Kapoor, of a Princeton center for international negotiations, in which he referenced his book, *Negotiating Internationally: The Art of Networking*.[1] Ashook inspired us with his spreadsheet for tracking a negotiation. We then developed our templates of Sheets One through Five based on our experience with negotiating.

There are two things we found in Ashook's work that are always beneficial. One is to juxtapose the objectives of each party to the shared objectives. Keeping track of where everyone wants to go with individual interests helps in many ways. It indicates where differences might surface. The common ground is made clear. For disputes, a retreat to the common ground can reestablish rapport to resolve the difference.

TEMPLATE 7-2.

NEGOTIATION PREPARATION—SHEET ONE

OPPORTUNITIES
(COMPLETE SHEETS 4 & 5)

OUTCOMES

PLAYERS

DEAL INTELLIGENCE

YOURS

THEIRS

SHARED

CONFLICTS

YOUR MUSTS

THEIR MUSTS

SHARED MUSTS

MUSTS IN CONFLICT

YOURS
NAME　　TITLE

THEIRS
NAME　　TITLE

BACKGROUND NOTES
PROFESSIONAL　　PERSONAL

INFORMATION NEEDED/SOURCE

SOURCES

CONTACT RECORD

Date　　Location

Date　　Location

Date　　Location

☑ = PREPARED
☐ = NEEDS MORE WORK

The other benefit we've found useful in Ashook's work is his emphasis on networking. You and associates in your firm should discuss what is happening. Your collective view may be influenced by being too close to the situation, so also check with others to see how they see things. Validation or invalidation of your interpretations may follow. Either is useful information. In networking, listen to others' viewpoints, but separate fact from opinion and get information from more than one source before reacting.

The Template

The next paragraph begins a step-by-step instruction for the negotiation template's completion. This is a basic foundation that can be adapted to subsequent negotiation situations, e.g., disputing resolutions, and managing new growth or acquisitions by the shared venture.

After completing the review of the negotiating template, we will return to the matters of dispute management and exit strategies as discussion points in negotiation.

Each subheading refers to a section for the page in the template. Instructions are outlined by the section in the template.

SHEET ONE

Opportunities

Opportunity is the shared ambition between you and the other parties. It defines what is to be done.

For major plays, opportunities will be derived from analyses on Sheets Four and Five. Sheet One is completed by reviewing and summarizing these sheets. Sheet One is kept on top to provide a focus during negotiation discussions.

In any case, consider an opportunity to be the potential that exists in you, your potential partner, or from your synergy. It is important to set priorities. It is difficult for most people to track more than 3–5 issues in human communication. The complexity of negotiation makes tracking issues even more complex. *Focus on the two or three key opportunities.* It is easier to begin where things are clear to both parties, of interest to both parties, and where success can be had easily. You can always build on the success by pursuing additional opportunity.

Listed on the following page are categories of typical growth opportunities:

VALUE-ADDED GROWTH ALTERNATIVES
- Optimization of Value Chain
  - ⇒ Operations (SCATs)
  - ⇒ Invention-Innovation-Customer Delivery (Silo Crushing)
  - ⇒ Logistics (Order Processing & Material Handling)
- Share Expansion
  - ⇒ Capture
  - ⇒ Break the Rules (Make the Pie Bigger)
- Entry
  - ⇒ Technology Development
    [Improvement to Innovation]
  - ⇒ Service Enhancement
    [Bundling to Virtual Value Chain]
  - ⇒ Financial Engineering
    [Risk Management to Derivatives]
  - ⇒ Channel Access
  - ⇒ Globalization
- Acquisition
- Privatization
  [National Assets & Intellectual Property]

Examine priorities from all perspectives: yours, theirs, what is common to both, and where you disagree. Keep this sheet in front of you in the negotiation process. Check the accuracy of your perceptions. Note any shifts in attitude or position.

Recognize what you have heard as their view. Request any clarifications or corrections.

Offer your position directly, followed closely by what you see as shared interests. Again, invite validation. Then call out your view of where differences of opinion exist at this point in time. Invite them to do the same.

- *TIP:* Most people find flip charts to be an effective tool for negotiation. A simple format for this portion of discussion is to list your interests, their interests, and then circle agreement or enclose in boxes the areas where views differ.
- *TIP:* Don't type early notes . . . get the flip charts reduced. This ensures better impact and fewer disputes over what is remembered (everyone fears the editor).

Reference

1. Kapoor, Ashook, *Negotiating Internationally: The Art of Networking,* Recallmed Ltd., Hangon Kirjapaino, Finland, 1991.

CHAPTER 8

Negotiation Outcomes

Outcomes are what you need to accomplish at this point in time in the negotiations. They focus in on the current expression by both parties as to what must be done to continue exploring the relationship.

Look for deal killers—things you will never be able to accept. Listen for the same reaction from your potential partner. Express reservations early on—there's no use in kidding yourself or them.

Look for opportunities—Use flip-chart listings of interests and indicate shared views and where there is disagreement. Keep stressing, "At this point in time, we are just beginning to explore what is important. If we continue a meaningful dialogue, we will determine when and where it makes sense to collaborate."

Players

Keep track of who is involved, what they do and what you know about the other side. Distinguish between what you know about them as individuals and what you know about them as key players in their organization.

Deal Intelligence

Deal intelligence helps you *track what you need to know and from whom* you are most likely to discover answers. Keep track of with whom you investigate answers and when.

SHEET TWO

Orchestration

Orchestration, as seen in Template 8-1, outlines the steps you need to take to initiate contact and conduct early meetings.

The contact letter invites involvement for mutual brainstorming. It leads to the rapport/explore conversation in which you listen to the potential partner and share visions of what is possible.

The focus letter sets things in motion to explore the priority opportunities. It defines what you want to talk about and offers an expressed invitation to do so.

Typically, negotiation begins with the meeting the focus letter defines. *Plan the meeting carefully.* Draft an agenda. Use a simple "problem-solving" model, as depicted in Figure 8-1, to flesh out the opportunity and put forth a vision of interest to both parties. Here is a good format to use:

- Define the opportunity
- Describe how things are NOW
- Define a VISION of success: Yours, Theirs, Shared
- Identify OPTIONS for getting from where things are NOW to achieving the VISION
- Describe potential BARRIERS to success
- Test OPTIONS against BARRIERS and the extent to which they realize the VISION(S)

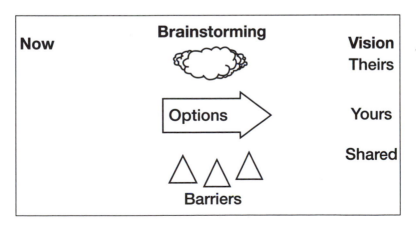

Figure 8-1. Problem-solving model.

TEMPLATE 8-1.

NEGOTIATION PREPARATION—SHEET TWO

ORCHESTRATION

ACTIVITY CHECKLIST
☐ CONTACT LETTER
☐ RAPPORT/EXPLORE CONVERSATION
☐ FOCUS LETTER
☐ NEGOTIATION

☐ AGENDA

☐ AUTHORITY LIMITS

☐ CREATE RIGHT ATMOSPHERE

EFFECTIVE COMMUNICATION

MUTUAL UNDERSTANDING
☐ ☐ ☐ ☐ ☐

DEMONSTRATE LEARNING
☐ ☐ ☐ ☐ ☐

GOOD USE OF QUESTIONS
☐ ☐ ☐ ☐ ☐

GOOD USE OF WRITTEN RECORD
☐ ☐ ☐ ☐ ☐

RELATIONSHIP REVIEW

NETWORK FEEDBACK
☐ OPPORTUNITY

☐ WATCHOUTS

☐ YOUR PROCESS OF WORKING TOGETHER

VALUE-ADD SERVICES
☐
☐
☐
☐
☐
☐
☐
☐
☐
☐
☐

Before engaging the partner, find out what your authority is. There are four general types:

- **Plenipotentiary**—Able to negotiate fully without checking with others
- **Delegate**—Able to negotiate to predetermined terms
- **Representative**—Able to explore but must seek others' approval
- **Observer**—Unable to negotiate but able to listen and convey interests of others, even act as sponsor

Think about what atmosphere will be most conducive to success. Spell it out to yourself and make it happen. There is a time and a place for everything. Timing can be important and it is influenced by what else is happening between parties, national or market events, potential partner's moods, and the opportunity to avoid distractions, etc. Envision what you think will get things off to a good start.

Effective Communication

This section prompts you to think ahead about: what needs to be *mutually understood;* how you can *demonstrate* what you have *learned* about the partner or from the partner; how best to *use questions;* and what you will do to keep a *written record* of the meeting (don't forget tips about the effectiveness of flip charts and reducing them as a meeting record).

Relationship Reviews

Relationship reviews remind you to look at how individuals are reacting to what is happening, as well as to consider the position of the other company. Both levels of involvement offer perspectives and they will not always be compatible. Projects outside your partner's strategic direction will probably not get off the ground. An individual on the other side may see personal goals being met and pursue an opportunity without the necessary support in his/her organization.

Be careful not to waste time and energy on personal initiatives lacking company support. Deals are made by people who represent their organizations. This is not always a rational process. Furthermore, people leave the organization. You must *steward continuity on both sides of the table.* At the end of the day, the deal must be responsible to the requirements of the two institutions which will be partners.

Network Feedback

Network feedback invites you to get others' views. This is important for intelligence gathering, to gain insight to both the process and to what is being negotiated, and for introducing objectivity. It is very easy to become overly involved in the deal making and to fail to see the opportunity for what it is, or to assess how it is seen by others—bankers, competitors, others in the partnership, and so on.

Look for advice on how the opportunity can play out for both sides, and solicit watchouts about people, the process being used, or the deal itself.

Your network can include a wide variety of roles, e.g., others in the partnership, colleagues, bosses who serve as coaches, vendors or contractors with unique vantage points, regulators, the trade—as well as professional advisors, such as accountants, lawyers, engineers, and consultants.

SHEET THREE

Sheet Three, as seen in Template 8-2, is the record of the negotiation. It includes:

☐ Agreements reached in the meeting. Listed below are potential areas for simple agreement. Some are key to effective operation.

Agreement Topics

- Who operates what
- Operator authorities
  ⇒ Budget
  ⇒ Business plan
  ⇒ Compensation for staff
  ⇒ Operating competencies
  ⇒ Hire/fire
  ⇒ Credit
  ⇒ Operating parameters
  ⇒ Operations audit/access
- Dispute resolution (internal, requiring arbitration)
  ⇒ Negotiation choices
  ⇒ Arbitration choices
  ⇒ Mediation choices
  ⇒ Litigation domain preference

- Exit terms
- Professional services
- Governance
  - ⇒ Autonomy (clear management control)
  - ⇒ Flexibility
  - ⇒ Direction for the pursuit of business development, strategic planning, market planning
  - ⇒ Sponsorship
  - ⇒ Transparency
  - ⇒ Oversight
- Intent to own (termination by acquisition)
- Technology transfer
  - ⇒ Train
  - ⇒ Share proprietary information
- Organization
  - ⇒ Structure
  - ⇒ Role expectation (assignment letters for key positions)
  - ⇒ Communication norms/teamwork
- Scope of rights/disclaimers
- Exclusivity
- Geographic scope
- Duration
- Royalty rights
- Testing and acceptance
- Warranties
- Technical assistance and training/obligations/performance warranties/maintenance support obligations
- Cross-license rights
- Rights to use new inventions
- Title
- Acquisition of supplies
- Cooperative advertising and market database management

Work carefully with your legal experts before, during, and after the negotiation. The task of the legal expert is not to do the deal. Their job is to:

- Advise on what is legally possible.
- Counsel you on how to express agreements to maximize your legal return while minimizing your risk to liability.
- Ensure proper regulatory and recording compliance in the appropriate jurisdictions.

It is your task to determine economic value, operating terms, and market positions. What the legal expert proposes may unwind the deal. Understand the legal expert's intent but make your own decisions.

There are very good lawyers who are also good deal makers. When your lawyer becomes your deal maker, it may be prudent to hire another legal expert to perform oversight. It may be a good idea to scrutinize the lawyer/deal maker as you would a project manager or enterprise unit leader.

People who relegate the details to tax and legal experts often return to the closing to find a different deal—for the good or bad. Surprises at closing can kill a deal. With or without your experts, be clear about:

☐ **Action plans** that both sides agree to make happen
☐ **Follow-up** you need to make as a result of the meeting
☐ **Feedback from your network** on what happened in the deal meetings

For smaller initiatives, optimization within the value chain, such as a Supplier-Customer Action Team (SCAT), Sheets Four and Five, in Templates 8-3 and 8-4, respectively, are typically tailored to interface opportunities. The processes and dimensions for optimization are much like those found in design work for continuous improvement and innovation.

Once opportunities are identified, they should be evaluated and rank-ordered. There is normally resistance to quantifying costs and value expected. Nonetheless, quantification is needed to contrast opportunities, measure progress, and educate employees about decisions based on value. Following are criteria others have found useful:

OPTIMIZATION OPPORTUNITY: EVALUATION CRITERIA

- SVA (or Option Pricing or Equity Cash Flow)
- Cost of Improvement
- Payback
- Expense vs. Capital Funds
- Available Talent to Execute
- Urgency as to Need for Effective Operation
- Window of Opportunity
- Easy-to-do—a "Quick Hit"
- Time to Complete
- Image to Others
- Demonstration Project

(text continued on page 123)

Template 8-2.

Negotiation Preparation—Sheet Three

Agreements

Mutual Action Plans

Follow-Up

Network Feedback

TEMPLATE 8-3.

NEGOTIATION PREPARATION—SHEET FOUR

INTERNAL REQUIREMENT

$ _____ CAPITAL INVESTMENT

$ _____ ANNUAL CASH COMMITMENT

	1Q	2Q	3Q	4Q

SVA $ _____

ROI _____ %

SHARE _____ %

YR1	YR2	YR3	YR4	YR5	YR6	YR7	YR8	YR9	YR10

SHARED ANNUAL COSTS

	VALUE		COST/YR.	
	OURS	THEIRS	OURS	THEIRS
□ CAPITAL				
□ TALENT				
□ FACILITIES				
□ EXPENSES				
□ PROMOTION				
□ CUSTOMERS				

TERMS & CONDITIONS

□ RIGHT OF FIRST REFUSAL ON: _____

□ TECHNOLOGY TRANSFER: _____

□ EXIT CONDITIONS: _____

□ WARRANTS: _____

□ LIABILITIES: _____

□ INTELLECTUAL PROPERTY MANAGEMENT: _____

□ PROFIT-SHARING OR PRICE PARTICIPATION: _____

□ OTHER: _____

OPPORTUNITY (RANK ORDER)

□ PRIMARY SALES _____

□ SUPPLEMENTAL SALES _____

□ NETWORKED SERVICES _____

□ IMPACT TO COMPETITIVE CAPABILITY _____

GROW BUSINESS

□ LOCATION EXPANSIONS

□ SERVICES

□ DATABASES

□ FINANCIAL ENGINEERING

□ INTERCONNECT AGREEMENTS

□ TECHNOLOGY DEVELOPMENT

INTERNAL REVIEW   DATE

□ REGION   _____

□ LLC   _____

□ CORPORATE   _____

(text continued from page 120)

Sheets Four and Five are for major plays. They are used to provide exacting assessments of opportunities.

SHEET FOUR

The Internal Requirement Section defines the organizational performance expectations:

- Annual cash commitment, displayed by quarters
- Capital investment
- NOPAT (Net operating profit after taxes)
- Cost of capital
- Return on investment (ROI), forecast for five years with an assessment as to when the initial payback is complete
- The Shareholder Value Added (SVA) for the project. We recommend use of EVA™ (see "Valuation Models" inset).

   Others have taken a similar tact and used a generic label, SVA for shareholder value add. We are strong advocates of EVA but realize other valuation techniques and methods may need to be understood. Partners may use different models, or prospective partners and targets may provide different modes in information gathering. Further to the point, competitors may have a different intent and use different models. An excellent resource is a book by Copeland, Koller, and Murrin, of McKinsey & Company: *Valuation,* 2nd edition, John Wiley & Sons, 1996.
- Share

   No undertaking of alliances, joint ventures, or partnering is to be used to defeat anti-trust laws in the U.S. or other anti-competition laws elsewhere in the world. Particular care must be taken to evaluate compliance. Bruce Metge and Andrew Nathanson, et al., address this issue with suggestions on how to differentiate strategic alliances from JVs, and properly formulate strategic alliances. Included are case law references and a review on alliances in the U.S. Department of Justice Antitrust Division's International Operation Guidelines. Good legal counsel, as evidenced by their article, is desirable.[1]

VALUATION MODELS

Shareholder Value Added, or SVA, is growing popular among Wall Street analysts. Their enthusiasm influences how senior managers and boards view performance so the interest in SVA cascades into the corporate world. Long disenchanted with accounting principles to arrive at value, executives are shifting to an economic view of value. Why so? Accounting can distort value through manipulation. Accounting's view tends to focus too narrowly on today and does not support value creation typical for R&D, start-ups, marketing and advertising, and alliances. These efforts take time for value to accrue. Good projects never get launched because of initial negative cash flows—though in the long haul, they may create substantial value.

One presentation of SVA is EVA, a trademark of the firm Stern Stewart & Co. in Chicago. Evolving from the University of Chicago over the last 30 years, EVA has soared in popularity, for it has the highest correlation to Market Value Added (MVA) yet developed. As such, it promotes an understanding of what can be done in an organization to create shareholder value.[2]

SVA is a management tool. Discount SVA and you have the NPV of discounted cash flow. NPV helps value capital projects but does little to guide how value is managed along the way. The difference is in the use. SVA helps managers evaluate opportunity, execute strategy and measure performance. Incentive compensation can be set with it. The result is that managers are motivated to act like owners.

The three principles of SVA are:

- Innovate so current capital is fully utilized. Continuous improvement projects and transformation are encouraged because they yield value results with little or no additional capital
- Eliminate projects which do not exceed the cost of capital
- Invest capital where increased profits will more than cover the charge for additional capital

THE FORMULA

NOPAT – (Capital [Equity or Debt] × Cost of Capital) = SVA
Where NOPAT is net operating profit after tax
SVA is not without controversy. Two issues are debated. One is that accounting information can be adjusted to perform like SVA—in this case, why do the work of SVA? The reason is project valuation is only one of the uses for SVA. SVA can be used to assess value creation across

---

THE FORMULA (*continued*)

---

the life of the capital investment. This means SVA is a performance measurement for tracking progress to the forecast value. The other debated point is market share. Gary Hamel contends that market share is a better predictor of wealth creation.[3] To look only at SVA could cloud judgment. This debate is easily resolved, however. Market share and net income constitute materiality. Profit above the cost of capital is real value. That is SVA. On the other hand, market share creates value if margins from growth are not sacrificed. If you are smart, pursue share to get more of the SVA available.

SVA is a performance tool. Decisions can be evaluated. Reward can be aligned. SVA demonstrates that it is useful to apply debt in realizing growth. Another SVA premise is that less than full ownership (JVs) is beneficial. SVA is higher when less of a firm's total capital is placed at risk on a single project. Spreading the capital around by using partners to share risk yields greater access to more gallons. LLCs which avoid growth or dilute value with premature distributions or poor projects can be determined with SVA. The best partnership is the one with the best SVA performance since value creation is the goal.

Stern Stewart offers software and courses on SVA. See their website for course schedules and to download a demonstration program, at www.sternstewart.com.

For high-value ventures, work more than one case for internal discussion. Possibilities include:

- **Aggressive**—Exploitation beyond goal achievement
- **Desired**—Recommended for goal achievement
- **Minimum**—Bootstrap to initiate program for goal achievement
- **Broker**—Set Action into motion to benefit from others' goal achievement

Shared Assets

Shared assets list *what both sides must put forth* in the deal. This includes capital, people, facilities, expenses and customer bases. Each is assessed in terms of overall value and cost per year.

Terms and Conditions

Following are terms and conditions frequently found in partnering agreements. Additional terms and conditions can be determined by reviewing the "Agreements" column on Sheet Three (See Template 8-2, page 117). This review for Sheet Three includes a lengthy list of possible terms and conditions. They may apply here.

Right of first refusal defines future growth opportunities that you envision as possible extensions to the primary basis for partnering. This provides two advantages. One is that the partner must declare the intent to enter another business. If competitors are nurturing a deal with the partner, the partner must declare its interest. The second advantage is that you have a chance to participate first.

Exit conditions help you think ahead, "How do I get my money out of this venture?" and "Under what circumstances would I want to move on?" This also reminds you to declare what you would do if the partner were acquired—in particular by a competitor—or entered into an agreement with others impacting this deal but under terms or with parties unacceptable to you. Options for exits include selling to a strategic buyer—a leveraged buyout (LBO).

An LBO involving employee ownership funds can access discounted federal guaranteed loans—an approach known as an employee stock ownership program, or ESOP LBO, merger for cash or stock, or put forth an offering.

There are two basic kinds of offerings, private placement memoranda (PPM) to sophisticated investors, and initial public offerings (IPO) to stock exchanges. Exits can be generated by stock swaps, royalty positions on future revenues, license agreements, and other instruments representing rights to earnings or gains.

Warrants describe obligations and how they get managed.

Liabilities describe risks and how they get managed. The ones of greatest concern are based on regulatory requirements. The most impacting in recent times are environmental and health hazards. Litigation in the areas of product performance and human resources are included among the high risks which cause deals to come undone. Human resources include regulatory compliance in fair treatment, and the administration of pension plans. On the following page is a quick checklist:

LIABILITIES CHECKLIST

- Environmental Liabilities
- Financial Problems
- Criminal Involvement
- Litigation (Product, Fair Treatment)
- Antitrust/Competition Rules
- Cultural Rigidity
- Consumer Liability
- Transportation
- Patent Infringement
- Pre-Existing Conditions
- Databased Access, Storage Security
- Right to Privacy
- Indemnification of Partners
- Hidden Contracts
- Labor Contracts and Employment Agreements
- Product/Service Warranties, Guarantees, Pledges and Commitments
- Non-Compete Restrictions
- Judgments (e.g., required access for audits)

Intellectual property terms address copyrights, licenses and patents—how revenues and rights related to intellectual property will be managed. This is an area of increasing sophistication and complexity. Trade agreement, levy, and protection for the markets of concern are important variables to consider. In the end, multiple sovereignties may need to be operated in, and one chosen for administration of primary ownership.

Profit-sharing and *price participation* address how the pie is divided.

Organizational Opportunity

This section is important because it reminds you of possible elements to the deal. Equally important, it invites a rank-order of importance. Negotiators need to be clear on relative trade-offs among the various opportunities. *In the actual negotiation process, it is important to know what is most important and needs protection as well as what can be sacrificed.*

Michael Hudson, president of Allison Engines, the U.S. subsidiary of Rolls-Royce, posits the three basic reasons for partnering:

- Access to markets
- Capital formation
- Capturing synergies between firms

Following are possible "currencies" in ventures:

- Money
  ⇒ Cash Flow
  ⇒ Foreign Exchange
  ⇒ Debt Management
  ⇒ Equity Instruments
- Assets
  ⇒ Raw Materials
  ⇒ Inventory
  ⇒ Facilities
  ⇒ Equipment (e.g., IT, Packaging, Transport)
  ⇒ Databases
  ⇒ Locations
- Property Rights
  ⇒ Tangible (See Assets Above)
  ⇒ Intellectual (e.g., Copyrights, Patents for Technology/Business Analysis)
  ⇒ Commercial Agreements
- Channel Access
  ⇒ Delivery Logistics
  ⇒ Distributor System (or Characteristic)
  ⇒ Retail System (or Characteristic)
- Talent
  ⇒ Leadership
  ⇒ Technical
  ⇒ Marketing and Sales
  ⇒ Research and Development
  ⇒ Administrative
  ⇒ Public Affairs
  ⇒ Contract
- Other Partners/Commercial Relationships (e.g., Franchise, License Agreement, Import/Export Registration)

Keep as much as possible in consideration. "Grow Business" opportunities can often serve to educate partners on what is possible. They also can be distractions which you assert but easily sacrifice to achieve a more important end. Following are potential contributions prospective partners can make to growth:

- Expand Current Base
- Accelerate Business Results
- Reduce Risk
- Avoid Diluting Focus
- Complement a Capability
  ⇒ Financial Engineering
  ⇒ Market Entry
  ⇒ Market Development
  ⇒ Channel Access
  ⇒ Globalization
  ⇒ Technology
  ⇒ Talent
  ⇒ Infrastructure
  ⇒ Capacity to Produce
  ⇒ Technology Transfer
  ⇒ Value-Adding Services
  ⇒ Privatization Access/Rights
  ⇒ Maintenance and Warranty Support

The *internal review* reminds you to communicate results to decision makers or to seek the appropriate sponsorship or approval.

SHEET FIVE

Growth plan highlights list the key steps needed to make things happen. A share projection forecast for five years is included.

Any *price model* to determine sharing should be indicated so that quick references can be made in negotiation discussions. Databases pertinent to the price model should be referenced.

A *deal structure* helps to keep in mind that several possibilities exist for formulating a partnering arrangement. The negotiator's preferences should be indicated. On page 131 are possible configurations:

TEMPLATE 8-4.

NEGOTIATION PREPARATION—SHEET FIVE

☐ **GROWTH PLAN HIGHLIGHTS:**

VOLUME PROJECTION

YR1	YR2	YR3	YR4	YR5

EBITDA PROJECTION

YR1	YR2	YR3	YR4	YR5

☐ **STRUCTURE:**

☐ **FINANCING**
   ☐ SOURCE:
   ☐ KEY CONTACT:
   ☐ TERMS:

☐ **PARTNER VALUE-ADD**
   ☐ OPERATIONS INNOVATIONS
   ☐ SITE DEVELOPMENT
   ☐ FINANCING
   ☐ OTHER (EXPLAIN)

☐ **DOCUMENTS REQUIRED:**

☐ **ACQUISITION VALUE-ADD**
   ☐ OPERATIONS INNOVATIONS
   ☐ SITE DEVELOPMENT
   ☐ FINANCING
   ☐ OTHER (EXPLAIN)

Possible Business Relationships

- Investment
- Strategic Purchase of Another (Ally to Acquire)
- Merger with Another
- Joint Venture
- R&D Consortium
- Franchise
- License Agreement
- Preferred Provider
- Life Cycle Management Partner
- Simple Contract Provider
- Industry Group

Partnering value-add services are the services relevant to the deal. Each is assessed for value. As with the various opportunities on Sheet Four, these factors need to be compared on the preparation sheet so that trade-offs among the alternatives can be valued, rank-ordered and handled appropriately in the negotiation.

REFERENCES

1. Metge, Bruce, Esq., Andrew Nathanson, Esq., Mintz, Levin, Cohn, Ferris, Glovsky and Popeo, P.C., "Strategic Alliances Under the Antitrust Laws," Boston, 10196 Website entry, http://www.mintz.com/newspubs/antitrust/antt1096.htm

2. "Best Practices: Debate: Duking It Out Over EVA," *Fortune,* August 4, 1997, p. 232

3. Ibid., p. 232.

CHAPTER 9

Managing Disputes

In negotiation, you are smart to set the boundaries for managing disputes and exits. Our discussion of disputes will cover the nature of disputes, options for their resolution, the special case of intellectual property, cross-border sensitivities, and alternatives for making an exit.

Most anything can cause a dispute in a partnering relationship. Most times, by-passes in human communication, aggravation of the differences between parties, or declining performance of the parent or the shared enterprise are to blame.

Regardless of the cause, mechanisms to resolve disputes should be worked out ahead of time. These have the potential to work the problem closest to the point of origin and quickly restore harmony. Malcolm Law, at Exxon Chemical Company, describes dissolution terms within the initial agreements to be very useful. He offers that such agreements are analogous to prenuptial agreements—in the worst case, as a means to end a conflict or simply because it makes sense for a party to leave the relationship. An exit with sound dissolution terms, then, does not necessarily bankrupt the venture.

In negotiation, a mechanism should be defined with its own terms and conditions for re-calibrating if circumstances warrant adaptation. Lock in to a process. The process to alter the process should also be defined. Then what you have is a cue and a process for resolving disputes, rather than to have disputes linger on and continue to distract.

Secondly, the flexibility to adapt the process presents a beginning point for discussions about adaptation, when warranted. This is just enough rigor to ensure timely action. There is flexibility to respond to whatever the reality in operations may be in the future.

In a dispute, there are five elements: 1) the personalities designated to represent parties, 2) the firms in which value is created, 3) the value to the firms and their shared enterprise, 4) the power to act as individuals or firms, and 5) the legal entitlements of all those involved: people, firms, or communities. It is important to understand all the elements and how they interact.

Personalities run the gamut. People can be of all types and inclinations. Capturing roles, responsibilities, the manner in which people involved are rewarded and recognized, and their intentions will guide prediction and help address expectations in any conflict resolution.

Firms possess intentions and act on the marketplace. These, along with what value they possess, can be subjects to disputes, i.e., assets, knowledge, access and talent. Usually, you judge the firm by the statements of its representatives. Care needs to be taken to validate both the support for the direction taken by the representative and for the representative's influence in the firm.

Power in the marketplace is determined by networks accessing influence, brand identification, market share, material wealth, net income, and growth opportunities. Entitlements are determined by agreements such as purchase orders, commitments and contracts, or the applicable laws.

The nature of disputes is to devote attention to symptoms of deeper-rooted problems. Full resolution will be served by examining expectations around the dispute from the perspective of the five elements. These reveal at least the *who* and the *what*. Surfacing an all-around look is likely to surface the "real" *why*. In the end, the discussion helps lead to more than a band-aid solution and prevents future disputes.

Following is an illustration of the value in being thorough and transparent. The tranparency evolved over time and was built by a foundation of thorough inquiry on the five elements.

WAR STORY

The Empire Had No Clothes

The situation involved a multinational and its foreign company partner. Their joint venture was in dispute over a major equipment purchase. There were strong personality differences which defeated honesty and led to a phony openness. Each side tried to outmaneuver the other, professing candor and hurt feelings for transgressions all the way.

The firms were clear on intent and shared intent. Both parties wanted to be able to compete in a tough international market. The hidden agenda for the multinational was to assign as many charges to the JV as possible and to siphon income from the government's backers in the international financial community.

The covert ploy of the government's representative was to appease the backers and accrue points for the government. Should this mean a three- or four-percent increase in cost to operate, this would be an acceptable surcharge for feathering their political caps as individuals.

In the contract, both sides held equal power in making any decision. The power of knowledge was very different. The multinational did work in many nations and knew how international financing may carry expectations for favor within political systems. The government's representatives knew more about how to make things happen with the government, and, as expected, had better "assets" among government decision makers. In particular, the government's people had strong relations with bureaucrats and import authorities.

The multinational eventually learned to pair two personalities in a "good cop-bad cop" team. They removed the bad cop from their immediate presence but he attended key meetings. The good cop strengthened friendships with government players. The good cop opened the session, reinforced the bad cop's objections with more subtle statements, and closed each session. The team developed an agenda to expose what was happening in the political behavior. Their objective was not to stop it altogether. They wanted it checked in the specific case, and limited for any future major equipment purchase. This is what was accomplished in the end.

The journey to their agenda began by getting intimate with the divided government team to gain information. Things moved along by positioning the issue on a meeting agenda with another topic. The other topic's resolution was anticipated to aid the government's spirit of nationalism and policy for full employment. A quid pro quo with respect to the equipment issue requiring the multinational's best benefit on this topic, if called for under explicit terms in the contract, would cause the government hardship in the media.

The meeting was held and a problem-solving approach was indicated. Lower-level staff from the multinational put forth histories of payback in other projects. Their presentation revealed what had been learned from the divided government team. During an early break, the good cop let it be known that he could anticipate that a complete loss on the equipment issue would elicit resistance to the "slam dunk" anticipated on the second topic. The tone was set for another level of disclosure, but in a comfortable way. Understanding was expressed for political decisions.

There was internal debate in sidebars and in the mainstream meeting among the government members. Pretty soon it became apparent to the government that there was a need to do something to appease the multinational. This was confirmed over lunch by the good cop. In the mainstream meeting, it was reported by lower-level staff that there were inadequacies in the favored vendor's equipment. The good cop hushed this and another multinational staff member hinted at a compromise: "Let this one go, but make the other two purchases according to the original plan."

Both sides discussed the solution. The suggestion became the decision and it was held as a precedent in the worst case for future differences on major equipment purchases. The debate, both sides felt, threatened the joint venture's existence, and it was set aside.

MORE THAN ONE WAY TO RE-SKIN A CAT

There are several alternatives for dispute resolutions which can be specified in the start-up agreement. We recommend specifying that operators propose a conflict resolution technique. It is not easy to impose a specific mechanism. Encouraging operators to create a means to restore harmony, however, is possible. The contractual imposition ensures that it is done.

To the benefit of the shared enterprise, problems are first dealt with by those closest to where they are felt. Clarifying and minimizing owners' involvement on the front end further prevents disagreements since meddling is limited. Having specific contractual terms permits operators a means for surfacing abuse by an owner.

When serious issues surface, internal or external to the operation, it is smart to have a quick-to-apply resolution process. This can mean negotiation, mediation, or arbitration. The objective is to avoid litigation.

Mediation employs third-party facilitators to guide the discovery of shared interests and other common ground to restore harmony. Arbitration can be binding or non-binding. Arbitration is lengthy and costly, involving more participants in the process. The benefits of arbitration are specialist involvement—usually, the involvement of someone knowledgeable of the industry or an expert in arbitration, confidentiality in contrast to going to public courts, the avoidance of facing precedents in courts, and the right to stipulate substantive law (pursuit of rights) but to accept adjudication under different procedural law.

There are many sources of arbitration and accepted norms. Productive referral can lead to industry specialists and established norms. Examples of resources for the latter are the International Commercial Code in Paris and the World Intellectual Property Organization's Arbitration Center in Geneva.

We advocate negotiated solutions through regularly scheduled owner meetings when operator resolution breaks down. This tends to work better if it is facilitated but does not take on the legalistic tone found in traditional mediation. Failing this, we recommend that the start-up agreement addresses arbitration. The faster it kicks in, the better it will be as a deterrent. The threat of arbitration can motivate the use of negotiation.

Arbitration carries several questions. Each situation must assess what is best. Do you assign arbitration as binding or not? Is a single arbitrator used or is a panel assembled? How are substitutions to be picked if changes in availability occur? Is there a pre-selected slate from which an arbitrator is chosen, or is there simply a pre-selected, rank-ordered list? What expertise is most important? If there is a panel, is everyone a voting member: commercial, legal, technical? For global agreements, where is the court of venue if all else fails? What are the norms for the venue in arbitration? For example, on the European continent, practice promotes independent judgment, and Anglo-Americans invite experts to be persuasive.

Mediation and arbitration are the early phases in alternative dispute resolution (ADR). These are modified judicial settings, more costly and rigid. They go by different names in different jurisdictions. The aim is to remain outside of the courts. A few years ago we met with a major global accounting firm. Their revenues were annually in the billions of dollars from handling dispute resolutions for their clients. The money paid to arbitrators, attorneys, and accountants can be quite high. The rigidity of the process can also impede future business relations for the venture, for those ventures continuing after a dispute.

Todd Carver and Albert Vondra wrote this observation about the ADR in 1994:

> . . . The bad news is that ADR, as currently practiced, too often mutates into a private judicial system that looks and costs like the litigation it's supposed to prevent.
>
> . . . The good news is that a number of companies have learned to use ADR effectively, and those companies are in fact reaping ADR's predicted benefits: lower costs, quicker dispute resolutions, and outcomes that preserve and sometimes even improve relationships.
>
> . . . At Chevron, for instance, ADR-based mediation of one dispute cost $25,000, whereas mediation through outside counsel would have cost an estimated $700,000 and going to court as much as $2.5 million over a period of three to five years. . . .

Carver and Vondra detail several reasons but focus on this as a key explanation: "Without the commitment of top management, ADR quickly turns into litigation-in-disguise. . . ."[1]

When it is all said and done, and no resolution exists, litigation is the end of the line. This is very costly and risks precedents of even greater proportion. In the discussion to follow on exits, we talk about ending a relationship. Sometimes a smooth exit is preferred to litigation or a litigation-based separation. Exits, of course, can accrue earlier through negotiation, mediation or arbitration, or through another ADR.

INTELLECTUAL PROPERTY RIGHTS: HEAD GEAR FOR ALLIANCES

Intellectual property is growing more complex. A matter as much of trade policy and agreement as it is of law, intellectual property is complicated by advancing technology, and the fluid nature of Internet exchanges across borders. Further, political and commercial tensions disrupt standards in what is protected. In the setting of the agreement for the joint enterprise, here are the issues to address:

INTELLECTUAL PROPERTY QUERIES

- What metrics will demonstrate the value contributed across time?
- What medium of value extraction will be best—royalty, license, lump sum payment, stock exchange, etc.? How is the medium shared?
- What can be done to credit and appropriately value intellectual property imbedded in other, future technologies?
- How to protect and maximize value in shared interests—now and in the future? Is there an issue on protection internal to the partners? If so, how is it managed?
- Where technology improvements are frequent, obtaining access to the future is essential—how do you avoid exclusives for initial prospects?
- How do you bundle for the alliance or de-bundle to permit other relations?
- How do the collateral issues get managed—reinvestment in innovation, the relationship of shared technologies to other technologies of the parties, sales database access, and marketing agreements?

These are interactive influences which must be tracked and clearly defined to avoid tensions and conflict. Where intellectual property is at issue, more time and effort need to be given. You need to think this out ahead of time.

WAR STORY

Is It Just a Rabbit or Do We Have a Pregnant Bunny?

A high-tech media application was set for negotiation. The inventor had done his homework. He knew the application on its own had high potential. However, he felt he could extract greater value by selling interest in the media technology to each of the various applications, i.e., military, aerospace, medicine, entertainment, agriculture, and industrial arts. His choice is in sharp contrast to most inventors who sell the base device, permitting others to extract the value from tailoring applications to a sector.

Never go to the negotiation without being prepared. Know your value. Know how to extract value—as a single product or combined with others. Bring terms to the negotiation for getting at intellectual property which are thought out ahead of time. Your preparation will allow you to explore the subject with others from a position of confidence and comprehension.

CROSS-BORDER SENSITIVITIES: SOMETIMES ROAST MONKEY IS ROAST MONKEY

In addition to trade agreements' impacts on intellectual property, there are several terms and conditions applicable in cross-border agreements:

CROSS-BORDER ISSUES

- Show respect for the sovereignties involved—this includes their community and cultural norms, regulatory and contractual law, and applicable levy. Choosing a venue may be a part of the dynamic for selecting a sovereignty. Sensitivity should be given to levying, licensing, and permitting to conduct business, trade policy, and trade agreements. Consideration should be given, as well, to ensuring mutual respect with other sovereignties of key markets or suppliers, security for conducting business, and infrastructure.

(continued)

CROSS-BORDER ISSUES *(continued)*

- Protection of undisclosed information such as trade secrets
- Control of anti-competitive practices , e.g., in contractual licenses
- Right to information
- Enforcement
- Remedies

Discussions on the front-end will not only avoid problems down the line but will also serve to educate those not familiar with preparing thorough agreements in cross-border situations. Do not count on those with prior cross-border experience. The risk is that they use paradigms of exploitation. Traditional views of underdeveloped countries do not fit emerging economies. This is what some are trying to convey by saying the days of the multinational are giving way to the global firm. This is something we support in its reality. Too often the re-labeling is only repackaging.

In the exploratory and negotiation discussions in cross-cultural situations, extraordinary effort must be made to ensure that communication is complete. It is prudent to test for understanding. This is very true when translators are involved. Hire translators who are of the country, but who have lived in your country and are familiar with business idioms and non-verbal communication in both cultures.

Summarize ideas frequently. Reinforce with written words—key words on paper while the conversation is on-going. Flow diagrams, for instance, often break through language problems when the sequence of events is made clear. Icons can also reinforce or supplant the need for the spoken word.

Avoid using questions that can be answered with a "yes" or "no." Make certain you get complete answers which clearly indicate positions taken. Slow the rate of speech for people listening to you in their second language or to make translation easier. Keep an eye to non-verbals.

Read about the stereotypical differences between your culture and the other person's. A good tool is Frank Acuff's *How to Negotiate with Anyone, Anywhere Around the World*. The stereotypical is not to be expected in everyone, all the time, but it will suggest sensitivities, or heighten your awareness to differences.

WAR STORY

Tarzan No Eat Jane or Boy . . . Cheetah Is a Different Story

A group of expatriates, together having experienced every continent, were reminiscing in Colombia. Several war stories had been retold when the eldest spoke.

"I remember coming here after World War II and traveling the Amazon looking for oil and negotiating access from the local people. We got back to some pretty raw country and a tribe spotted us. They were more curious than spooked by us. We were more frightened than curious. They had an uncanny way of just appearing in the jungle, like in the old Tarzan movies.

"Anyway, we were invited to the village for dinner. Our guide's English was not that good. Best we could figure out his advice was, to stay alive, do not offend. Eat what they ate and show you are pleased. We thought he said they had been cannibals or were. His verb usage was not clear.

"The meal was served. The center piece looked like a baked human baby. We all turned green. This caught the chief's eye who told the guide to explain it was monkey. That didn't help a lot."

Know your local customs and be yourself. Common sense will guide you as well as anything. Anticipate less intolerance of you, and more acceptance. Use the knowledge of culture to understand others rather than be a phony mimic. In all, the cross-border experience is rich and fun.

Some of the most exciting and interesting deals will be internationally oriented. As is obvious, cultural differences can present challenges. Given the globalization of business, appreciating differences and knowing how to resolve conflicts are extremely important. We talked to Willis Brown, president of Hughes Mid-East, Ltd. Willis was a vice president at McDonnell-Douglas when they defeated Airbus and sustained aircraft purchases for his firm by King Fahd of Saudi Arabia. The transaction was built on Willis' great respect for the king, and his ability to establish a trusting relationship. In the grand scheme of things, Willis was effective at securing the necessary government support for the deal from the late Secretary of Commerce Ron Brown.

We asked Willis what two or three things would defeat a global strategic business relationship. Willis replied, "Deals usually go sour when the partners have management style differences or the trust element is lost." In a nutshell, Willis' global experience is much like other executives we interviewed—learning that there are differences across cultures, but that the basics are the same.

Willis pointed out that in developing economies,

> . . . The biggest cultural issue seems to be trust. This comes through relationship building which takes time and effort. Potential partners will want to know who they are dealing with, not just the company name. In many countries throughout the developing world, there are just a few families that control business and commerce. Often these groups control entire segments of the economy and their wealth is considerable.
>
> If one is looking to link up for a megaproject, then it is advisable to find a large local conglomerate for financial and political considerations. The merchant families in this area are very accessible and always on the lookout to link up with reputable U.S. firms. One note of caution is that once you are in these relationships, it is sometimes very difficult to dissolve, so choose carefully! In some countries, the law prohibits the dissolution of a partnership or agency without the concurrence of the local partner.
>
> Strategic relations can be an ideal way to expand globally but it should be used along with other methods of market penetration. Partnering may not always be advisable. There may be instances where it is desirable to go it alone on the strength of the company in other geographic locations, and on the international reputation of the firm. It will really depend on the type of business, the customer, and country laws, etc.

Willis noted his involvement with a European partner which was a love/hate relationship. They provided the legal means to do business and have political clout. On the other hand, they often overstated their capabilities, and wanted to take the lead when they did not have the ability. All in all, he concludes, "The vision of global expansion has to be tempered with the reality that everyone does not think or act the same, and a partner's true motivations may be very different."

EXIT STAGE RIGHT!

Exit means how you will leave the partnering relationship. This is an economic value question. How will you extract value? When we advise people to address the question of exit on the front end, corporate staff and managers are appalled. Investors and entrepreneurs are nonplused. Investors and entrepreneurs want to know how they will get rich. Do you expect to sell to a strategic buyer? Sell to your partner(s)? Sell to employees and managers? Will you consider a placement of some sort? A private placement to sophisticated investors—an initial public offering to a stock exchange? Does it make sense to initiate a royalty, a license, or a franchise?

We coach clients to be defining about exits in three ways. First, under what terms and conditions will you leave the partnership? Say it up front and be clear as to the tolerance of all parties. Secondly, express when and how you would either invite or accept an offer to leave the partnership. Explain how you think value will be extracted throughout the partnership and at the moment of withdrawal. Third, under what conditions and with what mechanism will you be willing to grow out of the current relationship and evolve to something else—expansion of current business, or entry to new business?

In the exit discussion, be clear about what you want should your partner leave the relationship. Do you want the opportunity to buy out your partner? Are there parties you would find unacceptable as a new partner? How will liabilities be handled? What do you want in terms of notice or other involvement in the process? Do you need assurances—like an escrow account or other guarantees—to accept an out?

The greatest benefit to the exit discussion is the focus it brings to value. Better metrics evolve from the discussion. Participants learn the risks, opportunity costs, and value-add requirements. The view of the venture then is not that of a corporate home, a function, or a facility. The new venture is an enterprise, in pursuit of its own vitality for making money.

REFERENCES

1. Carver, Todd B., and Albert A. Vondra, "Alternative Dispute Resolution: Why It Doesn't Work and Why It Does," *Harvard Business Review*, May-June, 1994, p. 120–121, 123.

PART THREE

Making It Happen

CHAPTER 10

Closing and Implementing the Deal

The negotiation may take multiple sessions to complete and be an iterative process whereby positions are agreed upon but approvals must be obtained. Preliminary agreements and follow-ups to get information or test sensitivities with others outside the room are drafted, improved, and drafted again. Guidance from others is incorporated or challenged. Then there is the continuous validation process achieved by maintaining network inputs.

In some cases, it may be appropriate to conduct a "pre-due diligence." This step has the objective of learning details to confirm elements of the negotiation before moving further into the process. Like the eventual due diligence to validate the agreement, there is a checklist to follow. The checklist should be tailored to each situation with careful review by accountants, lawyers, tax experts, human resource specialists, and environmental and technical specialists appropriate to the technology. Our suggestion for building the checklist is the intensive business review found in Chapter 2, Template 2-1.

In the logistics for negotiations, be electronically prepared. The virtual office should be your tool kit. Have the capability to prepare agreements, print them out, and fax or e-mail them to experts like lawyers who may be far away. Do not permit experts' schedules to get in the way. Have them available in the room or on-line, as is most appropriate to the deal—not at their convenience.

In the layout, have space to meet together and meet apart. Do not use self-linking laptops. Be very mindful of cyber theft—it is a stark reality. This is not to say that your prospective partner cannot be trusted. Those outside the deal—competitors, venture investors, media—might learn useful information to compete against the new entity or to interfere with getting the deal done in order to get in the deal themselves, to break news you want kept quiet, to delay the new competitive force, or to extract value in stock speculations of the parents.

After all the agreements are aligned to reality, and approvals won, then the deal closes. The real work now begins. First there is the development of a business plan and the orchestration plan to make it all come together. A successful negotiation is one that creates an enterprise which in turn creates economic value for shareholders, and provides a life worth living for all of the participants.

When the deal closes, a celebration is in order. Invite all the stakeholders, not just the ones who attended the negotiation. Start the venture with everyone feeling good about the new beginning.

Reflection

For the most part, we are more alike than different. When Gary was a child traveling across cultures, the world was still rebuilding from the trauma of World War II and developing nations were struggling amidst trade barriers and their own inefficiencies. Times have changed, however. The middle class existence is very much a commodity among urbanites the world over. People want their children fed, clothed and educated; they aspire to meaningful work; and they enjoy a good movie with a Coke and hamburger afterwards.

As we negotiate, we should remember that we are all people. Each wants our uniqueness respected and we share many ambitions, though styles may differ. We want the same things. The appeal for a fair deal is thus more universal than our prejudices may allow.

By the way, billionaires are commodities, too. They are all quick of mind in perceiving opportunity and ask good questions about how their money is to be used. Culture and personal eccentricity may carve unique images but, at the end of the day, they are shrewd in their judgment of value. They expect to be treated fairly. If we are to be clever in negotiation, let us be like them.

IMPLEMENTATION

Warp Speed!

Gene Rodenberry's imagination created *Star Trek's* Captain Jean-Luc Picard for us. Envision the good captain standing on the bridge of the *Starship Enterprise,* looking forward into the universe. Without turning to face his Number One, he simply commands, "Make it so."

To listen to the comments in and around the time of deal closings, it seems that most investment bankers and deal-making lawyers, as well as senior executives, think this is all it takes to implement complex business strategies. We've often heard comments like, "They'll figure it out." "Good people always get things done." "Why can't they just make the deal work?" "What is wrong with those people, can't they get along?" "Why don't they just follow our plan?" "Five or ten years ago, I would be done by now."

There is more chaos than needs to be. There is also a great deal of tension. The distractions dilute value. Sometimes, value is destroyed by the messy beginnings. Maybe there would be more effort made to properly orchestrate business, were it realized how much value is lost. Better yet, the loss should also be measured and published.

On a more positive note, we have witnessed implementation which not only fulfilled the deal maker's planned implementation, but also achieved new insight beyond the plan anticipated at the time of closing. The better approach was conceived after the partnering was agreed upon. Sooner than anyone expected, results were accelerated and new business realized. A rare event, it should be the dominant pattern in business. Seeing what can be done makes it difficult to accept less. The comparative advantage is only achieved with good planning and effort.

Entering the 21st century, we need to carefully orchestrate making partnering relations happen. Simple or complicated, we need to plan and achieve a new level of precision. All value must be extracted to sustain a firm's ability to compete on a global basis. Any value left on the table will be grasped by others. The effect is either that others will compete against you better, or that you will not be rewarded with future capital investment.

Investors will not support your firm if you allow value to slip through your fingers. Others who do not make the same mistake will be more attractive. What saves most firms is that many others make the same mistake. The difference today, in contrast to a decade ago, is that someone in the market with you, or a new entrant, will eventually figure out what to do. At that moment, the bar is raised in your market contests.

We examine implementation with a precision possible only with adaptation in business landscapes, and enabling emerging strategies to succeed. Three broad topics are explored:

- The settings in which you will orchestrate
- The processes for implementation
- The means for shared owner relations

Settings for implementation include an array of new beginnings: product launches, projects, mergers and acquisitions, the start-up of new facilities or ventures, and reengineered units. Value-chain optimization, a function of more than one process in the array, represents settings from supplier-customer action teams to internal partnering to customer intimacy. Growth initiatives are complicated settings which may overlap with new beginnings, or link new beginnings with expansion of current business.

Processes for implementation are highly interdependent. Communication, design, learning, application, stewardship, and leadership are orchestrated into mosaics for change. Attention is given below to broad change strategies which leverage most, if not all, of these processes.

Shared owner relations addresses the level of involvement owners should have in partnering, methods for sponsoring shared endeavors, and how to complete an owner audit. The owner audit is gaining new attention as a tool for reluctant activists among institutional investors, and passive investment fund managers. The owner audit validates management's assumptions and strategies, or points out what else should be done. The owner audit can be an effective catalyst for transformation, and facilitate important strategy initiatives.

Settings for Implementation

Given that partnering is an underpinning to nearly all aspects of business, there are numerous settings in which implementation of partnering agreements occur. Following each overview of the major partnering settings, there is a brief based on our experiences identifying the key participants with essentials for success and watchouts. The most varied category of settings is new beginnings.

Capturing global markets and orchestrating across multiple borders makes product launches highly complex. As a new beginning for a partnership, the emphasis is primarily a new product or service for an existing channel. New channels or channel entrants may be a part of the new beginning.

New Beginnings: Product Launches

Participants:

- Firm
- Channel

Essentials:

- Prepare a detailed landscape of the launch to plan and orchestrate; track interrelationships across and within channels.
- Establish relationships in advance within the communities, channels, and markets important to expediting the launch.
- Permit flexibility among regions to address local market characteristics. Do not vary so greatly as to create cross-border purchases among channels of different regions.
- Design incentives based on total value-chain performance of the new product—this encourages optimization.
- Predetermine value of value-added services.
- In preparation, determine interactions and interdependencies in value among new product and existing products; develop optimization scenarios prior to launch negotiations.
- Ascertain global regulatory environment and approach in sequence determined by cascading acceptance and need to access a particular region.
- Establish a crisis hopper—convey to staff and channel the importance of a timely response to problems. Give user complaints the highest priority. Be transparent and do not hide product performance difficulties. Compensate and take action to restore confidence.
- Where there are questions about consumer acceptance, sponsor advertising* and consumer education through channel partners—pursue local solutions (*includes channel decision to use national campaigns).
- In go-direct initiatives, media and logistics are the partners. Base a portion of their compensation on product performance. Carefully align campaigns to local norms. Tailor logistics to local infrastructure.
- When competition is amidst a parallel launch, keep track of the competition's progress. Anticipate that the competitive environment may invite irresponsible behavior from them or your allies. Move quickly to address any dysfunction.

(continued)

New Beginnings: Product Launches *(continued)*

Watchouts:

- Do not ignore your technical staff's cautions regarding performance, use, or storage of the product.
- Do not outsource key steps in your manufacturing and delivery functions which bottleneck or directly impact end users. Packaging, storage and handling, in particular steps just prior to user acquisition, should be stewarded for careful handling.
- Do not assume that one regulatory agency's acceptance within a country guarantees others' acceptance.
- Do not drop your vigil because you successfully transfer product to a channel intermediary. Steward performance to end users.

Complexity accelerates when the product in the launch is highly regulated such as hazardous materials, medical wastes, medicines, foods, and the like. Entry licenses and regulatory acceptance may need to run in sequence or be in parallel, depending on the circumstances. In some cases, starting with the European Union or with U.S. environmental regulatory agencies, acceptance gains credibility in other regions of the world. Even when there is no special regulatory or trade issue, the process can still be complex.

Packaging and labeling, channel management, and the logistics infrastructure all must coordinate across cultural and language barriers. Currency variations influence pricing and, when not well thought out, invite cross-border purchases and other value-diluting trade practices. Many people with numerous expectations ride the business landscape of a product launch, further complicating the process. The launch represents a myriad of partnering dynamics up and down the value chain, each needing to be understood and effectively managed.

Projects of any sort involve internal partnering, and work with contractors and vendors. The more identity there is with the project among participants, regardless of their role, the better it may be for project success. Exxon was among the first to assign contractor staff to project management teams to provide seamless contribution. Heretofore, it was unheard of to use the "best player" if it meant subordinating Exxon staff to a contract project engineer or manager.

From small projects to mega projects worth billions of dollars, there are multiple agendas to manage and put into the field. Several years ago, concurrent effort became an important learning agenda for engineers. Working parallel accelerated progress. Keeping the points of overlap among multiple segments of work increased the complexity in project management.

Projects create new beginnings and the buzz of activity encompassing a project is difficult enough to plan, monitor, and implement. Multiple owners provide a means to share risk but may also send mixed signals—imposing even more top-down direction. Owner disputes can have as their effect the kind of delay associated with frequent design changes by technical specialists. The result is the same—a change order to the plan of action.

In a similar vein, project design and execution may require multiple parties to complete the task (see **New Beginnings: Projects** below). Should any party over-focus on their individual task, there is a good chance the overall project will be impaired. Building team effort is important to allay these concerns. Reward, in part, should function from total project success to properly align interests.

The complexity in projects grows with the project's scope, the crossing of borders, the resistance of the community, as well as the number of parties involved or impacted. Important work can be done to enroll broad support across relationships for the action plan.

New Beginnings: Projects

Participants:

- Owner(s)
- Financial Backers
- Prime Contractor(s)
- Subcontractors in Design, Procurement, Construction, Project Infrastructure
- Community Sponsors or Interest Groups

Essentials:

- In the case of multiple owners, a means to agree upon directions and corrections among themselves before issuing change orders

(continued)

New Beginnings: Projects *(continued)*

- Shared vision of success and interpretation of the project landscape among owners and contractors
- Provide timely communication and project stewardship information to stakeholders—inside and outside the project community
- Pursue a thorough understanding of the project landscape with special attention to investment vulnerabilities
- Teamwork among design, procurement and execution—whether they are internal functions or subcontractors and prime contractors
- Align some or all of reward for all parties to final completion
- Create transparency among players with respect to progress, costs and vulnerabilities—offer an invitation with appropriate access to influence outcomes with insight

Watchouts:

- Frequent change orders
- Disputes among owners which drift to project management
- Project wind-down—the hesitation to complete because there is no next project or the identity with the project has grown too strong
- Competition among parties
- Indifference to community expectations

There are strong similarities in the integration of different work cultures into an alliance, and melding firms in mergers. In mergers and acquisitions, new beginnings are fostered by new owners and the involvement of two or more independent work cultures. It is popular now to ally to acquire or divest prior to the final merger.

Ashlish Nanda and Peter Williamson examined how joint ventures could be used to facilitate restructuring:

> When seeking to sell businesses such as these, the restructuring CEO faces two fundamental issues. One is how to convey what the business is worth to a potential purchaser: to make the unknown known. . . .
>
> The second issue is how to maintain the health of the business during the process of selling it. . . . Labeling a business "for sale" may result in distracted employees and distrustful customers, distributors, and vendors. . . . [1]

McKinsey consultants Joel Bleeke and David Ernst studied the evolution of strategic alliances to determine how they may evolve into acquisitions and have written a book on the subject, *Collaborating to Compete: Using Strategic Alliances and Acquisitions in the Global Marketplace.* They observed, "The key to understanding whether an alliance is likely to lead to a sale is to project how bargaining power will evolve." They posit several types of alliances. Two types are probable to end as acquisitions: alliances between a strong player and a weaker one in which, as the old song says, only the strong survive; and alliances between two strong players in which differences surface, and one side or the other exits.[2]

The logic usually pursued in merger integration is to take the best of both worlds and create a new one. This is often the result but rarely does the result come close to realizing the very best of the firms merged. One firm will dominate and subordinate the other(s). In doing so, some good attributes get lost. Why? Integration does not even approach being a rational process unless there is strong leadership, capable facilitation, and a knowledge of how to blend work systems and cultures.

In a merger, an internal partnership is being fused. It requires independent parties to come together and make a business work. All parties have their agendas and methods of working through them. This is highly complex, and like most forms of alliances, the probability for failure is high.

New Beginnings: Mergers and Acquisitions

Participants:

- Multiple Firms

Essentials:

- Assess the cultural compatibility among players.
- Have owners choose and announce the leadership tier prior to or immediately after the announcement of closing.
- In a timely manner, resolve decisions about who will leave, and who will stay in what roles.
- Demonstrate strong leadership to focus on the future together and to promote letting go of today and the past.

(continued)

New Beginnings: Mergers and Acquisitions *(continued)*

- Provide strong leadership statements as to why the new entity offers hope.
- Work hard to promote shared experiences among all tiers of leadership and key opinion leaders representing others in the firm. Planning sessions, technology exchange conferences, learning seminars and simulations all create contact with the chance for meaningful interaction and informal discussion.
- Pick accounting, human resource management and information technology solutions and do not try to meld what should not be mixed, nor operate in parallel. All things being equal, toss a coin.
- When multiple facilities need consolidation, take the opportunity to experiment with virtual organizations.
- Excluding trade secrets and other proprietary information, be transparent to stakeholders about progress, problems and challenges— if a mistake is to be made, overcommunicate.
- Establish a crisis hopper and sustain it for more than a year after closing. Do not let things fall through the cracks. In particular, be customer responsive.
- Leadership should put the spotlight on customer responsiveness above getting organized—organization is a never ending story. When people take their eyes off the market road they may have a tragic accident. The fate of the firm is at risk.
- Assemble an infrastructure according to market requirements.
- Marry firms because they will create new business.

Watchouts:

- Do not permit rumor to go unchallenged.
- Do not forget investor relations.
- Do not permit investor relations to preclude timely communication to customers and employees.
- Move quickly when the market requires it; go slowly when the issue addresses internal convenience.
- Do not create entities without the capability to invest in new business and innovation.
- Unless consolidation or access to a key business advantage is the motive, avoid pairing with weak players.

New beginnings are most often envisioned to be the start-up of new businesses or facilities. Start-ups are not always a function of partner-ing among owners. We will focus only on those for our remarks. Starting up is challenging enough. Adding the complication of multiple owners makes this more demanding. Product launches, as noted above to be complicated partnering settings, are often embedded in start-ups. Put it all together, and the chance for turbulence is very good. Start-ups are not always chaotic but they are always complex.

New Beginnings: Start-ups

Participants:

- Multiple Owners

Essentials:

- Before start-up, all owners need to walk the facility/organization with management to see firsthand what is about to begin.
- Start-up responsibilities should not end with turnkey solutions from contractors, vendors, or advisors. Be messy—offering overlapping and continuing assistance for a transition period following the days of start-up.
- Owners should be provided timely information about progress, and provide only unified directions through appropriate channels.
- Managers should sustain a holistic view of their business landscape and include its review in the information shared about progress.
- A crisis hopper should be established to focus on customer responsiveness and address internal difficulties.
- Invest in learning and preparation for all those inducted to the venture—special operational or technical training will need to be strongly supported for new people. In transnational situations, look for nearby cross-border operations to be used as training facilities or sources of trainers. Operations in neighboring states can be effective models or demonstrations.
- Marketing and sales should establish special relations with customers regarding start-up, and keep customers informed of progress as well as any problems—including soliciting their problems.
- Celebrate milestones and build identity with a tradition in the new organization for recognizing positive steps and accomplishments.
- Proactively sponsor and propagate the start-up organization's performance.

(continued)

New Beginnings: Start-ups *(continued)*

- In the partnering agreement, be explicit about services, and for what price, which are provided by one of the partners; predetermine dispute resolution procedures to minimize controversy should differences result.

Watchouts:

- Do not permit concerns about start-up and production schedules to dilute learning in preparation for start-up.
- Within the projects, do not suppress or otherwise delay in surfacing concerns and issues.
- Avoid criticizing operators and partners for their mistakes. Concentrate on getting things back on track. Remember, before it is all over, there will be blame enough for everyone.
- Do not encumber the new organization with too many rules and policies.
- Do not bequeath policy as owners—the new entity must find its own way in the marketplace.
- When adding needed capacity to a system, do not encumber the new organization by subordinating its performance to other locations— permit it to carry its own weight when it is able and to pursue its limits.
- Do not rush within an industry to add capacity when you know it will soften industry value-add and price, or misuse capital. Instead, pursue partnering in facilities in combination with value-added service or performance additives. That is, differentiate after that point in production where excess capacity may be created.

Partnering dynamics have new beginnings within reengineered, redesigned, or transformed organizations—whatever the term of the day. There is, of course, the internal partnering, and we address this in the discussion on design. Again, we focus on the setting in terms of external business relations.

Change is necessary and it has some element of turbulence. It is a problem when not properly managed or taken to extremes. Turmoil is induced with change, and disruption is a byproduct of change. The effect on partnering can be both good and bad. Partnering is an organizational change dynamic like any other. Innovation is more likely under a general atmosphere of change. The innovation invites partnering, and strengthens competencies for strategic business relations.

Change can present an intent to reform reputation in partnering, as well as impacting new and existing relations with credibility.

On the other hand, turbulence can disrupt existing relationships. Existing partnering links to the old rules and power structure. We have witnessed in some organizations undergoing transformation that partners were played down in importance, altogether dismissed, or the tie was otherwise broken. Although the partners were adequate performers, the new regime did not want a tie to providers—even customers—brought forward by the old regime.

Worse yet, under the guise of new cooperation, the new regime simply supplants old partners with their own cronies. This is not genuine transformation behavior but it does occur. The offset is a judicious review of relation transition during a transformation. Otherwise, valuable assistance is lost, precious information to the firm is now outside the firm's control, or seeds of a bad partnering reputation are planted.

More than once, we have been offered penetrating insight into a firm by the victims of a corporate coup. The victim did not violate any confidentiality; the proclivities of personalities were simply revealed. You see, everyone knows how to play along with a phony when it is in their interest. When it fits their need, however, they avoid future relations and talk.

Transformation in the early stages will examine the base businesses. The result might be decisions to consolidate or exit from a business. In the latter case, spin-offs are not unusual. In all cases, owner transitions occur. There can be important impacts to partners. The capital structure may be diluted by a spin-off and preclude growth. Or corporate R&D may no longer be available or as available to the partnership. Consolidation may preoccupy capital for a period of time to the exclusion of growth in partnerships. Changes in ownership may establish relationships with third parties that are unacceptable to partners. The reverse can be true for partnerships strengthened by the change. The question then becomes if "credits" are to be given to the partnership—literally and figuratively.

The point is, transformation changes may change partnerships in important ways. Given that most transformations have the ambition to improve flexibility and access to opportunity through partnering, the partnering agenda needs thoughtful attention and stewardship.

New Beginnings: Reengineered Units

Participants:

- Owners
- Value-chain partners
- Customers

Essentials:

- In the review of the business landscape for transformation, current and future partnering should be treated as a major work dynamic with the likes of finance, human resources, technology, and marketing.
- Existing partners should be invited to briefings on the transformation and given special contacts to report changes in business relations— good or bad—that they attribute to the transformation.
- Customers should be briefed on the transformation, kept informed throughout the process and given special contacts for feedback.
- Prospective new partners and customers should be considered for attendance in briefings and planning sessions about the transformation. They may offer alternatives for the transformation if given the opportunity to have a say early on.

Watchouts:

- Do not permit patronage to disrupt value-added relationships during transformations.
- Do not permit internal development to obscure or impair your customer focus amidst a transformation.
- Deploy third-party assessment to be joined with internal feedback from contact with customers and partners so as to determine your partnering reputation. Watch out for declines in reputation attributed to the transformation and act on the information.

Value-chain optimization ranges from supplier-customer action teams (SCATs) supporting your mission to internal partnering to customer intimacy. These are addressed elsewhere in our discussion. For now, we examine what it means to strengthen partnering in the value-chain setting.

In the complexity of a value chain, the first objective is optimization. This requires exacting data and information technology to derive best decisions among all-too-numerous choices. Accurate data is a function of method and trust. Strong relationships among partners will create the better databases. It makes possible cooperation in information technology choices permitting the use of the improved databases.

The value chain is always in need of innovation and growth. In the turbulence of global markets, the patterns for success are not always straightforward. For these reasons and more, value-chain partners should jointly examine the complications and address leverage points with an open mind and fair play.

In openness, creative alternatives will more easily surface. The candor promotes understanding, accelerates the determination of bottlenecks and fosters emerging strategies for pursuing mutual interests for the future. It is easier to launch into a supportive atmosphere in which new patterns accelerate or achieve dominance because of the support offered by partners.

Value Chain: From SCATs to Internal Partnering to Customer Intimacy

Participants:

- Owners
- Value-chain partners
- Customers

Essentials:

- For the areas of genuine overlap, act as partners and be transparent to both optimize and pursue patterns for growth.
- Build on successes in the areas of overlap before attempting to reach further up the value chain.
- When necessary, use confidentiality and operating agreements to protect sensitive information and encourage the sharing of information.
- As part of the landscape for value-chain reform and improvement, carefully examine the business landscape to produce a sound linear workflow supported by databased intelligence of actual use.

Watchouts:

- Do not permit squabbles over information technology to delay or preclude meaningful optimization—consider the use of "canned" packages to gather momentum.

(continued)

Value Chain: From SCATs to Internal Partnering to Customer Intimacy
(continued)

- Do not become so overwhelmed by optimization that growth is ignored or stymied by stinginess.
- Do not become overzealous about partnering in ways that risk trade secrets and proprietary information, or inappropriately outsource sensitive steps in manufacturing or logistics.
- Do not forget about what is yours and what is theirs. Skip Kersey at Exxon's Baton Rouge refinery captures the situation for his organization with this metaphor: Partnering is like an hourglass. It narrows at the point where things pass from one to another. The subject of partnering then is the neck.

Growth of any sort may involve partnering. Internal cooperation among technical, marketing/sales and manufacturing/service is key to determining customer interests and needs—known or unknown to the customer. Research for new products and services can be driven by marketing, sales, and operations inputs.

Inputs are received directly from the customer, or gleaned from observations about the customer. On the other hand, research may be the point of origin for a product or service. In this case, acceptance will need to be nurtured. Marketing, sales, and operations will be needed to convey the possibility to the customer. Their early involvement will facilitate their ownership for the new product or service, enhancing cost efficiencies in addition to customer acceptance.

Customer intimacy is paramount to all other issues and relationships. What growth is possible without customers? Growth has another audience—investors and other financial backers. The backing of financial partners and one's supply chain will be critical to success. Like customers, backers are best brought along with an idea or innovation through close contact with the development process. Again, acceptance is fostered, and their involvement will sponsor enthusiasm.

Growth is exciting and hope-inspiring. The fervor, however, can be a source of imprudence and wastefulness. What usually happens is that in the excitement, good business practices are subordinated in favor of momentum. Unchecked reality in growth, or growth for growth's sake, is dysfunctional for the firm.

What is most important is real growth—that which creates value. For many years, and it is still prevalent today, expanding markets without regard to cost, payback, or future earnings took place. This is why, for some people, materiality should be defined as market share and net income. Growth is both of these—not one or the other. This view weds the debate between the marketing theorists and the economic value advocates. There are more complex issues involved but the simple, most important lesson is that growth is *not* growth if it does not create value.[3]

Growth

Participation:

- All possible parties

Essentials:

- Growth should be based on a thorough understanding of the business landscape, in particular, your own self-reflection of strengths, competencies, vulnerabilities, and leverage in the marketplace.
- At the onset, growth objectives should be clearly stated and mutually agreed upon by all investing parties.
- Growth should be carefully defined as to resources required and participation commitments—now and in the future.
- Growth is best orchestrated when there is a specific charge or assignment to pursue the growth initiative at hand. Any future growth the venture deems probable for marketplace success, and investors are willing to support, should be included in the mandate for growth. The additional encouragement should be contingent upon demonstrating value-add in the initial growth prospect. This requirement stifles jumping from project to project, and avoiding responsibility for value-added performance by constantly engaging in new activities.
- Growth partners will accomplish more if they empower the joint effort to function as an enterprise unit, and pursue financing and partnership relations as an entity.
- Build structures whereby a royalty or passive ownership is expected for new future opportunity.
- Anticipate that growth will tax resources and talent until properly established and staffed.
- Complete a thorough and well-thought-out joint business plan.

(continued)

Growth (*continued*)

- Define terms and agreements for sharing future direct and indirect revenue streams, including but not limited to licenses, franchises, intellectual property rights, royalties, services and outsourcing.
- Outline options for each growth venture so as to avoid a "drop dead" decision at the first supplemental growth opportunity.
- Bundle your products with others and your own to extend access to a market or new technology.
- Treat internal product line bundling like an external partnership—be respectful, responsive, and pursue issues and opportunities on their business merits.
- Look for opportunities in which you are a platform to future opportunities.
- Treat exits as alternatives rather than as emotional ends or battles.
- Spend time understanding partners and customers, and waste little time on internal disputes—resolve them and get on with the business of making money.
- Forever and always, think globally and respect the local business culture.

Watchouts:

- Do not permit growth to distract from the smooth functioning of existing business.
- Avoid partnerships with uncertain business plans and ambiguous requirements for additional investment.
- Do not assume that a joint effort formed for growth is guaranteed to succeed again. Be a good banker and require a business plan to decide about the next venture.
- Do not pursue growth with unworthy business partners—in the end, the cost is too high.
- Do not permit your good reputation to be associated with shallow growth prone to either failure or liability.
- Do not enter into growth in controversial arenas for your core business. Do not get involved or sell your rights to access these pursuits.
- Be mindful of partnering which may change your core business' share and risk anti-competitive regulatory rebuke.
- Do not bundle core business products with joint growth initiatives without strong cause and the ability to exit at your inclination with your core product in tact.
- Do not assume that all distribution networks will have sufficient infrastructure or will behave in the same manner.

Each implementation setting has its own unique set of characteristics and circumstances. As a business landscape is concocted, care must be taken to address the setting as a source of influence to decision making. Appreciate and understand the nature of change in the setting, including what fosters change and what are the typical sources of resistance, its history for implementation, and the standout characteristics of leaders who advanced in earlier attempts in the setting.

Implementation Processes

To build order in chaos for achieving a complex business solution, there is a need for multiple methods in multiple events scheduled over time. Order begets order. Surrounding people with a change conveys a message about the intent to change. The message is that the change is genuine and it precludes turning back to the old way of doing things.

Just conveying that change is genuine is difficult in business, given the flavor of the month approach for introducing new programs by senior management. A partnership is a relationship, not a program. No new vocabulary is essential. Hard work is.

There are six processes available to business change: *communication, design, learning, application, stewardship,* and *leadership.* We define each as it generally applies to partnerships. Then return to integrated strategies. Included are templates and briefs. Our encouragement is to take these as grand strategies you will need to carefully adapt to the setting and nature of your partnership.

Communication is a broad term. Here we mean the conversations, large and small, formal and informal, held with a wide variety of stakeholders to get across what the partnership is about. The communication serves to announce, educate, or explain. Explanations serve to reinforce the education in application or politically support messages of persuasion concerning the partnership.

The communication will need to be a conversation to procure feedback. At a very minimum, feedback lets you know where you stand. More importantly, it tells you where people are so you may begin where they are, not where you want them to be. Precision in reaching people is important in the early days of announcing a partnership.

Feedback begins the adult process of building ownership. The tête-à-tête is important in the learning and testing of ideas. Feedback pegs progress and points out where to go next. In partnerships, it is important to demonstrate openness to establish an atmosphere for building trust. Inherent to the conversation, then, is a dialogue which is just beginning and must operate the venture.

Design is the purposeful structure of work, including the financial foundation, organization of roles and responsibilities, and the work practices and systems. For the 21st century, design invites choices to create the right patterns for a life worth living at work and the creation of value. These ends are no longer to be at the opportunity cost of one or the other. They are interactive and interdependent choices essential for success. In place of just letting things happen or continuing past practices, 21st century design challenges both continuous optimization and patterns of increasing returns serving value. In this way, continuous improvement and innovation is realized.

Learning was examined at length in our previous book *The Nature of Chaos in Business: Using Complexity to Foster Successful Alliances and Acquisitions.* Learning in a nutshell is the means to awareness and action. Learning builds understanding and acceptance. Awareness from understanding transforms into an interest in taking responsibility for results. Learning empowers by yielding skills and competencies. The outcome is the power to act—self-confidence intertwined with capability and motivation. The only thing missing is the opportunity. The communication about the partnership should make the opportunity known.

Application is putting the new relationship to work. What is difficult for most is the transition period. Much of what has been the case before the relationship is still in effect. Even for new relationships starting afresh, the slate is not completely clean. Whatever the person was doing before makes up their habit and thought process influencing choices involving the new relationship or role.

Application is about trying something new and gaining mastery at it. There can be trial and error, and a need for on-line coaching to make application go smoother. Effective coaching rarely comes naturally to people. Either people arrive to the task with prior experience as effective coaches, or an investment is made to develop their understanding of adult learning.

Tolerance for error is needed in the work relationship as learning occurs. Quick response is needed to correct problems before they cause performance difficulties or become habit. A quick response is possible with close contact and good relations with those responsible for getting the job done.

Progress needs to be tracked for discerning where more effort is needed, and when newly established work systems are ready to stand more on their own—making it possible to move your scrutiny to where it may next accelerate progress. Application requires the ability to push ahead while keeping an eye on the target ahead. Monitoring permits you to check the map periodically to understand where you have been as well as where you are headed on the business landscape.

Application embodies the understanding and skill from learning and rides on the quality of ongoing communication. Application is making the design work, and fine-tuning when it does not. Application harvests the value in the done deal.

Stewardship was a mystery until we spent time at Exxon. Stewardship there carried the meaning we intend for today. Stewardship is monitoring progress and performance, being held accountable, and asking where next for what purpose. The interest shown by owners and hierarchy offers a challenge and can show caring for at least how money gets used if not the quality of life in doing the work. We advocate both accountability and recognition; our Exxon experience varied but at the best of times did include both.

Regardless, stewardship is also the work of doing the assessment so that reporting to others, hierarchy, peers, and your own team can be complete. It makes corporate contributors do what entrepreneurs do because they are owners: look hard at what is and what is not, then figure out how to get there.

Stewardship includes the plan that voices the ambition which should be the stretch. Ventures should demand the best you can be, and if that is not enough, the market will not reward you or your backers. This realism evades large organizations until they treat businesses as entities and not accounts. Accounts get funded and their stewards are transferred, at times regardless of performance. Being challenged by others to achieve is important as are others' timely feedback and reward to you. The best reward is a piece of the action and earning it yourself.

War Story

The Stewards Are at the Helm

In time, large systems can become rigid and can put the emphasis on control over value. This dysfunction was called to our attention by a major oil company attorney lamenting a decision not based on good law or sound business, but in his and our eyes, the convenience of middle managers not being accountable to shareowners. Were it their own money, the decision would probably have been different.

The lament from long ago begged the question, where are the geniuses and cowboys who found the oil or closed the deals that made the company great? How were they replaced by "stewards who are like the servants on an old steamship liner? They take care of their people in the cabins assigned to them and little more."

In the case causing the upset, there was incredible effort made to report the loss in exacting detail but little insight offered for alternative solutions, or the courage to fight. This is not stewardship for us. The company may be different today but this bureaucratic proclivity of large systems continues through to today in any large organization.

What has been described is being a steward. Stewardship for us, on the other hand, is in the psyche of ownership.

We could level this same scrutiny at any oil company. For example, on a hunting trip, an outstanding and brilliant marketing manager for another major oil company told of his early days in retail gasoline stations. The emphasis then was on beauty and cost-cutting. The best districts, as reviewed and judged by senior management, were granted the budgets and capital to grow.

Understanding this, the young district manager purchased potted plants from a nursery and rented flatbed trucks. He had enough great plants to enhance only two stations so that they looked fantastic. With dozens of stations in his area, however, this was problematic. As the tour of senior managers went to one location, the plants at a previous stop were loaded and transported to the next station on the tour. Every station toured was beautiful. One senior manager, according to the now

(continued)

> ### War Story (*continued*)
>
> embellished story, noted the cleverness of using potted plants to add to the image.
>
> In both cases, the ongoing transformations of these firms is aimed at eschewing these behaviors. Sadly, they continue not only in the major oil companies but also in most large firms. The morals for our war stories are simple: Reality and transparency are critical to stewardship. And yes, leadership is not made up of review and pretense.

Stewardship is the challenge: to perform on commitments, to explain what is or is not happening, and to move on to the next agenda. It is a process of knowing the business landscape and saying how you will act out on it. It is planning, monitoring, and paying the toll of defeat or reaping the reward of success. Stewardship is the entrepreneurial spirit of responsibility and risk taking. This can be found anywhere entrepreneurial personalities exist. This can be found anywhere entrepreneurs are encouraged . . . from Exxon to the Mom 'n Pop store.

Leadership is a process and a role. In firms, the greatest emphasis is on hierarchical roles vested with responsibility for results. While responsibility should be shared throughout the organization, leadership is the role all stakeholders hold accountable for progress. Leadership, in the hierarchical sense, possesses decision-making authority over resources and the use of talent. Leadership sets a direction for others to follow. How well leadership performs is evaluated in the acceptance of others for the direction offered. Leadership typically influences through how rewards are managed, and how career opportunities are assigned.

Leadership as a process is found in the spirit of every person. Leadership includes self-initiation—the ability to understand and act on the understanding. Leadership, however, does not end there. Leadership as a process extends again to the person's ability to persuade others to accept a direction to follow. The leadership process can shift the point position among personalities within a situation. Group dynamics can be influenced by what choices individuals make, and the patterns they set for others to follow. The complexity in leadership as a process is how acceptance moves from compliance to conformity to commitment among the players and the dominant patterns.

REFERENCES

1. Nanda, Ashish, and Peter J. Williamson, "Use Joint Ventures to Ease the Pain of Restructuring," *Harvard Business Review,* November-December, 1995, p. 119.

2. Bleeke, Joel and David Ernst, "Is Your Strategic Alliance Really a Sale?" *Harvard Business Review,* January-February, 1995, pp. 99–103.

3. "Debate: Duking It Out Over EVA," *Fortune,* August 4, 1997, p. 232.

CHAPTER 11

The Grand Strategies for Change

Orchestration is oversold as a leadership challenge; it takes very little brilliance—just timing, diligence and persistence. It involves learning and then putting learning to practice. There are attempts to pull back to old ways that must be met with the courage to confront the fallbacks and resistance to change. The pace is never ending and the ability to hang in there makes the difference. Orchestration is high-energy and fast-moving. At times only adrenaline grants survival. Great satisfaction is derived from making it happen.

Telling the people who are the stakeholders for the change is not enough. They need an explanation of the new partnering arrangement. After announcements and time for the new circumstances to soak in, there is a need for dialogue and education. Then comes practice and on-line coaching. The process needs constant attention to remain vital.

Just when you think things are done, a cycle seems to begin again. Shortly thereafter, you realize this is not a cycle but a new dynamic for getting the job done. The bar has been raised. One thing which greatly helps in change work with partnering is the expectation of multiple parties. One side or the other will always be interested in progress and insist that the bar stay high on the standards. Internal change does not have the luxury of this impetus to momentum.

Here is the normal sequence of events: design, communication, more design, implementation concurrent with learning, application, and stewardship. Throughout, there should be leadership. Even with the iterative step for design, this is too linear. The mentality is to get everyone through this as though the process were a car wash: leadership drives the car through so you can vacuum the communication, dust off the design, spray on the learning, dry down the application, and polish the stewardship.

Running a New Play Pattern

We coach clients to not fall into this conventional pattern unless it makes sense. Here are inquiries we use to challenge conventional wisdom:

- Do the stakeholders with whom you are communicating know enough about the subject to understand what you are saying? If not, how can you best educate them? Which one will work best—one-on-one coaching, simulation, war room briefing, seminar, written communication?
- How can you design this organization or work system such that, at your level, you have done what you need to do but can now delegate to those closer to the work—influencing them further by the charter you give them to complete the design or through your stewardship of their design.
- What learnings will advance the communication, design, and application?
- In the beginning, you do not want to let things fall through the cracks, so what do you need to steward at the onset and how frequent should this be?

In Figure 11-1, you see a global transgenics launch and a related large-account management process. While this focuses on a 15-month period, three years of work brought the effort forward. In terms of orchestration, we will discuss how a successful launch was achieved.

Outlined are key points to announcing partnering:

- Explain and put emphasis to the business intent for partnering. Provide the scope of anticipated revenues.
- Brief your people on what is in it for your firm and anticipate what partnering might mean to prospective partners or does mean to partners.

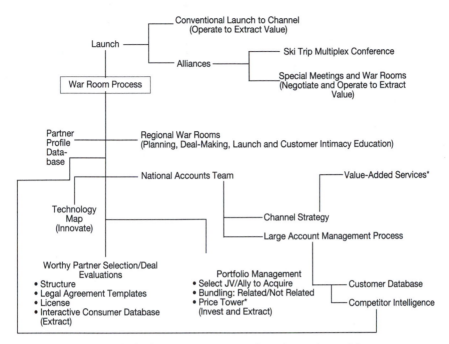

Figure 11-1. Global transgenics product launch and large account management.

- Explain where the product of the partnering sits in the firm's portfolio—who is responsible for what duties.
- Indicate honestly what might be the impact—good or bad—to the people in your firm. Give a sense about when this all will occur and how they can learn more.
- Provide an answer line for feedback. (Clients have found it useful to request any street talk heard by anyone, anywhere in their work or home life which is pertinent to the breaking news. One important learning is that people low in the hierarchy may have friends and relatives in high places in organizations who see the opportunity at play in the marketplace).

War Story

Magic Beans

Earlier work began with a company strategy for their global region. The strategy created an initiative to improve the way in which national marketing and sales offices interfaced. The sales organization and the channel were redesigned. This effort led to a customer intimacy strategy about the time the international corporate office was sanctioning and supporting transgenics launch projects.

The customer intimacy strategy unfolded with an alliance complex systems workshop and planning session. Senior management and staff were briefed on alternative alliance structures, purposes, and currencies used to formulate them and value-added contributions. They began to outline applications for their strategic plan.

The primary transgenics for the region were being prepared for launch in the region at this time. The transgenics launch was determined in the alliance planning to be the best alternative for reconstituting reputation and establishing a stronger partnering image.

War rooms were conducted to ascertain a partnering strategy. Sound progress had been made on technical stewardship, legal agreements, and regulatory interfaces in the major global markets prior to the war rooms. These efforts were coordinated and examined for overlap as part of the partnering strategy. Action plans for a launch team, advertising and other elements for launch implementation were deployed.

In parallel but interconnected to the launch, the national accounts management team and a special subteam of senior management pursued the customer intimacy strategy. A large-account management system was developed, supported by a new customer database and commercial intelligence. Both of the support systems were deployed in the alliance strategy for the launch. A partner profile database was added to business intelligence. Eventually, both efforts integrated at the point of contact with customers and key partners.

War rooms were used to assist learnings in simulations and seminars. They supported customer meetings and negotiations. Multiple war room sessions were conducted to enroll the entire national sales forces and glean their inputs to their local strategy. This led to still other war rooms for efficient and expeditious planning with channel partners.

In all, a very complicated process was streamlined and expedited. A new reputation was established for partnering. A pipeline successfully opened for multiple products in more than one technology, in addition to financial engineering services.

All this was accomplished with worthy business partners in several global markets. Turbulence in the form of resistance to the product was overcome. Reforms were made to the channel requiring value-added service for reward, and databased negotiation for deal making. War rooms served to get the job done quickly while providing both an atmosphere for creativity and a process for keeping a focus on business.

The orchestration was an iterative approach in which communication, design, learning, application, and stewardship occurred in sequence and, in parallel, these dynamics were made to support one another. They were also scheduled to be repeated as a means for bringing other people up to speed: owners, employees, customers, partners, and regulators. There was a clear beginning and apparent success in application. What happened in-between was not always logical, and was at times messy and turbulent, but was always focused to the end result.

Specific methods of communication used help us with guidance and templates for what you might consider. First is communication. General communication was offered to all internal stakeholders at the onset. Top-down communication was fast-moving and accurate. That is, the word got out to the teams directly involved and to other employees.

In routine announcements, newsletters, bulletins and like e-mail, employees are kept informed about business, in general, and about specific plays such as the transgenics launch. The business objective with technical information about the product—that which would invite customer interest—is provided with key milestones. If appropriate, confidentiality is noted.

In the case of presentations or mention as a staff meeting item, these face-to-face interactions offer important opportunities for dialogue, and should be pursued. For these interactions

(continued)

War Story (*continued*)

to be meaningful, investment needs to be made in presenters and leaders. Talking points and Q&A guides may seem like overkill. The chance that miscommunication can disrupt partnering is too high to not make sensible investments in understanding.

Generating feedback was important in the transgenics launch. The competitor database was grossly incomplete. Inputs were needed. Requesting feedback in announcements and bulletins accomplished two tasks: one is that people not always directly involved on the project felt involved and reported what they knew. The other task completed was that sales people were stimulated to think more about the launch with customers. Although they may not have talked it up, they kept an ear to conversations for the transgenics, took note of it, and then made certain the team knew. Good data came forward from both sources.

Communication to the work force—our client's and later their partners'—grew in intensity when briefings were conducted in a war room format. A departure from the dull sessions, the war rooms, with walls filled with drawings and key discussion points, and multimedia presentations, captured their attention and stimulated excitement. Though these sessions were only a day, they included meaningful debate and participation in action planning.

The general outline for war rooms to brief others went like this:

- Product launch objectives
- Product key characteristics
- Product launch issues: briefing and discussion
- Problem-solving discussion for select issues: plenary session to demonstrate, followed by small groups
- Small group reports to plenary for review and discussion
- Next steps overview

This is a simple approach of inform, demonstrate what you want from the group, give them a chance to have their say and determine inputs, and then end with a clear statement of what is to be done after the meeting.

Communication throughout does not depend on announcements and e-mail alone. Good dialogue needs to take place among internal and external networks. The objective is keep a pulse on the firm, the partnership, and the marketplace.

Communication to brief owners, customers, and partners should not vary greatly. The difference is in terms of what is appropriate to the relationship. There must be a business purpose for sharing the information if it is not a part of the overlap in responsibilities.

An important involvement tool for owners and backers, as well as for your best and most trusted customers and partners, is the invitation to strategic planning. Select briefs or summary briefs can be shared and meaningful discussion held. Do not position these at the end of your process. Their inputs can open doors you did not anticipate or raise important sensitivities.

Expect that whatever is shared goes to the street. This does not mean that you should not proceed. It means that you should be thoughtful about what takes place. Do not permit teleconferencing or virtual participation. This puts the links too far out of control. We know of cases where competitors were silently scripting inputs for others to mention. Keep the boundary tight and the contact visible.

Special meetings are appropriate for owners and customers and should not be cookie-cutter in fashion. You may begin with a core format but design each to its circumstance. This can be done in large forums with a clever use of agenda. For example, the customer ski weekend referenced in Figure 11-1 had two formats. One format was a one-on-one meeting with a customer. The other invited several.

Special one-on-one meetings were held while general sessions were conducted. Each customer had access to sessions, with some repeated across a schedule matrix. More importantly, topics were presented to preview concepts in conversations before one-on-one sessions were held. Then sessions were conducted regarding more detail, probable agreement areas, or how to's. In place of several meetings, only one was conducted. More members of the firm had to participate to make this logistically possible. A serendipitous benefit was that it forced delegation and involved lower-level staff in meaningful contact with customer leadership. This later proved to be a real edge over competitor sales organizations.

Architecture for Partners

Design is the most complicated of the processes and volumes have been written to describe how to proceed. There are fundamental issues to the conduct of design for partnering organizations. We will address these and the related core "work systems" that are important to the smooth operation of partnerships.

- All parties need to actively participate in the design. This is less of a problem than just five years ago. Nonetheless, now that the parties are in the room, the emphasis shifts to establishing a level playing field for participation in discussion. Invite everyone's expertise and experience to the debate. Decision making, however, is a function of ownership and does not necessitate a level playing field when the vote is taken.
- The initial design should be for a start-up organization which itself engages in design to flesh out the details. Until operational, it may not be possible to consider every need of the partnering entity.
- Establish a separate entity whenever possible. If the alliance cannot stand alone as a business unit, establish it as a joint team. Designate a leadership structure. Most claim there should only be one leader. We differ on this issue, and suggest a panel of managing directors representing owners' interests. The CEO role can rotate among them. For a long-term venture, this can involve a year to 18 months.
- Design the owner interface. Address emergency contact, planning, periodic review, and owner audits—organizational and commercial, as well as financial. Strive to minimize interference.
- Be clear on selection practices and how members of the joint operation are terminated. For larger concerns, in particular in emerging nations where nationalism can flare from time to time, set employment policy at the owner level but leave the day-to-day decisions to operators. Regardless of size and scope, the leadership selection and termination practice should be defined.

Do not set up autonomous operators who are able to dominate owners by playing them against each other with the clever use of a rigid, protectionism policy. Instead, treat leadership as any senior management responsible to a board. This is especially true when an owner provides the talent for senior management.

- Develop a joint business plan and have it serve as the basis for design. The test of the design is its ability to fulfill the plan.
- Require continuous improvement and innovation. Joint efforts should have the license to pursue vitality. That is, as they fulfill their plan and expansion, or as other growth is deemed possible, they should be permitted to explore.

- For more casual shared efforts, such as melding databases, forming supplier-customer action teams, or granting access to customers, develop key contacts for all participants to the agreement. Require timely communication among them and to sponsors.
- Regardless of the size, shape, or form of alliance, assign a senior management team from the enterprise unit or from corporate to steward the relationship. Expect the same from the other parties. This should involve a risk taker and a decision maker. Provide them access to reward based on the relationship's EVA.
- Align the reward of participants—direct employees, contractors, or owners—to the economic value-add performance of the strategic business relation.

For joint efforts creating business units, we recommend the partnering unit and not mirror-image owners unless they are of a high performance design. Owned by one party or many, an organization should be optimized and should achieve a high-performance capability.

More and more joint efforts are taking on their own destiny as an organization and executives from sponsoring organizations are acting as board directors. This elevates the importance of the design process in building strategic business relations.

In recent years, the "hub and spoke" and constellation designs are frequently seen in value chains. The "hub and spoke" represents a core operation which tolerates different practices among spokes, eventually bringing each spoke to a core, overlapping set of characteristics. Characteristics vary by value opportunity and industry.[1]

Constellation is the position of a firm with multiple entities in pursuit of one or more commercial advantages based on size, composition, internal competition, or collective governance. Examples include Asia Link, a constellation of Asian advertising firms integrated across regions as a virtual competitor for global firms such as Ogilvy and Mather, and Saatchi & Saatchi; WorldPartners, AT&T's global telecom venture; Delta Airlines' global partners initiative; and Bank of America with its original sixties-era (and now antiquated) BankAmericard credit card association.[2]

Heretofore, senior management and central planning staffs serve as the focus point for partnering. As more and more value extraction for a firm is dependent on partnering, special roles and organizations are created. This is more involved than the faddish relabeling of logistics and marketing roles as strategic alliance managers.

Some firms are creating roles, teams, or units responsible for coordination of all partnering. The objectives are to ascertain and optimize cross-commitments, improve understanding of partners and prospective partners, and advance sophistication in partnering competencies. We anticipate shortly after the turn of the century that the role of Chief Alliance Officer may evolve.

Reginald Jones, Ken Brown, John Harbison, and Peter Pekar offer illustrations of "collaborative core" solutions. They observe, " . . . we have been droning on about building a centralized alliance capability—what we call a collaborative core. . . . Unfortunately, there is no definitive study or argument to be made: living on the front edge of the learning curve, after all, does not lend itself to strong documentation. If you want indisputable support for building a collaborative core, you'd better wait a few years. . . . "

They cite case illustrations for their collaborative core: Fuji Xerox, in which things began in a regional office but were brought under the auspices of a corporate alliance director; Apple Computer, which rotates field managers to head alliance development; and Andersen Consulting, which deploys alliance directors to set strategy across alliances in addition to facilitating particular relationships.[3]

There are many more configurations available for organizing partnering internally or with others, depending on circumstances and opportunity. As in any design dynamic, your imagination defines the limits of what is possible in design. The best designs are tailored to the value to be extracted and the related optimal operation.

We recommend that partnering organizations, in particular, be innovative in work design. Partnering ventures must be as sleek as possible and innovative to avoid the pitfalls of multiple owners or multiple parties in operation.

What follows are design templates for core work systems. Though the principles detailed apply to any organization, they are tailored to partnering organizations. The briefs are based on over 100 high-performance designs around the world. Each presents a definition of the work system, tips for effective designs, watchouts, and case illustrations.

The core work systems are interdependent. As shown in the following puzzle diagram (Figure 11-2), all the pieces come together to make optimization of work flow possible. The presence of one helps make others happen. It is important to recognize that you may not be able to start all the core work systems at once. In start-up situations, starting with all core work systems in place is easier to accomplish. Melding organizations in alliances or merger integration, however, makes this more difficult.

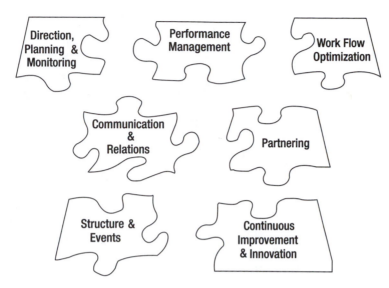

Figure 11-2. Puzzle diagram.

Before presenting the design briefs, we align the core work systems for high performance to the broad categories used to define the business landscape and provide organization to the Intensive Business Review. This is given to help people understand what work systems to think about when movement occurs in the business landscape (see Figure 11-3).

Landscape Category	Core Work System
Investor Relations	Planning & Monitoring
Value-Chain Management	Work Flow Optimization
	Continuous Improvement & Innovation (CII)
Financial Engineering	
Direction & Growth	Planning & Monitoring
Learning & Orchestration	Performance Management
	Communication & Relations
	Structure & Events
Partnering	Partnering
Technology	Information Technology
	Continuous Improvement & Innovation (CII)

Figure 11-3. Core work systems.

Table 11-1. Interdependencies among core work systems

	PLANNING & MONITORING	PERFORMANCE MANAGEMENT	WORK FLOW OPTIMIZATION	COMMUNICATION & RELATIONS	PARTNERING	CONTINUOUS IMPROVEMENT & INNOVATION	STRUCTURE & EVENTS
PLANNING & MONITORING	HOPE & CONFIDENCE	Aligns learning & reward of individual with business intent	Makes a bureaucratic process easier to administer	Gets the work out faster with higher credibility & specificity to role	Grounds the intent in reality on a real-time basis	Points out where next technically	Provides media for offering & reinforcing intent
PERFORMANCE MANAGEMENT	States what is a priority & evidences progress	ADAPTATION TO MARKET & PERSONAL BENEFIT FROM MARKET	Removes obstacles to performance	Expectations are clear & validated	Highlights performance impact to end results	Offer challenge & personal growth	Clear responsibility for timely response
WORK FLOW OPTIMIZATION	States what is a priority & evidences progress	Establishes the learning agenda for new technology	OPTIMIZATION	Makes it easier to accept changes (trust)	Makes linkage to 3rd parties more efficient	Reduces steps or substitutes with better systems	Make change happen easier & faster
COMMUNICATION & RELATIONS	Clarifies what messages are important & offers a means for judging what is a priority	Interacts around harmony management	Makes it easier to record into & share it	CIVILITY & HARMONY	Extends internal competencies to 3rd parties	Challenges with new requirements	Reduces time spent to accomplish linkages
PARTNERING	Chooses where in the market the business will make its play	Builds the competency for customer responsiveness	Smooths interaction & makes process efficient	Brings the market into focus on a daily basis	SUSTAINED BUSINESS & GROWTH	Creates growth conversations with 3rd parties	Reduces time to accomplish
CONTINUOUS IMPROVEMENT & INNOVATION	Indicates area for stretch & sets level of reinvestment	Establishes the learning agenda for new technology	Makes more time available for creativity	Surfaces ideas faster & credits more fairly	Links improvements & innovation to market	COMPETITIVE EDGE	Ensures fair play in idea management
STRUCTURE & EVENTS	Sets the mission around which orchestration functions	Provides justification for living the orchestration	Reinforces, takes less time for events to work, & reduces the need for structure	Reinforces lead control & work responsibility	Forces inclusion of 3rd parties in partnering	Challenges with new requirements	CONTINUITY, STABILITY & MEANINGFUL INVOLVEMENT

Table 11-1 demonstrates the interdependencies among core work systems. In the cells cascading from the upper left cell along the diagonal to the lower right cell, the contribution of the work system to the partnership is identified.

To aid in setting priorities for implementation, a high-performance work systems audit is presented before the design briefs. This audit is a good supplement to an intensive business review in support of cultural due diligence. The audit reviews five high-performance characteristics: mission-driven, commercially astute, empowered talent, technologically advanced, and open communication system. A sample of such an audit can be found on pages 203–205.

Outlined next are the design briefs for core work systems. A template is presented indicating what should be included in the core work system. For each core work system, tips for implementation, watchouts for application, and case illustrations are provided to guide development and implementation. Select briefs are more involved and sub templates are offered for more detailed understanding.

The briefs are arranged in this order:

1. Direction, Planning & Monitoring and Metrics
2. Work Flow Optimizaton
3. Communication and Relations
4. Performance Management
5. Continuous Improvement and Innovation
6. Partnering
7. Structure and Events Orchestration

Briefs are provided to design teams, cross-sections of leaders, contributors and customers, for the tasks of tailoring application to the firm's needs, building on the briefs to create unique solutions, integrating core work systems into a total organization, and orchestrating start-up and development.

(text continued on page 205)

BRIEF: DIRECTION, PLANNING & MONITORING AND METRICS

TEMPLATE 11-1: DIRECTION, PLANNING & MONITORING AND METRICS

DIRECTION
- VISION (BLUE-SKY VIEW OF FUTURE)
- INTENT (MISSION & STRATEGY . . . TESTED WITH REALITY)

PLANNING & MONITORING
- INVOLVEMENT (MEANS FOR COMMUNICATING & SOLICITING INPUT WHICH LEADS TO 1) A DIALOGUE ON HOW BEST TO RUN THE BUSINESS; 2) PARTICIPATION WHICH BUILDS COMMITMENT TO INTENT AND STRATEGY; AND 3) A STIMULUS FOR CONTINUOUS IMPROVEMENT AND INNOVATION)
- CRISIS HOPPER (MEANS FOR RESOLVING UPSETS WITH MINIMUM DISTRACTION)
- STEWARDSHIP (MEANS FOR PERIODIC MONITORING OF PROGRESS WITH BOTH OPENNESS FOR NEW INITIATIVES REQUIRED FOR MARKET RESPONSIVENESS AND LINKAGE WITH REWARD & RECOGNITION TO ENCOURAGE THE RIGHT CONTRIBUTION)

METRICS
- ECONOMIC PERFORMANCE (SVA—SHAREHOLDER VALUE ADDED)
- EARNINGS BEFORE INTEREST, TAX, DEPRECIATION, AMORTIZATION (EBIT DA)
- PRODUCTIVITY
- CASH MANAGEMENT
- COST EFFICIENCY
  - ⇒ BUDGET VARIANCE
    - + GENERAL
    - + TRAVEL
    - + CONSUMABLE
    - + CONTRACTS
  - ⇒ COST OF REWORK
  - ⇒ COST IMPROVEMENT IDEAS & INNOVATION
- QUALITY
  - ⇒ COMPLETENESS
  - ⇒ TIMELINESS
  - ⇒ CONSISTENCY/RELIABILITY
  - ⇒ CUSTOMER COMPLAINTS, SATISFACTION
  - ⇒ INNOVATION
- EMPLOYEE SUPPORT
- MARKET PERFORMANCE (MATERIALITY: NET INCOME AND SHARE)
- CUSTOMER RESPONSIVENESS
- COMMUNITY REQUIREMENTS

ROLE EXPECTATIONS STATEMENT OVERVIEW
- KEY TO HABIT CHANGE AND PARADIGM SHIFT
- DEFINITION OF HOW CHANGE IMPACTS EVERYONE
- BASIS FOR ROLE IMPROVEMENT AND FEEDBACK
- ORIENTATION TO WHAT ARE THE NEW PRIORITIES FOR THE BUSINESS
- EXPRESSED IN SIMPLE TERMS FOR CLARITY
- FOUNDATION FOR FUTURE PERFORMANCE

ROLE EXPECTATIONS STATEMENTS
- RESPONSIBILITIES: CUSTOMER, OPERATING, BUSINESS, ORGANIZATIONAL
- OPENNESS
- FREEDOM TO OPERATE
- ACCEPTING CHANGE—FLEXIBILITY, MANAGING IDEAS
- SELF-INITIATION
- TEAM WORK
- QUALITY
- LEADERSHIP
- JOB KNOWLEDGE, SKILL, CONTINUOUS LEARNING

TEMPLATE 11-1: DIRECTION, PLANNING & MONITORING AND METRICS *(continued)*

TIPS

DIRECTION
- DIRECTION DEFINES BUSINESS PURPOSE AND INTENT FOR SUCCESS
- DIRECTION SHOULD BE A FUNCTION OF ALL STAKEHOLDERS: BANKERS, OWNERS, CUSTOMERS, EMPLOYEES, VENDORS, CONTRACTORS AND REGULATORS AMONG OTHER COMMUNITY INFLUENCES
- ONCE THE NICHE IS DETERMINED, THE CUSTOMER SHOULD BE THE FOCUS OF DIRECTION
- DIRECTION SHOULD LEVERAGE THE CAPABILITIES OF OWNERS, R&D, MANUFACTURING AND CHANNEL TO RESPOND TO CUSTOMER-DRIVEN OPPORTUNITY
- DIRECTION SHOULD ADDRESS BUSINESS GROWTH THROUGH EXPANSION TO CURRENT BUSINESS INNOVATION TO LEAD CUSTOMERS OR ACQUISITION
- DIRECTION SHOULD BE BASED ON CAREFUL THOUGHT TO EXIT STRATEGY—PARTIAL AND COMPLETE (I.E., CIRCUMSTANCES WHICH WOULD PROMPT EXIT, ANTICIPATED METHOD, ETC.)
- DIRECTION SHOULD BE BENCHMARKED AGAINST COMPETITION AND SUBSTITUTION THREATS (THINK ABOUT WHAT THE COMPETITION COULD DO TO YOU OVER THE NEXT THREE YEARS TO SHARPLY DISADVANTAGE YOU. THINK WHAT YOU COULD DO TO THEM.)
- DIRECTION EXPLAINS AMBITIONS AND OFFERS HOPE AND ASPIRATIONS TO STAKEHOLDERS
- DIRECTION DEFINES MISSION (PURPOSE), VISION (FUTURE VIEWS), STRATEGY (HOW TO GET THERE) AND, OCCASIONALLY, PHILOSOPHY (VALUES AND NORMS)
- DIRECTION SHOULD OFFER AN INDICATION OF HOW CULTURE SHOULD BE OR WILL EVOLVE— INCLUDING THE AMBITION FOR CONTINUOUS IMPROVEMENT AND INNOVATION
- DIRECTION NEEDS TO BE THE GUIDING LIGHT TO EXPECTATIONS FOR CONTRIBUTION AND THUS PROMOTE SELF-INITIATION

PLANNING & MONITORING SYSTEM
- BUILD ON CURRENT SYSTEMS
- EXPECT 2–3 CYCLES BEFORE SMOOTH APPLICATION AND BROAD INVOLVEMENT
- INVOLVEMENT CAN BE MANAGED TO OBTAIN INPUT AND DIALOGUE WITHOUT COMPROMISING PROPRIETARY ACTION PLANNING
    ⇒ PRE-WORK WITH EMPLOYEES, BANKERS, CUSTOMERS, VENDORS, REGULATORS
    ⇒ TWO-STEP ANALYSIS SESSION BY SENIOR MANAGEMENT. PERMITS REVIEW OF GENERAL DIRECTION BEFORE FINALIZING
- PLANNING CYCLE SHOULD INCLUDE MULTIPLE STEWARDSHIP REVIEWS TO MONITOR PROGRESS AND DETERMINE ANY NEED TO MODIFY PLANS
- PLANS SHOULD INCLUDE STRETCH EXPECTATIONS
- BROAD INVOLVEMENT IS DESIRED TO PROMOTE OWNERSHIP, INFORM PEOPLE OF PROGRESS AND INVITE IDEAS FOR NEXT STEPS
- DATABASE MANAGEMENT SHOULD BE USED TO PREDICT TRENDS, ENHANCE FORECASTS' ASSUMPTIONS AND PLOT OPTIMUM SOLUTIONS
- GREATER OPENNESS INCREASES ACCESS TO IDEAS AND CHALLENGES
- PLANNING PROCESS SHOULD BE FUN AND INTERESTING TO CREATE ENERGY AND ENTHUSIASM
- PLANNING AND MONITORING SHOULD BE HOLISTIC AND COMPLETE
- PROCESS SHOULD INTEGRATE IDEAS ACROSS FUNCTIONS, OPERATIONS AND STAKEHOLDERS
- PLANS AND BUDGETS SHOULD BE ALIGNED SO "TWO" MASTERS ARE NOT CREATED
- ACTIVITIES-BASED COSTING PROMOTES A FOCUS ON RESULTS AND AN UNDERSTANDING OF HOW WHITE COLLAR STAFF ACTIVITY IMPACTS OPERATIONAL COST
- TREAT LEADERS AS CONSULTANTS WHO CAN OFFER ADVICE—NOT JUST BOSSES WHO MAKE DECISIONS
- PLANNING AND MONITORING SYSTEMS INCLUDE "CRISIS HOPPERS"
- ASPIRE TO AN INFORMATION SYSTEM WHICH PROVIDES REAL-TIME VIEW OF PERFORMANCE, CASH MANAGEMENT, AND CUSTOMER EXPECTATIONS

METRICS
- DETERMINE BEST FREQUENCY (DAILY, WEEKLY, MONTHLY, QUARTERLY)
- BE EFFICIENT IN STEWARDSHIP. THIS IS NOT A VALUE-ADDED STEP BUT AN OVERHEAD—UNTIL PEOPLE TRANSLATE PLANS TO ACTION

(continued)

TEMPLATE 11-1: DIRECTION, PLANNING & MONITORING AND METRICS *(continued)*

⇒ MANAGE TIME—EXPLORE ONLY VARIANCES, KEY ISSUES
⇒ USE ELECTRONIC DATA BASING FOR COMPARISONS, TRENDS, ANALYSIS AND "REAL TIME" REVIEW
• MAKE INVOLVEMENT MEANINGFUL
  ⇒ BE FOCUSED
  ⇒ OFFER CALIBRATION SO PEOPLE CAN UNDERSTAND THE MAGNITUDE OF THEIR EFFORTS
  ⇒ CONSIDER CONVERTING METRICS TO DOLLARS—PEOPLE CAN UNDERSTAND THEIR
    INFLUENCE ON RESULTS EASIER
• SPONSOR CELEBRATION OF METRIC GOALS ACHIEVED
• BE COMPREHENSIVE
• INCLUDE ALL EMPLOYEES IN STEWARDSHIP OF METRICS TO BUILD UNDERSTANDING OF BUSINESS AND
  COMMITMENT
• MINIMIZE USE OF SOFT DATA (OPINION SURVEYS) AND WEIGHT THEIR USE ACCORDINGLY IN ASSIGNING
  REWARDS
• DATABASE METRICS AND TRACK RELATIONSHIPS
• USE DATABASES TO DEFINE OPTIMUM SOLUTIONS
• REQUIRE METRICS IN CAPITAL/PROJECT PROPOSALS

ROLE EXPECTATIONS
• DEFINE WHAT YOU ARE EXPECTED TO DO AND WHAT YOU EXPECT FROM OTHERS
• SHOULD NOT BE LIMITING TO CONTRIBUTION BUT DEFINE WHAT IS ESSENTIAL FOR MISSION SUCCESS
• ROLES BECOME "RUTS" WHEN THEY BECOME OVERLY ROUTINE AND PREDICTABLE. BUSINESS IS EVER
  CHANGING AND EXCITING—SO SHOULD PERFORMANCE EXPECTATIONS
• THE ROLE IS THE FOCAL POINT FOR THE ECONOMIC EXCHANGE BETWEEN EMPLOYER AND EMPLOYEE
• THE TREND IS FOR PEOPLE TO FOCUS ON MISSION AND BE LESS CONCERNED ABOUT GOING BEYOND
  ROLES TO DO WHAT NEEDS TO BE DONE. THIS PROCESS REQUIRES UNDERSTANDING BY ALL INVOLVED
  SO RISK IS NOT MISMANAGED NOR PEOPLE EXPLOITED
• BLURRING ROLES HAS LESS RISK IN DILUTING QUALITY OF CONTRIBUTION. TYPICALLY, IT IS
  ENCOURAGED WHERE GROUP EFFORT LEADS TO SHARED REWARD OR RECOGNITION—THAT IS,
  EVERYONE IS ENCOURAGED TO HELP SINCE ALL BENEFIT BY LENDING A HELPING HAND (ONE WHICH IS
  USEFUL IF PEOPLE KNOW WHAT THEY ARE DOING)
• EXPECTATIONS MUST BE JOB-RELATED TO BE LAWFUL
  ⇒ SKILL OR ABILITY
  ⇒ KNOWLEDGE
  ⇒ BEHAVIOR

WATCHOUTS

DIRECTION
• DIRECTION CAN BE TOO COMPLICATED AND DETAILED, RESULTING IN LIMITED UNDERSTANDING AND USE
• DIRECTION NEEDS TO BE VALIDATED FOR COMPLETENESS AND SPONSOR COMMITMENT
• DIRECTION CANNOT BE FIXED FOREVER. CHANGE IN MARKET MAY NECESSITATE IMPROVEMENT AND
  INNOVATION BUT . . .
• TOO-FREQUENT CHANGES IN DIRECTION DILUTE CONTINUITY AND HEIGHTENS ANXIETY
• DIRECTION NEEDS TO BE COMMUNICATED WITH MORE THAN ONE METHOD
• LEADERSHIP MUST REINFORCE DIRECTION, WALK-THE-TALK, AND STEWARD PROGRESS WITH STRETCH
  EXPECTATIONS BASED ON METRICS

PLANNING AND MONITORING SYSTEM
• AVOID BUZZ WORDS—USE EVERYDAY LANGUAGE
• KEEP PLANS EVERGREEN OR RIGIDITY WILL RESULT
• DO NOT PERMIT PLANS OR PLANNING ACTIVITIES TO BECOME ENDS UNTO THEMSELVES
• AVOID STRONG TIES FOR BUDGETS TO REWARDS. BUDGET "BUSTERS" MAY SERVE INCOME BETTER
  THAN "SCROOGES"
• STEWARD WITH INSIGHT AND ANALYSIS. AVOID TEDIOUS DETAILS BY EXAMINING VARIANCES AND
  PROMOTING DIALOGUE ON WHAT CAN BE DONE ABOUT VARIANCES.

TEMPLATE 11-1: DIRECTION, PLANNING & MONITORING AND METRICS *(continued)*

- In examining variances and what influences them, do not fail to ask how they can be eliminated
- Do not personalize databases. Keep them open within the organization to avoid fraud, "pencil whipping," performance data, and loss of information when people leave

METRICS
- Evolve understanding of metrics over time
- Do not begin with complicated metrics
- Do not count activities (unless they are clearly linked to a business outcome)
- Do not associate activities with rewards

ROLE EXPECTATIONS
- Formats for expectations should promote easy understanding
  - ⇒ Outlines
  - ⇒ Major themes in bold to stand out
  - ⇒ Easy to remember
- Roles should not become isolated from information about the business. They tend to lose meaning and interest
- In traditional organizations, people often over-identify with their role. This risks limiting involvement in the mission—the purpose for the role
- Expectation must be explained to be useful
- People must accept them as realistic, do-able and reachable
- Expectations can easily be forgotten or only partially enforced; leadership needs to keep attention to them

KEY DIRECTION TERMS AND THEIR USES

VISION
- Blue-Sky Projection of Future Possibilities
- Statement of Aspirations
- Represents Hope and Ambition
- Influenced by Stakeholders and Events in the Market Place
- General Outline of Characteristics: Commercial, Organizational, Technological

MISSION
- Purpose for existing
- Essence of the Business
- Tie-Breaker
- Short, Crisp, to the Point

PHILOSOPHY OF BUSINESS OR WORK
- Reflects the Beliefs, Values and Norms of How Business is to be Conducted
- Inspires Stakeholders
- Several Statements Describing the Emphasis Placed by the Firm on Work Life
- Sets Norms for Dignity and Respect
- Defines Ethics and Integrity
- Affirms Conformance with Laws

STEWARDSHIP
- Means for Tracking Performance on Metrics Against Goals, Plans and Budgets
- Sponsorship Affirmation and Insight or Redirection (Goals or Priorities)
- Database Management Most Relevant to Incentive Rewards

(continued)

TEMPLATE 11-1: DIRECTION, PLANNING & MONITORING AND METRICS *(continued)*

CONTINUOUS IMPROVEMENT AND INNOVATION
- MEANINGFUL EMPLOYEE INVOLVEMENT TO CONTINUOUSLY SOLICIT INPUTS AND COMMITMENT
- PRODUCT AND SERVICE INNOVATION
- OPERATIONAL EFFICIENCY IMPROVEMENT
* REINVESTMENT STRATEGIES AND ACQUISITION AMBITIONS
* ADVANCEMENTS RESULTING IN ZERO EFFECTS FOR HUMAN KIND IN TERMS OF HEALTH AND SAFETY

CRISIS HOPPER
- ADDRESSES MARKET UPSETS AND DISRUPTIONS; EMERGENCY RESPONSE; EXTRAORDINARY BUSINESS GROWTH OPPORTUNITIES; LEADER OR OWNER TRANSITIONS; EXCEPTIONAL REQUESTS FROM OWNERS, UPPER MANAGEMENT, CUSTOMERS, COMMUNITY OR REGULATORS
- PROVIDES TIMELY DECISIONS BY INVOLVING KEY PARTIES—LEADERS AND EXPERTS
- KEEPS ORGANIZATION ON TRACK WITH EXISTING PLAN AND MINIMAL DISTRACTION/USE OF RESOURCES, OR
- ORCHESTRATES A NEW AGENDA BECAUSE THE CRISIS REQUIRES A DIFFERENT PLAN OR SET OF PRIORITIES

CASE ILLUSTRATION FOR DIRECTION, PLANNING & MONITORING AND METRICS

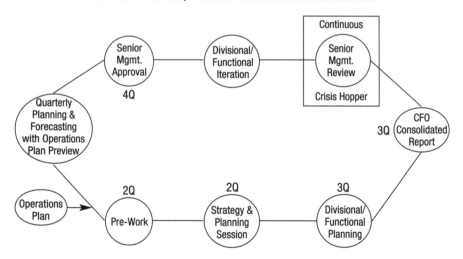

BRIEF: WORK FLOW OPTIMIZATION

TEMPLATE 11-2: WORK FLOW OPTIMIZATION

INFOTECHNOLOGY (IT) RECOMMENDATIONS
- IMPROVED USE OF CURRENT SYSTEM
- INCREMENTAL INVESTMENT
- REENGINEERING
- IMPLEMENTATION OF CURRENT PLANS

TEMPLATE 11-2: WORK FLOW OPTIMIZATION *(continued)*

WORK FLOW IMPROVEMENTS
- WITHIN SHIFTS
- BETWEEN SHIFTS
- BETWEEN OPERATIONS AND STAFF FUNCTIONS
- AMONG STAFF FUNCTIONS

TIPS

INFORMATION AND TELECOM SYSTEMS
- FULLY UTILIZE CURRENT RESOURCES
- DEVELOP KNOWLEDGE ON HOW TO USE TECHNOLOGY
- BE THOROUGH IN YOUR ASSESSMENT OF POTENTIAL IT USES:
    ⇒ INTERACTIVE MULTIMEDIA
    ⇒ EXPERT SYSTEMS
    ⇒ PERFORMANCE SUPPORT SYSTEMS
    ⇒ SENSING/ENVIRONMENTAL INTEGRITY AIDS
    ⇒ ELECTRONIC DATA INTERCHANGE (EDI) WITH CLIENTS, CUSTOMERS, ALLIANCES, REGULATORS AND EXECUTIVES
    ⇒ VIRTUAL REALITY
    ⇒ MODELING/SIMULATORS
    ⇒ ELECTRONIC COMMUNICATION (VOICE, FAX, E-MAIL)
    ⇒ TELECONFERENCING
    ⇒ VIDEO-CONFERENCING
    ⇒ ELECTRONIC BULLETIN BOARDS (PROJECTS, INFORMATION SHARING, INPUTS)
    ⇒ SCANNING/IMAGE PROCESSING/BAR-CODING
    ⇒ AUTOMATION/ROBOTICS
    ⇒ RELATIONAL DATABASES/DATA DICTIONARIES/OBJECT ORIENTED PROGRAM SYSTEMS
    ⇒ COMPUTER AIDED DESIGN
    ⇒ COMPUTER AIDED OPERATION
    ⇒ GROUPWARE
    ⇒ TASK MANAGERS
    ⇒ KNOW BOTS (SELF-INITIATING SEARCHES FOR TASKS)
    ⇒ FIBER OPTICS LINKAGE

WORK FLOW
- ELIMINATE DUPLICATION OF EFFORT
- MAKE CURRENT SYSTEMS WORK
- SEEK OUT SIMPLE, RELIABLE PATHS
- MAKE CERTAIN NOTHING FALLS THROUGH THE CRACKS

WATCHOUTS

INFORMATION AND TELECOM SYSTEMS
- AVOID USING MACHINES TO HANDLE INTERACTIONS WHERE CUSTOMERS ARE LIKELY TO BECOME IRRITATED, OR KEY PROBLEMS GO OVERLOOKED TOO LONG

WORK FLOW
- DO NOT LEAVE IMPRESSION OF TIME STUDY
- BE CLEAR. THERE IS MORE THAN ENOUGH WORK TO BE DONE. THE OBJECTIVE HERE IS TO DO WHAT VALUE-ADDS ARE NECESSARY AND TO ELIMINATE THE NONSENSE.

CASE ILLUSTRATION: WORK FLOW

WIRE DIAGRAM

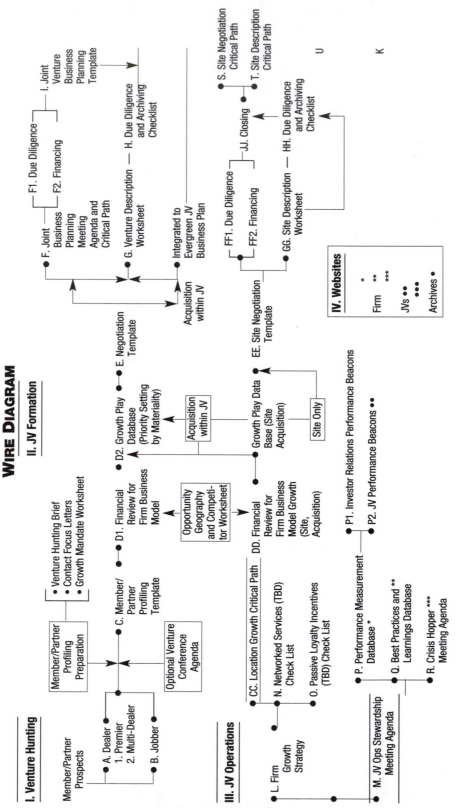

BRIEF: COMMUNICATION AND RELATIONS

TEMPLATE 11-3: COMMUNICATION AND RELATIONS
- OPENNESS
- TRUST
- HARMONY
- ADVICE GIVING
- NETWORKS FOR INFORMATION TO PERFORM JOB OR REPORT RESULTS
- WITHIN SHIFTS/TEAMS
- BETWEEN SHIFTS/TEAMS
- WITH STAFF FUNCTIONS/TEAMS
- AMONG STAFF FUNCTIONS/TEAMS
- WITH CUSTOMERS, OWNERS, AND OTHER THIRD PARTIES

TIPS

COMMUNICATIONS AND RELATIONS
- PRESENT MAJOR IDEAS MORE THAN ONCE WITH MORE THAN ONE METHOD
- KEEP A POSITIVE BIAS IN PRESENTATION
- INVITE QUESTIONS AND DIALOGUE
  - ⇒ STORY-BOARD MAJOR NEW THEMES FROM YOUR REDESIGN WITH BEHAVIORS
  - ⇒ DRAW WHAT IS DONE NOW
  - ⇒ DRAW WHAT WILL BE DONE IN THE NEW ORGANIZATION
  - ⇒ SHOW OUTCOMES FOR LIVING UP TO THE NEW EXPECTATIONS
  - ⇒ LINK TO MISSION, VISION, REWARD AND RECOGNITION
  - ⇒ SHOW AS EVOLUTION OF LEARNING AND HABIT-CHANGE FOR THE VARIOUS ROLES
  - ⇒ SIDE-BAR SOME GOOF-UPS
  - ⇒ SHOW FUN AND INTERESTING ASPECTS OF ROLES
  - ⇒ DEMONSTRATE THE INTERPERSONAL SITUATIONS DESIRED
- CREATE A PROCESS TO PROMOTE CONTINUOUS IMPROVEMENT IN RELATIONSHIPS AND COMMUNICATION . . . INCLUDES A DEFINED MEANS FOR RESTORING HARMONY EVERYONE IS RESPONSIBLE FOR

OPENNESS
- PROMOTE THE NORM IN WHICH FEEDBACK IS VALUED AS A GIFT
- MAKE SURE EXPECTATIONS ARE CLEAR
- PROMOTE THE RIGHT TO PRIVACY FOR WHAT ARE HOME LIFE ISSUES
- PROVIDE INFORMATION TO UNDERSTAND DIRECTION, CHANGE AND RESOLVE ANY DIFFERENCES
- OFFER INFORMATION TO INITIATE IN SUPPORT OF DIRECTION
- SEE THAT SUCCESSES ARE CELEBRATED
- PERMIT ACCESS TO INFORMATION—USED OR NOT

TRUST
- DEMONSTRATE COMPETENCE TO FOSTER CONFIDENCE (ESPECIALLY LEADERS)
- BE RELIABLE SO PEOPLE KNOW THEY CAN COUNT ON YOU
- SHOW YOU WILL ACT IN OTHERS' BEHALF—EVEN IF IT'S UNCOMFORTABLE FOR YOU

HARMONY MANAGEMENT
- HAVE DEFINED MEANS FOR RESTORING HARMONY WITH RESPONSIBILITIES SPELLED OUT IN ADVANCE
- DETERMINE THE BUSINESS RESULT IN JEOPARDY (MISSION)
- LEVERAGE THIRD PARTIES AS A CATALYST FOR TIMELY RESOLUTION
- SOURCE CONFLICT'S ORIGIN—JUST THE FACTS
- LISTEN TO ALL PERSPECTIVES
- FOCUS ON LEARNING—NOT FAULT-FINDING/BLAMING
- DECLARE COMPARATIVE ADVANTAGE OF HARMONY
- SET FORTH ACTION PLAN AND DEFINE MILESTONES FOR MONITORING PROGRESS

GENERAL TIPS FOR ADVICE-GIVING
- SEEK PROMISING OPPORTUNITY
- DECLARE EXPERIMENTS

(continued)

TEMPLATE 11-3: COMMUNICATION AND RELATIONS *(continued)*

- STAY ALIVE
- USE CONSULTING SKILLS
  - ⇒ DEVELOP RAPPORT
  - ⇒ LISTEN AND LEARN CLIENTS' NEEDS AND ASPIRATIONS
  - ⇒ START FROM WHERE CLIENT IS—NOT WHERE YOU ARE OR WANT CLIENT TO BE
  - ⇒ CONVEY YOUR POTENTIAL CONTRIBUTION CLEARLY AND SUCCINCTLY
  - ⇒ ASK MEANINGFUL QUESTIONS
  - ⇒ PROPOSE WHERE YOU VALUE-ADD
  - ⇒ ESCHEW JARGON AND OFFER PARABLES
  - ⇒ ILLUSTRATE OR DEMONSTRATE VALUE-ADDING
- START WHERE THE CLIENT IS—NOT WHERE YOU WANT THEM TO BE
  - ⇒ LISTEN
  - ⇒ GUIDE A SYSTEMATIC REVIEW: CURRENT SITUATION, BARRIERS, VISION OF SUCCESS, BRAINSTORM AND EVALUATE OPTIONS
  - ⇒ LEARN WHAT THEY KNOW AND HOW THEY THINK/EXPRESS IDEAS
- OFFER OPTIONS WITH RESOURCE REQUIREMENTS—RECOMMEND AFTER ALL OPTIONS ARE PRESENTED AND REVIEWED
- BUILD FROM A SUCCESS

NETWORKS
- LEVERAGE FOR BUSINESS GROWTH
- BUILD THEM BEFORE YOU USE THEM
- LEVERAGE MENTORS
- REVIEW AS A GROUP AND SHARE VARIANCES
- STRENGTHEN WITH OCCASIONAL TELEPHONE CALLS, VISITS, AND "UPDATES" CORRESPONDENCE
- MANAGE TIME IN EXPRESSING SELF AND OVERALL RESPONSIVENESS
- INVITE FEEDBACK
- ADAPT TO THEIR REQUIREMENTS
- CHALLENGE—BUT DO IT IN AN EVOLUTIONARY MANNER IF UNDERSTANDING IS MISSING
- SUSTAIN THE RELATIONSHIP IN YOUR NETWORK BY CHECKING PROGRESS/UPDATING

WATCHOUTS

COMMUNICATIONS AND RELATIONS
- DO NOT ASSUME MESSAGE IS UNDERSTOOD OR AGREED TO. CHECK BY ASKING FOR FEEDBACK
- DO NOT AVOID COMMUNICATION BECAUSE OF DISPUTES
- DO NOT PROMOTE RUMORS OR HALF-TRUTHS

OPENNESS
- NO HIDDEN TRAPS
- NO COLLUSION
- NO FRAUD OR ABUSE

TRUST
- TRUST IS EASILY LOST AND TAKES TIME TO BE WON
- DO NOT BE AFRAID TO CHALLENGE DISTRUST BY SETTING THE RECORD STRAIGHT
- DO NOT HIDE MISTAKES. IT'S BETTER TO ADMIT THEM AND MOVE ON

HARMONY MANAGEMENT
- DO NOT LEAVE HARMONY TO CHANCE
- DO NOT OVERWORK MINOR ISSUES
- BIAS IN CONFLICT RESOLUTION TOWARD ONE SIDE WILL BUILD RESENTMENT

TEMPLATE 11-3: COMMUNICATION AND RELATIONS *(continued)*

GENERAL TIPS FOR ADVICE GIVING
- DO NOT WORK UPHILL
- DO NOT ARGUE IF YOU CAN'T WIN

NETWORKS
- DO NOT OVER HARVEST
- PLAY GOD ONLY A LITTLE

SUB TEMPLATE: ROLE CLARIFICATION PROCESS

HIGH PERFORMANCE EXPECTATIONS

↓

ASSIGNMENT LETTER

↓

BOSS-SUBORDINATE DISCUSSION

↓

4-MONTH REVIEW DISCUSSION

↓

ANNUAL REVIEW
[WITH CONTINUOUS FEEDBACK (FORMAL/INFORMAL) AS WARRANTED]

SUB TEMPLATE: TRAINING AND DEVELOPMENT
- BUSINESS KNOWLEDGE, AWARENESS, AND STEWARDSHIP
- TEAM MANAGEMENT
- IT TECHNICAL SKILLS
- SUBJECT MATTER TECHNICAL SKILLS
- PARTNERING SKILLS

BRIEF: PERFORMANCE MANAGEMENT

TEMPLATE 11-4: PERFORMANCE MANAGEMENT
- EXPECTATIONS (SEE DIRECTION, PLANNING AND MONITORING)
- ROLE CLARIFICATION
- TRAINING AND DEVELOPMENT
- COACHING AND DISCIPLINE
- REWARD AND RECOGNITION

SUB TEMPLATE: COACHING AND DISCIPLINE
- EXPECTATIONS/ROLE CLARIFICATION/DAILY DIRECTION COMMUNICATION
- INTERPERSONAL FEEDBACK
- HARMONY RESTORATION PROCESS
- ONE-ON-ONE COACHING
- TEAM COACHING
- SUPERVISOR COACHING
- DISCIPLINE

Sub Template: Coaching

Coaching Style:
- Be Positive
  - ⇒ Look to help another
  - ⇒ Express feedback without sarcastic criticism
  - ⇒ Point out potential gain
- Use an appreciate/wish format
  - ⇒ Establish first how much you value the person
  - ⇒ Do not be rigid in use of the format. Be natural
- Check your perception with others
  - ⇒ Invite others to share opinions—whether they agree or not
  - ⇒ Invite feedback from others on your opinion
- Invite feedback. Help create a positive norm for feedback
- Before offering feedback, analyze the issue carefully
  - ⇒ Do not use unfair or discriminatory practices/language in expressing feedback
  - ⇒ Ask yourself, is this job-related? (If not, stop process . . . it would be illegal to continue)
  - ⇒ Reference general expectations, if relevant
  - ⇒ Clarify any related business strategy, priority or sensitivity related to observed behaviors, if relevant
  - ⇒ Deal with performance questions directly and in a timely manner

Coaching Process: Should be non-threatening and available from all employees or leaders to one another. This is true open communication and trust—elements of high performance organizations. Leaders in the beginning have to get the ball rolling and serve as role models. Effective coaching steps are to:

- Describe the difference between what is being done and what should be done
- Determine likely cause(s) for difference
  - ⇒ Skill or knowledge is lacking
  - ⇒ Nonperformance is easier
  - ⇒ Communication of expectation was not clear
  - ⇒ Conflicting instructions were given
  - ⇒ Performance has side effects—performance breakdowns exist
- Provide feedback
- Take action and monitor—provide feedback on progress
- Utilize employee assistance when available (provide telephone contact information and outline or services)

Coaching success is influenced by how you set up the dynamics and what issues are important. To assist you in preparing for coaching, consider these dynamics and issues.

Sub Template: Reward and Recognition

Wedding Cake for Reward and Recognition

| Profit-Sharing Bonus |
| Gain/Loss Sharing Bonus |
| Company/Unit/Group Incentive Bonus |
| Individual Incentive Bonus
Wage or Salary |
| Benefits |

Atmosphere
- Recognition on interpersonal basis
- Recognition with formal program

SUB TEMPLATE: REWARD AND RECOGNITION *(continued)*

TRENDS ARE:
- TO PAY FOR PERFORMANCE, IMPROVEMENT, EDUCATION (SKILL OR KNOWLEDGE), VERSATILITY
- TO PLACE SOME PAY "AT RISK" AS AN OWNER DOES WITH INVESTMENTS (E.G., SVA)

REWARD AND RECOGNITION (R&R) SYSTEM TEST
- GIVEN YOUR LIST OF PRIORITIES, WHAT CONTRIBUTIONS FROM INDIVIDUALS ARE NEEDED?
    - ⇒ HOW COULD YOU REWARD AND RECOGNIZE THESE CONTRIBUTIONS USING THE EXISTING R&R TOOLS?
    - ⇒ WHAT SLIGHT CHANGES IN ADMINISTRATION MIGHT IMPROVE THE IMPACT OF THESE R&R TOOLS?
    - ⇒ DRAFT A "BLUE-SKY" SCENARIO FOR THE EVOLUTION OF R&R TOOLS.
- GIVEN YOUR LIST OF PRIORITIES, WHAT CONTRIBUTIONS FROM GROUPS/TEAMS/UNITS ARE NEEDED?
    - ⇒ HOW COULD YOU REWARD AND RECOGNIZE THESE CONTRIBUTIONS USING THE EXISTING R&R TOOLS?
    - ⇒ WHAT SLIGHT CHANGES IN ADMINISTRATION MIGHT IMPROVE THE IMPACT OF THESE R&R TOOLS?
- DRAFT A "BLUE SKY" SCENARIO FOR THE EVOLUTION OF R&R TOOLS

IN ANSWERING THE ABOVE—DO NOT SET $ AMOUNTS OR %'S—THINK INSTEAD IN TERMS OF METHODS AND MEASUREMENTS; SET THESE LATE AFTER A MECHANISM IS DEFINED. UTILIZE SVA AS BASIS FOR VALUE-ADD MEASUREMENTS RELATED TO REWARDS.

TIPS

ROLE CLARIFICATION
- USE AN INTERACTIVE PROCESS: EXPECTATIONS, REVISIT AFTER 4 MONTHS, ANNUAL REVIEW
- USE ASSIGNMENT LETTER TO AVOID EVALUATION BUT OPEN DIALOGUE ON NEW EXPECTATIONS WITH AN ASSESSMENT OF CURRENT CAPABILITY
- CHALLENGE PEOPLE TO EXAMINE THEIR USE OF TIME . . . PROMOTE A FOCUS ON BUSINESS PRIORITIES
- INCLUDE A DIALOGUE ON RESOURCES AND SUPPORT AS WELL AS SETTING STRETCH EXPECTATIONS
- INVITE INDIVIDUAL TO STATE POSSIBILITIES FOR FUTURE AND THUS DEFINE NEXT STRETCH OPPORTUNITY
- OFFER OWN STRETCH CHALLENGE IN YOUR OWN ROLE DISCUSSION

TRAINING AND DEVELOPMENT
- INITIALLY NEEDS TO ADDRESS ONLY REDESIGN IMPLEMENTATION
    - ⇒ TEAM SKILLS/BUILDING (INCLUDES MEETING EFFECTIVENESS)
    - ⇒ INVOLVEMENT TEAM START-UP
    - ⇒ SPECIAL IT PROJECT
- NEEDS STEWARDSHIP BY TEAM
    - ⇒ PHILOSOPHY
    - ⇒ SET OBJECTIVES AND PRIORITIES
    - ⇒ SET BUDGET
    - ⇒ SET ACCESS RULES
    - ⇒ SET INVESTMENT PARAMETERS
    - ⇒ STEWARD PROGRESS AND IMPACT ON OUTCOMES
- TREND IS A 50-50 SHARED RESPONSIBILITY
- TREND IS TO INCREASE TRAINING INVESTMENT
- TREND IS TO HAVE A COMPREHENSIVE EDUCATIONAL PROGRAM: HPO, COMMERCIAL, TECHNOLOGICAL LEARNING OBJECTIVES AND PROCESSES
- IT IS A GOOD IDEA TO USE OWN PEOPLE TO DO TRAINING (ONCE THEY ARE COMPETENT):
    - ⇒ PROMOTES LEARNING FOR INSTRUCTORS OWN USE
    - ⇒ MORE AVAILABLE FOR FOLLOW-UP COACHING
    - ⇒ LESS COSTLY
- FOR COURSES OUTSIDE COMPANY:
    - ⇒ REQUIRE ATTENDEES TO EVALUATE
    - ⇒ HAVE ATTENDEES PRESENT HIGHLIGHTS TO LEADERS AND PEOPLE IN LIKE ROLES OR DUTIES RELEVANT TO TRAINING SO THEY ALSO BENEFIT FROM THE TRAINING/SUPPORT NEW METHODS
- REQUIRE VENDORS TO PROVIDE TRAINING
- TO A LIMITED EXTENT, USE TRAINING TO RECOGNIZE

(continued)

SUB TEMPLATE: REWARD AND RECOGNITION *(continued)*

- LEADERSHIP SHOULD STEWARD NEW IDEAS AND PROMOTE USE OR QUICKLY KILL THE INAPPROPRIATE
- TRACK ATTENDEE USE

COACHING AND DISCIPLINE
- BE LAWFUL
- BE FAIR
- BE CLEAR WHEN COACHING EVOLVES TO DISCIPLINE
- CONSIDER ORGANIZING MENTORING TO:
  - ⇒ PROVIDE CONSISTENT AND FAIR ACCESS
  - ⇒ DEVELOP OPERATIONAL, OWNER, CUSTOMER INTEREST IN EMPLOYEE
  - ⇒ MARKET SERVICES TO OPERATION
- RECOGNIZE MENTORING IS FUN
- FOLLOW GOOD COACHING PRACTICES
- SHARE SUCCESSES AMONG COACHES
- KEEP COACHING CASUAL AND DISCIPLINE FORMAL

REWARD AND RECOGNITION
- REWARD AND RECOGNITION ARE DIFFERENT WAYS TO ENCOURAGE FUTURE CONTRIBUTION TO THE MISSION OF THE ORGANIZATION
- REWARD IS PAY, BONUS, BENEFIT OR PRIZE FOR EFFORT. IT HAS ECONOMIC VALUE
- RECOGNITION IS PRAISE FOR EFFORT. IT HAS SOCIAL VALUE AND MAY LEAD TO CAREER OPPORTUNITY
- EACH PERSON HAS THEIR OWN PERCEPTION ABOUT REWARD AND RECOGNITION AND WHAT IS IMPORTANT. PEOPLE MAY VARY THEIR OPINION FROM SITUATION TO SITUATION
- IN HARD ECONOMIC TIMES—FOR SOCIETY OR PERSONALLY—REWARD TAKES ON GREATER IMPORTANCE
- FAIRNESS IS CRITICAL IN THE DESIGN OF REWARD AND RECOGNITION. UNFAIRNESS MAY TAKE AWAY FROM THE VALUE OF THE REWARD OR RECOGNITION
- THE CLEARER THE MEASUREMENT OF SUCCESS, THE EASIER IT IS TO OBTAIN ACCEPTANCE FOR REWARD OR RECOGNITION FROM THE INDIVIDUAL AND PEOPLE AROUND THE INDIVIDUAL
- CLEAR EXPECTATIONS ARE THE BEGINNING OF FAIR PLAY IN REWARD AND RECOGNITION
- THE TREND IN REWARD AND RECOGNITION IS TOWARD:
  - ⇒ TIME-ADJUSTED RESULTS
  - ⇒ DIFFUSION OF PERFORMANCE BONUSES FROM SENIOR LEVELS TO THE ORGANIZATION AS A WHOLE
  - ⇒ MULTIPLE STRATEGIES—COMPLEXITIES TAILORED TO INDIVIDUAL PERFORMANCE, NEEDS AND ASPIRATIONS—BUT REQUIRING BETTER KNOWLEDGE OF THE ECONOMICS OF THE BUSINESS
  - ⇒ MORE INCOME BASED ON PERFORMANCE RESULTS AND FEWER GUARANTEED PAYMENTS FOR HOLDING A JOB
  - ⇒ MORE ENCOURAGEMENT FOR LEARNING AND ADAPTING
  - ⇒ IMPROVED MEASUREMENT OF PERFORMANCE AND BROADER INPUT ON EVALUATION OF RESULTS—COLLEAGUES, DIRECT REPORTS, CUSTOMERS, SUPPLIERS, CONTRACTORS (360-DEGREE FEEDBACK)
  - ⇒ CHANGE
- MOST REWARD AND RECOGNITION SYSTEMS EVOLVE OVER TIME WITH EXPERIMENTATION AROUND BOTH METHODS AND THE BASIS FOR PERFORMANCE MEASUREMENT. DEVELOPING A PROCESS FOR EVOLUTIONARY CHANGE IS IMPORTANT TO ACCEPTANCE AND SUCCESS

WATCHOUTS

ROLE CLARIFICATION
- CAREFULLY PREPARE FOR DISCUSSIONS
- DO NOT LEAVE PRIORITIES AMBIGUOUS
- DO NOT DILUTE FOCUS BY SETTING TOO BROAD A SET OF GOALS
- BE REALISTIC

Sub Template: Reward and Recognition *(continued)*

Training and Development
- Do not be unfair—okay to "play" best player but they cannot absorb all the resources all the time
- Do not use vendors without checking them out
- Do not permit individuals to do their own thing. Either go to training at own election or avoid training

Coaching and Discipline
- Brief anyone who coaches on Equal Employment Opportunity (EEO) laws
- Do not count on employees to initiate coaching
- Prepare leaders to coach
- Carefully steward early coaching and discipline
- Keep personal issues out of mentoring
- Cultural Barriers exist to coaching
  ⇒ Feedback is seen as criticism
  ⇒ Criticism is a political put-down (there is a purpose to saying it at a certain time)
  ⇒ Criticism should be private
- When feedback is a new experience, it can be uncomfortable
  ⇒ Fear old wounds and issues will surface
  ⇒ Telling people something you think may not be acceptable is typically not fun
- Initial experiences go smoother with advance coaching and facilitation by a third party
- As with any feedback, take histories and moods into account
- Get help where it has been difficult

Reward and Recognition
- More reward does not necessarily mean better contribution
- More recognition does not necessarily mean better contribution
- Jealousy may influence the impact of reward and recognition, diluting their impact to encourage
- As a career system, reward and recognition are subject to laws and legal/administrative proceedings. Fairness is not optional
- Reward and recognition is an emotionally charged subject in design. It can detract from the total capacity to plan change
- Tax laws greatly influence decisions in reward and recognition—impacting reporting, withholding and rate of taxation

(continued)

Case Illustration: Performance Management

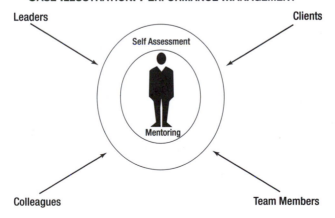

CASE ILLUSTRATION: REWARD AND RECOGNITION

DONALDSON, LUFKIN, JENERETTE: STOCK LOAN SBU
VALUE CREATION-BASED REWARD SYSTEM

	YEARS				
	85	86	87	88	89
INCENTIVE AS PERCENT OF SALARIES	23%	160%	250%	150%	143%
INCENTIVE AS PERCENT OF NET PROFIT	9%	25%	28%	25%	22%
RETURN ON REVENUE	43%	55%	57%	54%	56%

TOTAL STAFF = 8

MESA PETROLEUM CASE ILLUSTRATION

- **SBU BASED**
- **100% OF BASE PAY—POTENTIAL FOR BONUS**
- **PAYOUT SCHEDULE FOR 1009**
  - −30% 1/91   −25% 1/92
  - −25% 1/93   −20% 1/94

TYPICAL TOTAL COMPENSATION OF FIVE YEAR PARTICIPANT

1986 BASE $50,000   1986 BONUS $20,000
1987 TOTAL COMPENSATION   1987 BONUS $20,000
  $50,000   BASE
  $ 6,000   30% OF 1986 BONUS
  $56,000   12% INCREASE
1988 TOTAL COMPENSATION   1988 BONUS $20,000
  $50,000   BASE
  $ 2,500   5% BASE ADJ.
  $ 6,000   30% 1987 BONUS
  $ 5,000   25% 1986 BONUS
  $63,500   13.4% INCREASE
1989 TOTAL COMPENSATION   1989 BONUS $20,000
  $52,500   BASE
  $ 6,000   30% 1988 BONUS
  $ 5,000   25% 1987 BONUS
  $ 5,000   25% 1986 BONUS
  $68,000   7.8% INCREASE

1990 TOTAL COMPENSATION   1990 BONUS $10,000
  $52,500   BASE
  $ 2,500   4.76% BASE ADJ.
  $ 6,000   NEW BASE
  $55,000   30% 1989 BONUS
  $ 5,000   25% 1987 BONUS
  $ 5,000   25% 1987 BONUS
  $75,000   9.4% INCREASE

1991 TOTAL COMPENSATION
  $55,000   BASE
  $ 3,000   30% 1990 BONUS
  $ 5,000   25% 1989 BONUS
  $ 5,000   25% 1988 BONUS
  $ 4,000   20% 1987 BONUS
  $72,000   −4.0% DECREASE

Rice University, Executive Productivity Network Meeting (Spring, 1990)

BRIEF: CONTINUOUS IMPROVEMENT AND INNOVATION

TEMPLATE 11-5: CONTINUOUS IMPROVEMENT AND INNOVATION

- IDENTIFIES QUICK HITS AND PENDING ITEMS ACTION LISTS
  - ⇒ KEY PROJECTS OR MINI-STEPS TO DEMONSTRATE CREDIBILITY
  - ⇒ INTEGRATION OF CURRENT CAPITAL EXPENDITURES AND PROJECT LISTS
  - ⇒ ESTIMATES AT GROSSEST LEVEL (UNLESS DATA AVAILABLE)
  - ⇒ FUNDS FOR INVESTIGATING NEW METHODS, TOOLS, TECHNOLOGIES—NOTE IN BUDGET OR PROJECTS LIST
- ONGOING STRUCTURE FOR EVERGREEN RENEWAL OF CII

TIPS

CONTINUOUS IMPROVEMENT AND INNOVATION (CII)

- CII INCLUDES OPERATIONS IMPROVEMENTS AND BUSINESS/TECHNOLOGY INNOVATIONS WHICH CREATE OPPORTUNITY OR REDEFINE A PROCESS FOR BETTER PERFORMANCE
- DESIGN TEAM CAN INITIATE CII AND DEMONSTRATE ITS IMPACT
  - ⇒ BEST TO FOCUS ON JUST A HANDFUL OF "QUICK HITS" WHICH DEMONSTRATE THE VALUE OF CII AND SET THE BALL ROLLING FOR THE FUTURE
  - ⇒ "QUICK HITS" TYPICALLY ARE CHARACTERIZED AS BEING EASY TO DO, HAVING BROAD IMPACT AND REQUIRING LIMITED RESOURCES (TIME/MONEY)
  - ⇒ THIS FOSTERS A MECHANISM FOR CII; CII DEPENDS ON THE MIND-SET OF THE PEOPLE IN THE ORGANIZATION
- EXPECTATIONS FOR CII, LEADERSHIP STATEMENTS AND ACTIONS, AND REWARD/RECOGNITION INFLUENCE PEOPLE'S VIEWS OF CII
  - ⇒ PEOPLE WHO SEE CII AS PART OF THEIR JOB SEE LESS RISK IN CHALLENGING AND FIND RECEPTIVE ATMOSPHERE FOR IDEAS
  - ⇒ HOW LEADERSHIP MANAGES IDEAS HAS GREAT INFLUENCE OVER PEOPLE'S CHOICES FOR CII; ACTIVE ENCOURAGEMENT, PARTICIPATION IN PROBLEM-SOLVING, RECOGNITION OF IDEAS AND EXPERIMENTS (EVEN ONES WHICH DON'T WORK BUT ARE EXPLAINED AS TO WHY THEY WILL NOT BE SUPPORTED), AND CREDITING CONTRIBUTORS ARE LEADERSHIP ACTIONS FOR CII
  - ⇒ REWARDS AND RECOGNITION ALIGNED TO IDEA MANAGEMENT WILL SPONSOR CII
- SUCCESS COMES FROM THE BLEND OF BOTH MECHANISMS AND ATMOSPHERE
- DESIGN TEAM SHOULD SET A CRITERIA TO GUIDE A BALANCED ASSESSMENT OF OPPORTUNITIES AND ESTABLISH PRIORITIES, E.G.,
  - ⇒ RATE OF RETURN
  - ⇒ TIME TO PAY BACK INVESTMENT
  - ⇒ SIZE OF INVESTMENT (TIME/MONEY)
  - ⇒ OUTCOMES FOR STAKEHOLDERS
  - ⇒ CREDIBILITY TO STAKEHOLDERS
  - ⇒ PROBABILITY OF SUCCESS
  - ⇒ RANK-ORDER AMONG ALL CRITERIA
- DESIGN TEAM SHOULD INITIATE A LIST WHICH IS:
  - ⇒ KEPT "EVERGREEN" OVERTIME . . . UPDATED PERIODICALLY AND REVISITED AS TOP PRIORITIES ARE ACHIEVED AND THE "NEXT" TASK IS TO BE IDENTIFIED
  - ⇒ TRANSFERRED AS A RESPONSIBILITY TO A GROUP/TEAM AS DIVERSE AS THE DESIGN TEAM TO FULFILL THE EVERGREEN TASK
  - ⇒ FULLY INTEGRATED WITH THE CAPITAL/EXPENSE BUDGET PROCESS
  - ⇒ BASED IN PART ON BENCHMARKING OF COMPETITORS, ALLIED INDUSTRIES AND BUSINESS INNOVATIONS
- USE CII TO EDUCATE PEOPLE ON BUSINESS ECONOMICS BY SCOPING OUT OPTIONS AND THEIR COMPARATIVE BENEFITS/COSTS

(continued)

TEMPLATE 11-5: CONTINUOUS IMPROVEMENT AND INNOVATION *(continued)*

WATCHOUTS

CONTINUOUS IMPROVEMENT AND INNOVATION (CII)
- LEADERS CAN KILL CII BY:
- NOT CREDITING OTHERS OR TAKING ALL THE CREDIT
  ⇒ FAILING TO REWARD AND RECOGNIZE
  ⇒ CUTTING OF IDEAS WITHOUT AN EXPLANATION
  ⇒ NOT SUPPORTING IDEAS (EXCEPT THEIR OWN)
  ⇒ GIVING UP TOO SOON
  ⇒ ALLOWING OPERATING UNITS TO KILL IDEAS FROM OTHERS
  ⇒ TRYING TO ACHIEVE RESULTS WITHOUT MAKING INVESTMENTS OR DOING THE WORK
- CII WILL NOT PROGRESS WHEN PEOPLE HOLD ON TO THE PAST AND DO NOT PUT ENERGY INTO TRYING NEW THINGS
- CII CAN BE STOPPED WHEN PEOPLE REFUSE TO LEARN
- CII DIES WHEN NO ONE MAKES THE TIME TO REFLECT AND BRAINSTORM
- CII CAN BE SHANGHAIED BY PEOPLE DEMANDING A REWARD FOR ANY CII IDEA. CLEAR PARAMETERS ARE NEEDED TO AVOID THIS
- CII CAN BE UNDERCUT BY DYSFUNCTIONAL COMPETITION AMONG/BETWEEN TEAMS. AGAIN, CLEAR PARAMETERS ARE NEEDED

BRIEF: PARTNERING

TEMPLATE 11-6: PARTNERING

- SET COLLABORATION PHILOSOPHY AND STRATEGY
- PREPARE PARTNERING STRATEGY OR MECHANISMS:
  ⇒ CUSTOMERS
  ⇒ VENDORS/SUPPLIERS
  ⇒ CONTRACTORS
  ⇒ REGULATORS
  ⇒ COMMUNITY
  ⇒ INVESTORS/BANKERS
- DEVELOP MECHANISM FOR BENCHMARKING
  ⇒ COMPETITORS
  ⇒ SUBSTITUTION THREATS
  ⇒ ALLIED INDUSTRIES

TIPS

PARTNERING
- DESIGN TEAM SHOULD INITIATE CONSIDERATION OF HOW THE FIRM CAN ACHIEVE ITS GOALS BY COMBINING WITH OTHERS IN ALLIANCES. ISSUES TO BE CONSIDERED:
  ⇒ CHOOSING WORTHY BUSINESS PARTNERS
  ⇒ DEVELOPING THE CAPABILITY IN TERMS OF TALENT AND WAYS TO ORGANIZE WHICH TRULY PROMOTE ALLIANCES (MORE THE CONCEPT IN THAT NORMS AND PRACTICES ARE DEVELOPED THROUGHOUT THE ORGANIZATION)
  ⇒ MARRYING COMPATIBLE WORK CULTURES

TEMPLATE 11-6: PARTNERING *(continued)*

> ⇒ EXPRESSING ALLIANCE EXPECTATIONS (INCLUDING EXIT CIRCUMSTANCES AND TERMS) FOR POTENTIAL PARTNERS AND YOUR OWN SHAREHOLDERS
> ⇒ ALIGNMENT OF REWARD AND RECOGNITION TO PROMOTE ALLIANCES

- DESIGN TEAM SHOULD SPONSOR PARTNERING INTERNALLY:
  - ⇒ DESIGN EFFECTIVE HORIZONTAL RELATIONS AND FACILITATE THEIR CONTINUOUS USE
  - ⇒ DEMONSTRATE PARTNERING CONCEPTS AND DEVELOP THEIR APPLICATION TO ENSURE COMPETENCE WHEN APPLIED TO THE OUTSIDE
- DESIGN TEAM SHOULD OUTLINE A STRATEGY FOR EFFECTIVE PARTNERING WITH:
  - ⇒ CUSTOMERS
  - ⇒ REGULATORS
  - ⇒ VENDORS
  - ⇒ CONTRACTORS
- CUSTOMER INTIMACY IS A KEY LEVERAGE OPPORTUNITY FOR BUSINESS GROWTH. KNOW CUSTOMERS NEEDS/CIRCUMSTANCES SO WELL YOU CAN LEAD THEM TO YOUR NEW PRODUCTS/SERVICES
- REGULATORS MUST POLICE BUT INVOLVING THEM IN PLANNING AND PROVING YOUR DILIGENCE CAN REDUCE AUDIT REQUIREMENTS
- VENDORS/CONTRACTORS WHO OWN YOUR AGENDA FOR SUCCESS CAN HELP CUT COSTS (MOST WILL EXPECT TO SHARE IN SAVINGS)
- IN EXTERNAL PARTNERING, KEEP IN MIND:
  - ⇒ PEOPLE WILL JUDGE YOUR COMMERCIAL VALUE/LEGAL INTENT BY YOUR PARTNERING
  - ⇒ BEST TO PLAY THE BEST PLAYERS WITH OUTSIDERS
    - + PREPARED/INFORMED
    - + ABLE TO EXPRESS IDEAS
    - + NEGOTIATION SKILLS
    - + BE CLEAR ON AUTHORITY TO MAKE COMMITMENTS
- DESIGN TEAM SHOULD FOSTER BENCHMARKING OF COMPETITORS, ALLIED INDUSTRIES, SUBSTITUTION THREATS, BUSINESS INNOVATIONS BECAUSE:
  - ⇒ THEY ARE A SOURCE OF IDEAS
- NEED INTELLIGENCE ON WHERE OTHERS ARE IN THE MARKET . . . TO SEE OPPORTUNITIES TO WIN THEIR CUSTOMERS . . . TO SENSE THREATS TO YOUR MARKET SHARE

WATCHOUTS

PARTNERING
- INTERNAL COMPETITION INCREASES THE COST TO DO BUSINESS
- OTHERS WILL ALLY WHERE YOU WILL NOT—AND TAKE THE ADVANTAGE
  - ⇒ ALLIANCES GIVE YOU ACCESS TO OPM AND OPM MEANS MORE THAN "OTHER PEOPLE'S MONEY":
    - + "OTHER PEOPLE'S MARKETS" . . . ESPECIALLY FOREIGN
    - + "OTHER PEOPLE'S MEANS" . . . FACILITIES, EQUIPMENT, TECHNOLOGY
- ALLIANCES CAN BE DISGUISED TAKEOVER ATTEMPTS. KNOW THE DEVIL YOU COURT AND REMEMBER THE DEVIL IS IN THE DETAILS

BRIEF: STRUCTURE AND EVENTS ORCHESTRATION

TEMPLATE 11-7: STRUCTURE AND EVENTS ORCHESTRATION

- INVOLVEMENT ON WORK STRUCTURE
- ROLES
- TEAMS
- UNITS
- LINKAGES
  - ⇒ COMMUNICATION
  - ⇒ NETWORKS
  - ⇒ DECISION MAKING

SUB TEMPLATE: STRUCTURAL DEVICES

INDIVIDUAL ROLES
- LEADERS
- SUBJECT MATTER EXPERTS
- SKILL EXPERTS

TEAMS
- PART-TIME/FULL TIME
- TEMPORARY/PERMANENT
- SINGLE/MULTIPLE MEMBERSHIPS
- TYPES
  - ⇒ WORK (PERMANENT, FULL TIME)
  - ⇒ STANDING (PERMANENT, PART-TIME)
  - ⇒ BRIDGE (INTEGRATING STANDING TEAM)
  - ⇒ DIRECTION (LEADERSHIP-BASED BRIDGE TEAM)
  - ⇒ SPECIAL (AD HOC QUALITY/TASKS/PROJECT)

LINKAGES
- ROLE INTERFACES
- NETWORKS (OCCASIONAL, SHARED INTERESTS/RESOURCES)
- COMMUNICATION AND ELECTRONIC INTERFACES

UNITS
- PRODUCT/SERVICE/CUSTOMER
- MINI-ENTERPRISE OR SBU (STRATEGIC BUSINESS UNITS)
- CORE COMPETENCY
- FUNCTIONAL
- FACILITY
- REGION OR OTHER LOCATION-BASED

SUB TEMPLATE: ORGANIZATION DESIGN PLATEAUS

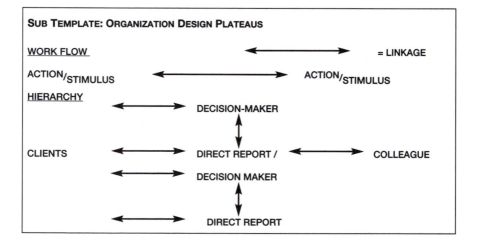

SUB TEMPLATE: INVOLVEMENT STRUCTURE

LEADERSHIP TEAM
"BROADLY INTEGRATES, MAKES DECISIONS, TAKES ACTION AND STEWARDS"

INVOLVEMENT TEAM
(CROSS-SECTION OF FIRM)
"INTEGRATES IDEAS AND OPINIONS ACROSS ORGANIZATION; FORMULATES RECOMMENDATIONS FOR POLICY/PRACTICE; FACILITATES HORIZONTAL RELATIONS AND TECHNOLOGY TRANSFER"

DAILY WORK TEAMS
EXECUTES CORE
COMPETENCIES AND INFRASTRUCTURE
SUPPORT ACTIVITIES

SPECIAL TEAMS
PERFORM STUDIES AND
PROJECTS

"ACTION"

SUB TEMPLATE: STRUCTURE CRITERIA

(CRITERIA FOR STRUCTURE TO ACCOMPLISH)
- SUPPORTS THE BUSINESS INTENT . . . MISSION
- UTILIZES EXISTING TECHNOLOGY . . . ACCOUNTING FOR ITS EVOLUTION
- MAY INITIALLY BE A TRANSITIONAL STRUCTURE TO FACILITATE ACCEPTANCE AND UNDERSTANDING—LATER EVOLVING TO THE VISION
- BRINGS MEANING TO WORK
- PROMOTES MUTUAL RESPECT
- OFFERS OPEN COMMUNICATION—PEOPLE CLOSEST TO A DECISION HAVE ACCESS TO THE INFORMATION REQUIRED
- SPONSORS MEANINGFUL INVOLVEMENT IN THE BUSINESS
- RETAINS ONLY AN ESSENTIAL HIERARCHY
- LEVERAGES CORE COMPETENCIES FOR GROWTH
- LEADS TO OR ACHIEVES THE NEAR-TERM VISION
- PROVIDES MOMENTUM AND PROCESSES FOR CONTINUOUS IMPROVEMENT AND INNOVATION
- DEMONSTRATES THE CHARACTERISTICS OF HIGH PERFORMANCE
- ESTABLISHES THE CORE WORK SYSTEMS

WATCHOUTS
- STRUCTURE IS THE MOST SENSITIVE ISSUE. IT:
  - ⇒ IMPLIES STATUS
  - ⇒ CALIBRATES MAGNITUDE OF CHANGE IN PEOPLES' MINDS
  - ⇒ DISTURBS RELATIONSHIPS
  - ⇒ CREATES RELATIONSHIPS
  - ⇒ MAY REQUIRE MORE EFFORT
- PEOPLE JOCKEY FOR POSITION OR TURF
- STRUCTURE MAY BE TOO COMPLEX TO UNDERSTAND
- STRUCTURAL CHANGE DOES NOT NECESSARILY HELP RELATIONSHIPS FUNCTION BETTER
- SOME WORK OR TASKS MIGHT GET OVERLOOKED AND FALL THROUGH THE CRACKS . . . ALL SUSTAINING AND NEW WORK MUST BE ACCOUNTED FOR IN THE NEW STRUCTURE
- STRUCTURE IS GIVEN GREATER ATTENTION THAN OTHER ESSENTIAL SYSTEMS, E.G., PERFORMANCE, PLANNING AND MONITORING, ETC.
- WHEN TRANSITIONS ARE NOT MADE, CHANGE EFFORTS CAN BECOME TOO ABRUPT
- STRONG TENDENCIES MAY EMERGE TO GET THINGS BACK TO THE WAY THEY WERE

(continued)

SUB TEMPLATE: STRUCTURE CRITERIA *(continued)*

- CATALYSTS MAY FAIL TO CONTINUOUSLY CHALLENGE THE ORGANIZATION TO FULFILL THE DESIGN IMPLEMENTATION INTENDED
- ORIENTATION AND ASSIMILATION TO THE NEW ORGANIZATION MAY BE UNDER-DEVELOPED OR POORLY CONVEYED
- PLANS ARE NOT MADE TO HANDLE CRISIS
- SPONSORS AND LOCAL LEADERSHIP ARE POORLY PREPARED FOR TRANSITION

SUB TEMPLATE: EVENTS ORCHESTRATION
- ANNOUNCEMENT
- CELEBRATION
- TEAM LEARNINGS
- TEAM DEVELOPMENT
- COACHING
- IMPLEMENTATION STEWARDSHIP
- SPECIAL TECHNICAL EDUCATION: IT ENHANCEMENTS
- INITIATE COMPETENCY EDUCATION
- INITIATE SPECIAL SKILLS EDUCATION

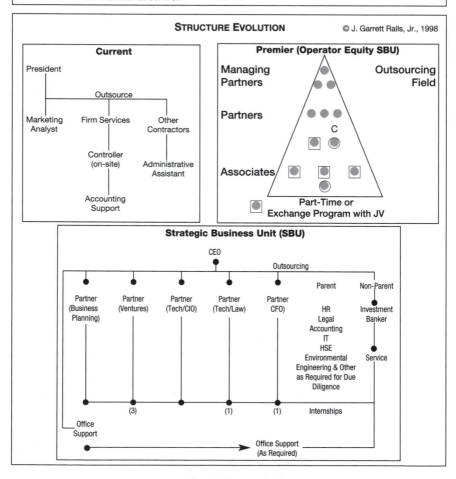

STRUCTURE EVOLUTION   © J. Garrett Ralls, Jr., 1998

CASE ILLUSTRATION: STRUCTURES

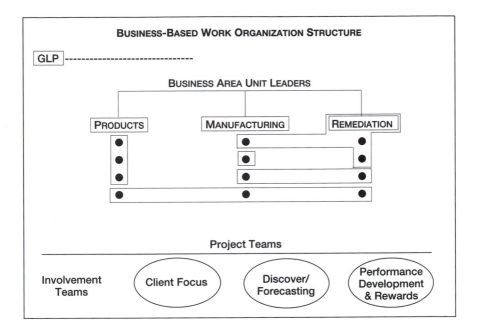

SAMPLE AUDIT REVIEW

HIGH-PERFORMANCE ORGANIZATION (HPO)

AUDIT	PRIORITY	
		MISSION DRIVEN
❏	❏	• ALWAYS IMPROVING SVA FOR OWNER(S)—NOW AND IN THE FUTURE
❏	❏	• POSSESSES A SENSE OF URGENCY TO ACHIEVE MISSION
❏	❏	• MAKES DECISIONS AND RESOLVES DIFFERENCES BY FOCUSING ON OPPORTUNITY
❏	❏	• VALUES BOTH RESPONDING TO CHANGE AND PERSISTENCE IN INTENT
❏	❏	• PURSUES GROWTH TO "MAKE THE PIE BIGGER"
❏	❏	• FOCUSES ON THE HERE AND NOW AND ENVISIONS A POSITIVE FUTURE
		COMMERCIALLY ASTUTE
❏	❏	• ACHIEVES MATERIALITY (NET INCOME AND MARKET SHARE) AND BUILDS NET WORTH
❏	❏	• UNDERSTANDS THE CUSTOMER, THE CUSTOMER'S BUSINESS AND ANTICIPATES NEEDS
❏	❏	• ABLE TO LEAD CUSTOMER TO NEW PRODUCTS/SERVICES TO SECURE BUSINESS AND PURSUE GROWTH
❏	❏	• UNDERSTANDS THE MARKET AND AGGRESSIVELY PURSUES OPPORTUNITY WITH PURPOSEFUL STRATEGY
❏	❏	• REMAINS ALERT TO THREATS AND DISTRACTIONS
❏	❏	• BENCHMARKS THE COMPETITION, CONTRACTORS, VENDORS, AND THEIR DIRECTION
❏	❏	• EMPHASIZES SPEED AND QUALITY IN MARKET RESPONSE
❏	❏	• SEEKS OPPORTUNITY WITH A GLOBAL PERSPECTIVE AND KNOWS HOW TO SUCCEED IN DIFFERENT CULTURES
❏	❏	• REMAINS ALERT TO CHANGES IN PUBLIC MOOD AND TASTES, TECHNOLOGY, AND ORGANIZATIONAL PRACTICES
❏	❏	• ALL LEVELS APPRECIATE THE CONCEPT OF ADDING VALUE

(continued)

HIGH-PERFORMANCE ORGANIZATION (HPO) *(continued)*

AUDIT   PRIORITY

EMPOWERED TALENT

AUDIT	PRIORITY	
❑	❑	• GIVES PEOPLE WHAT THEY NEED TO SELF-INITIATE
❑	❑	• SEES PEOPLE AND ORGANIZATION AS THE CATALYSTS FOR INTEGRATING COMMERCIAL OPPORTUNITY AND TECHNOLOGY TO CREATE A DYNAMIC ENTERPRISE
❑	❑	• ENABLES PEOPLE TO KNOW THE BUSINESS AND SELF-PRIORITIZE AND TAKE ACTION
❑	❑	• VALUES PRUDENT RISK OVER DELAY
❑	❑	• MEANINGFULLY INVOLVES PEOPLE AT ALL LEVELS IN PLANNING AND DECISIONS RELATED TO HOW THEIR WORK GETS DONE AND WHAT IS POSSIBLE
❑	❑	• CREATES AN ENVIRONMENT FOR CHALLENGE AT WORK AND A LIFE WORTH LIVING
❑	❑	• INVITES PARTNERS AND COMMUNITY TO JOIN IN ACHIEVEMENT

TECHNOLOGICALLY ADVANCED

AUDIT	PRIORITY	
❑	❑	• VALUES TECHNOLOGY FOR WHAT IT MEANS TO RETURN ON INVESTMENT RATHER THAN AS AN END UNTO ITSELF
❑	❑	• STAYS ABREAST OF TECHNOLOGY ADVANCES IN OWN INDUSTRY, ALLIED INDUSTRIES, CUSTOMERS' INDUSTRIES, SUPPLIERS' INDUSTRIES, AND ADMINISTRATIVE SERVICES
❑	❑	• FOSTERS AWARENESS AT ALL LEVELS OF CUTTING-EDGE INNOVATIONS AND PLANS PARTICIPATION AT THE OPPORTUNE MOMENT
❑	❑	• APPRECIATES SUCCESSFUL TECHNOLOGY IMPLEMENTATION IS OFTEN A FUNCTION OF HUMAN ACCEPTANCE
❑	❑	• WEIGHS INVESTMENT DECISIONS IN TERMS OF ALL EXISTING TECHNOLOGY, MAINTE-NANCE CONSIDERATIONS, OPERATIONAL REQUIREMENTS, AND FINANCIAL ENGINEERING

OPEN COMMUNICATION SYSTEM

AUDIT	PRIORITY	
❑	❑	• PROMOTES TRUST THROUGH MUTUAL RESPECT, CANDOR AND SHARING OF IDEAS AND OPINIONS
❑	❑	• PROVIDES A TRANSPARENT VIEW OF INTENT AND ACTIONS APPROPRIATE TO STAKE-HOLDERS' NEED FOR COMMUNICATION
❑	❑	• CREATES AN ATMOSPHERE IN WHICH CHALLENGES TO IDEAS AND OPINIONS ARE EXPECTED AS WELL AS SUPPORT FOR DIRECTION TAKEN
❑	❑	• ENCOURAGES FLEXIBILITY AND ADAPTABILITY TO RESPOND TO CHANGING OPPORTUNITIES AND CONDITIONS
❑	❑	• PROMOTES SYSTEMS THINKING FOR CREATIVITY AND TO MINIMIZE TURF DISPUTES
❑	❑	• HAS A POSITIVE BIAS FOR SUCCESS
❑	❑	• VIEWS DIFFERENCES AND CONFLICT AS SOURCES OF CREATIVITY
❑	❑	• IS ACTION-ORIENTED
❑	❑	• PROVIDES FREQUENT FEEDBACK TO ASSESS PROGRESS, MOTIVATE, AND JUDGE THE NEED TO CHANGE
❑	❑	• ESTABLISHES EFFICIENT STRUCTURES WITH MINIMUM BUREAUCRATIC PROCESSES TO ACHIEVE BUSINESS RESULTS
❑	❑	• EXPECTS EXCELLENCE THROUGH INDIVIDUAL EFFORT AND TEAMWORK
❑	❑	• FOCUSES CHOICES ABOUT INFORMATION-SHARING AND DECISION-MAKING ON THE WORK TO BE DONE
❑	❑	• EMPHASIZES POSITIVE ATTITUDES OVER FAULT-FINDING OR BLAMING
❑	❑	• EMPLOYS CONTROL SYSTEMS ONLY TO DEMONSTRATE AN HONEST PERSON IS HONEST
❑	❑	• REQUIRES SHARED RESPONSIBILITY AND PROACTIVITY
❑	❑	• HAS CONSISTENCY BETWEEN ACTIONS AND WORDS
❑	❑	• VALUES AD HOC RESPONSES TO BUSINESS NEEDS OVER INTERNAL CONSISTENCY

		HIGH-PERFORMANCE ORGANIZATION (HPO) *(continued)*
AUDIT	**PRIORITY**	
		CONTINUOUSLY IMPROVES AND INNOVATES
❏	❏	• INVESTS, INNOVATES, IMPROVISES, AND CONTINUOUSLY IMPROVES TO ACHIEVE COMPETITIVE ADVANTAGE
❏	❏	• APPRECIATES VALUE OF FORMULA: INCREASED $ = GOOD IDEAS + OWNERSHIP
❏	❏	• SEEKS BROAD PARTICIPATION IN CAPITAL INVESTMENT PLANNING/IMPLEMENTATION
❏	❏	• CELEBRATES RISK-TAKING AND REWARDS ACCOMPLISHMENTS
❏	❏	• CREATES FAITH IN CHANGE BY LOADING EXPERIMENTS FOR SUCCESS AND/OR MOVES QUICKLY ON OBVIOUS OPPORTUNITY
❏	❏	• DOES NOT OVERCOMPLICATE CHANGE
❏	❏	• VALUES STEP CHANGE OVER INCREMENTAL GAIN
❏	❏	• PURSUES AN INTENT TO WIN TODAY AND TOMORROW
❏	❏	• TAKES AN "APPRECIATE-WISH" VIEW OVER EVALUATING OR BLAMING
❏	❏	• VALUES CII AS A DETERMINANT OF SUCCESS
		PARTNERING
❏	❏	• CAREFULLY CHOOSES AND PRIORITIZES POTENTIAL PARTNERS
❏	❏	• CLARIFIES ROLE EXPECTATIONS—INTERNALLY AND EXTERNALLY
❏	❏	• BUILDS BUSINESS ON KEY ACCOUNTS AND OPPORTUNITIES WITH HIGH POTENTIAL
❏	❏	• LEVERAGES PARTNERS' EXPECTATIONS TO DO WHAT IS RIGHT
❏	❏	• LEADS PARTNERS TO A "BIGGER PIE" BY EXPANDING BUSINESS OR LEVERAGING RELATIONSHIP FOR NEW ENDEAVORS
❏	❏	• LIVES TO THE SPIRIT OF AN AGREEMENT CREATED WITH INSIGHT TO MUTUAL OPPORTUNITY
❏	❏	• EXISTS RELATIONSHIPS IN A MANNER TO MAXIMIZE VALUE AND SET PRECEDENT FOR FUTURE PARTNERING

(text continued from page 181)

REFERENCES

1. Games-Casserves, Benjamin, and Simon Krieger, "The corporation is dead. Long live the constellation," The Alliance Analyst, www.allianceanalyst.com, June 10, 1996, p. 1.

2. Games-Casserves, Benjamin and Simon Krieger, "The corporation is dead. Long live the constellation," The Alliance Analyst, www.allianceanalyst.com, June 10, 1996, p. 1.

3. Jones, Reginald, Ken Brown, John Harbision, and Peter Pekar, "Arguing the collaborative core," The Alliance Analyst, www.allianceanalyst.com, April 29, 1996, p. 1.

CHAPTER 12

Learning in Orchestration

Learning is constant in organizations. Every meeting, conversation, individual work assignment and pause to reflect may lead to learning. The greater attention, however, is to structured learning—seminars, technical training, simulations, and computer-assisted learning. The popularity of learning broke at the beginning of this decade as the means to transform organizations. People who learn are better able to adapt.

Nothing is truly new. The learnings were taught before. The difference is the endorsement to invest time and money in learning. The objective for investment, therefore, is adaptation to the pressure of globalization and advancing technology.

The slicing of the learning melon is three-way. One slice is about relationships. Primary is the bond between worker and firm. The aggregate of workers into teams forming internal partnerships is another bonding. This evolves to what most people label as partnering—collaboration external to the firm.

Another slice is based on the patterns set by others—some of which may have altered the world and invalidated the learning offered. Seminar leaders show how others envisioned the need to change and acted on it. To generalize others' adaptations to one's own circumstance is precarious. Not only may the original applications have altered the business landscape and made the learning invalid, but there may never have been any chance for a fit. Benchmarks carry more weight as catalysts for possibilities to be tailored to the firm.

The other slice is a broadening in interests and knowledge. This is not to say that everyone is to aspire to a renaissance view in a world of highly specialized knowledge. It does demonstrate, however, that a single specialization is not enough in commerce. Financial engineers need cultural sensitivity. Lawyers must grasp technical aspects of intellectual property in diverse technologies such as advanced electronics, composite materials and biotechnology.

A term or condition popular in one technology can set a pattern applicable to another. For example, the license agreements used in computer software sales was modified for application by farmers purchasing genes—nature's software—within seeds and plants.

Information technology specialists must grasp anti-trust laws and trade agreements. Take your experts with you to interpret. You will soon discover that you cannot comprehend your experts unless you possess base knowledge in their discipline.

Learning leads to action when individuals, regardless of reactions or restraints, decide to act, are allowed to act, or may be encouraged to act. Faced with the failure of traditional business practice, people are acting differently, organizations are transforming, and reward is more aligned at all levels to value-add.

Trends are moving in the right direction but it will still be some time before genuine high performance is a commodity in business practice. Many people can describe or teach about high performance. Few truly deliver. The greatest value-add of design is to bring the context of work into alignment with adaptive capability, reinforced by reward based on SVA.

A case illustration for orchestrating change is presented on the next page in the following matrix of learning, with the introduction of new work systems, technology, and decision-making.

For partnering efforts, we advise clients to develop relationship skills in human communication, teamwork, and group dynamics. These competencies facilitate internal collaboration and apply equally well in external partnering.

Outlined next are modules we generally recommend as a minimum for relationship development. They lead to joint team building, which is also outlined. If a partner has not made similar investments, provide sponsorship. Minimally, sponsor joint team building. There is good reason to do the preparatory modules with all sides participating. The shared experience strengthens team building and creates a common language for interpersonal communication, group dynamics, and conflict resolution. If you have not made the investment prior to partnering, wait and do it jointly. The modules are:

- Basic Human Communication & Adult Learning
  ⇒ Messages and Interference
  ⇒ Effective Listening
  ⇒ Feedback
  ⇒ Bypassing and Other Common Communication Problems
  ⇒ Personal Expectations and Backgrounds: What We Hear and Do Not Hear Because of Who We Are
  ⇒ Leveraging Differences for Creativity
  ⇒ Restoring Harmony and Conflict Management
  ⇒ Coaching and Mentoring
    [Experienced-based exercises, including simulations]
- Group Dynamics
  ⇒ Meeting Management—Time, Agendas, Follow-up
  ⇒ Social Psychology of Groups
  ⇒ Group Relations in Practice
  ⇒ Conflict Resolution
  ⇒ Creative Problem-Solving
    [Experienced-based exercises, including simulations]
- Team Building in Joint Efforts
  ⇒ Exercise: Create a cartoon about how you see the other party's organization: work systems, culture, etc. Send a message about 1) what you respect but do not want as a part of your joint effort, 2) what you admire about them and want as a part of the joint effort, 3) what they do and you don't want happening, and 4) what is missing about them you can address or just needs to be addressed because no party brings it forward.
  ⇒ Myers-Briggs Assessment of Styles
  ⇒ Personal Style Declaration—including what is right/wrong/fuzzy about Myers-Briggs Profile
  ⇒ Effective Use of Different Styles: Personal Action Planning
  ⇒ Matrix of Interpersonal Styles and Interactions
  ⇒ Team Work Action Planning
  ⇒ Performance Targeting and Team Metrics
  ⇒ Team Routines
    + Business Landscape and Continuous Improvement/Innovation Review Process

+ Communication with Owners
+ Routine Performance Stewardship of Business Plan
+ Harmony Management
+ Conflict Resolution
+ Cultural Integration Stewardship
+ Owner-Sponsor Review of Methods, Practices, and
  Action Plans

We recommend complex systems workshops to expose people to new possibilities (including benchmarks of competitors, allied firms, innovators in business from other regions or industries, and circumstances never yet applied); briefs on global markets and related societal trends: economic, political, social, and military; and each other's views and experience. Complex systems workshops permit debate and decision-making. Simulations and practice are very much a part of the sessions.

Complex systems workshops often include overviews of knowledge areas to promote broadening. The core topics are:

- Financial engineering—Valuation to derivatives to fund raising to currency management
- Pertinent technology briefs—Rarely are information technology and telecommunications omitted
- The new business law—International trade, intellectual property, and levy
- Complexity—The intersection of chaos and stasis

Learning takes place in meetings and conversations, as well as in individual work and reflection. It is much more than structured events like seminars.

When you learn within a context for application, use is easier and learning is retained. For this reason, it is important to both orchestrate learning on the job, even for seasoned players, and to promote coaching. Equally important is to create situations in which information and interactions about the information come together to raise the standard bar.

In these situations, the conversation around the issue is integrated with individual thought processes. At once, we sense, think, and act. In the blur of microseconds in which this occurs, individual reactions achieve insight by using what is in the head with what is in the room—others' ideas, information, and more. In a complicated and confusing world, you may not be able to keep everything in your head. You can leverage your context for work to support your coping with, or mastering of, complexity.

Leaders need to be prepared to coach and challenge, so learning reaches out of the seminar and into the work of the partnership. Leaders need to create environments and expectations to promote continuous adaptation. Learning, its application, and good analytics turn on access to information, knowledge, and self-initiation. Partnering will produce results where people are prepared and given the opportunity to apply what they know—not in a vacuum but with a market-based challenge from leadership and management.

In orchestration, we must remember lessons learned in building trust. Leaders who are trusted will have more opportunities to coach and mentor with results. Transparent organizations and partnerships will adapt faster by sensing the need to change and encountering less resistance—within, as well as with the outside.

Learning is leverage for making value creation happen. It is an important enabler, but not an end result. The value inherent to learning is a sunk cost in talent. If the talent leaves, the value is lost. Learning, thus, is an investment for shareowners value.

Application

Application requires a personal and firm agenda. On a personal level, the dynamics of learning, habit change, time management, and persistence animate application. For the firm, the following criteria give life to application:

- Stewarding progress closely against a plan
- Sensitivity to important reasons to adapt plans and action to changes in the business landscape
- Sponsoring communication and learning
- Consistency between statements and actions by leaders
- Extraordinary customer caretaking

In partnering, application is more than start-up or the transition period to follow. It is a day-in, day-out effort to make the relationship work. It moves along the landscape from a point of mutual exploration through a honeymoon period and on to a continuous engagement.

The mutual exploration begins before negotiation, and continues as the team managing the interface, as well as any operations team, get to know one another and begin work. Team building can accelerate and strengthen the process. What is most important is keeping clear about what is shared and not, how to manage boundaries, and being clear on how to restore harmony anywhere conflict may surface in the effort—all levels, interactions, and times.

The honeymoon is a time when mutual respect and tolerance of difference is granted before being earned. The earning of respect and tolerance matures in this time frame. The focus should be on tasks, quick resolution of differences, and the opportunity to prove one's competence and capability to facilitate in order to build mutual respect.

The relationship will be tested. No new relationship is without difficulty. How these situations are handled will set patterns for the future. Good habits or bad habits will be formed. The question of highest priority is whether or not the economic initiative of the partnering will set a pattern of dominance in the market.

Continuous engagement in a strategic relationship is routine and exceptional. The routine is found in making the relationship function to extract value. The exception is adapting to the changing landscape, sustaining harmony over dispute, and pursuing growth. As in any job, the monotony may dull senses and foment work habits serving the incumbent more than the firm. The benefit to partnering is that more than one owner is intent on extracting value and thus cares about what is happening.

The chances of a challenge for wasting time or resources is better with multiple owners. Implied is a higher level of scrutiny—which can at other times interfere with getting the job done. The difference may be, however, that there is always someone caring enough to ask with no additional involvement. One partner or another is willing to show interest. In single-owner situations, an enterprise unit can be ignored while upper management is preoccupied with their own matters, or while another enterprise unit needs attention.

Superior partnering will communicate in a timely manner and produce results to allay the possibility of owner concerns. The resulting alertness may begin by serving multiple owners and end with a heightened awareness of the business landscape. The vitality of the value is then served in the application.

Application is making it happen. To overcome resistance and set the new order for business, a mosaic of leadership, communication, design, learning, and application must emerge. Leadership sets the agenda for orchestration and provides the resources for action. Communication, as an application dynamic, informs and gathers information for precision in action. Design creates a context to guide and support application. Learning then builds skills and knowledge for action. Learning inspires contribution through understanding and encourages acceptance by building understanding.

Reexamine the transgenics launch diagram and envision how one event makes for or supports others. Do the same for the orchestration schedule illustration (Figure 12-1). In both cases, choices were made as to when things were done. Some work was done concurrently. Adaptation forces other work to occur. In the end, application was completed.

Stewardship

In application, there is the special dynamic of stewardship. Stewardship embodies recognition, the basis of reward; hope; the need to adapt; and the catalysts for discussions about "where next"—including the start of a growth agenda. Stewardship is a dynamic for coaching and directing—if necessary, caring and exploring alternatives for securing value.

There are three mechanical solutions which must be worked by the partners. One is agreement on how to track and measure progress in the business plan. We recommend that milestones across time be posted, quantitative metrics be monitored, and judgments be offered on soft outcomes.

Milestones provide cost and schedule reference points. They indicate if critical activities and events are occurring. The activity does not guarantee value. They indicate that work is headed in the direction set by the plan in some relation to the anticipated schedule.

Metrics are hard and fast outcomes. The measures of easiest discussion among partners are economic: cost, budget variances, SVA, net income, and capital management, by source—equity or debt. Sales, units or services delivered, inventory, production and more lead to economic outcomes. These are tracked to influence the course of action.

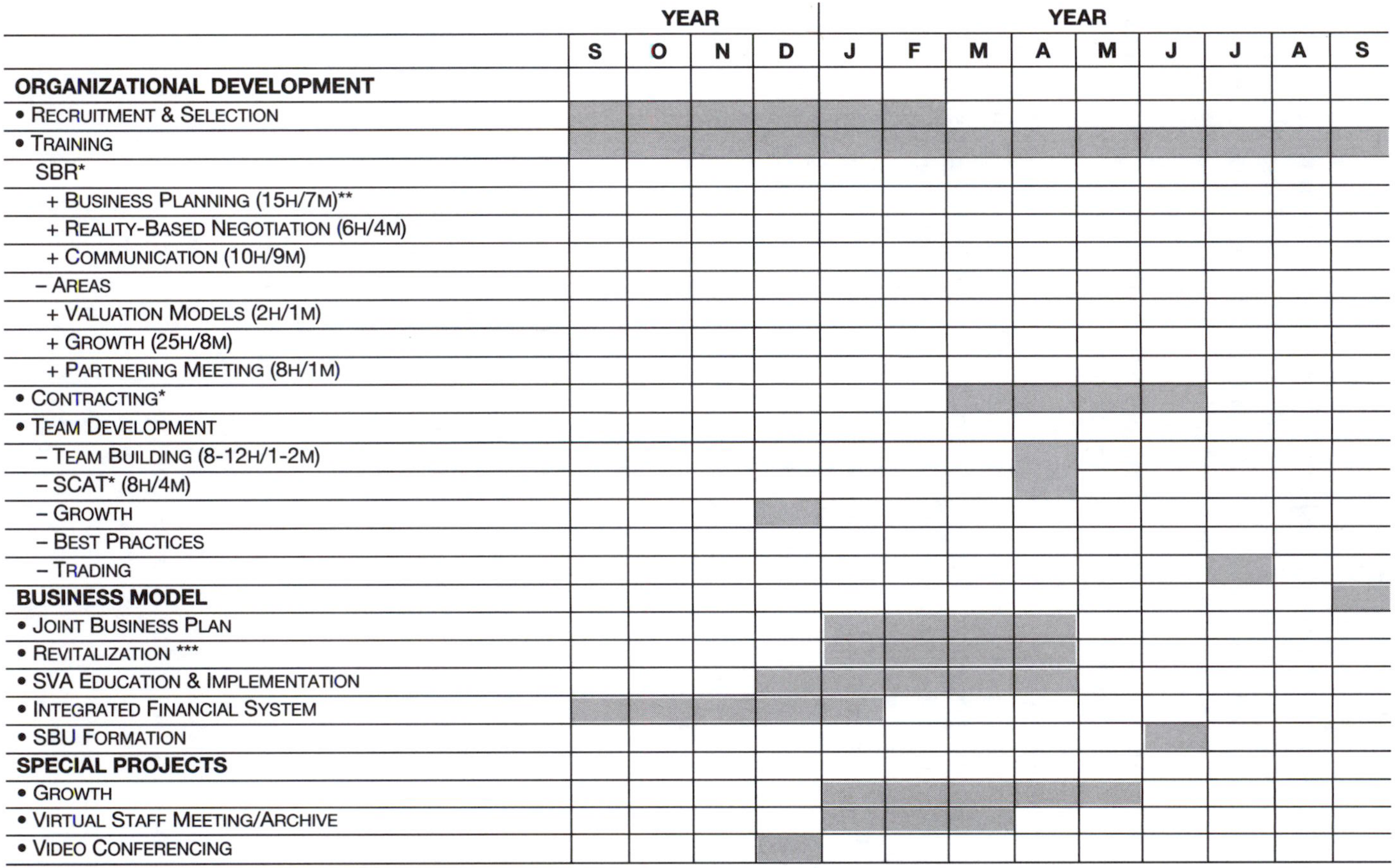

Figure 12-1. Orchestration plan.

People within the same organization will differ in interpretation of metrics and the chance for different paradigms of analysis among owner is good. Partnerships should attend to metrics in the business plan and base templates for stewardship of the business plan. The early agreement should define the means and frequency of review.

Reporting variances to plan ahead of owner meetings is smart. After any needed clarification of the reported figures, this permits agendas to focus on action plans operators propose as next steps and owner coaching. Arguing about reporting is a waste of time and an easy means for avoidance.

Qualitative reports on the integration of work culture, trends in the industry, competitor behavior, and the results of customer dialogues should be reported. In these observations may be important sensitivities affecting the business landscape. Though observation and opinion, they are catalysts in emerging strategies for harvesting value.

The second mechanical solution for partnering stewardship is defining circumstances warranting changes to the plan. Under what conditions and to respond to what kind of forces should the business plan be adapted? Agreeing in advance on the cues and the process makes it easier for decisions to be made when challenges to the plan surface.

The third mechanical solution is the nature of contact between owners and the shared effort. As previously indicated, it is smart to restrict involvement, as the tendency is interference. Clear, transparent steps for contact makes it possible for operators to challenge unwarranted involvement. This is important even when one of the owners is the operator. In this situation and in the early days of mergers, staff groups from corporate, in particular, may need to be reined in. A defined mechanism can always be enhanced at a later date. Better to begin with a straight-forward process that is public to all stakeholders.

An important process in stewardship is the conduct of the owner meetings. Better-performing partner relations use a board meeting format, though representation to the meeting may not be based on election by stockholders. Appointing key managers and staffs to act as directors for an owner organization matures their business acumen.

The character of the meeting should be one of sounding board in contrast to executive direction, strategy input, and approval of action plans. If the operator team for the joint effort cannot lead, get rid of them. Do not manage from the board. This is a sure sign of failure in the making.

Further to this point, operating tactics and work practices which creep into owner meetings then preclude genuine owner agenda items like financial engineering and growth. Failing to attend to the owners' work can delay or risk value.

Stewardship is the capstone to orchestration. It guides value creation and validates choices made for value creation. Stewardship of the business landscape sparks self-reflection and a survey of the market, both prompting growth. Stewardship restores focus in the fray of doing the work.

Owner Relations

Orchestrating effective owner relations in the 21st century will not be characterized as activism. Activism is today's cutting edge, and represents an accelerating transition from traditional corporate ownership to a new entrepreneurial spirit for complex systems.

Currently, more is said than done in creating entrepreneurial atmospheres. People are sometimes overwhelmed and confused by the complexity of these atmospheres. Many slip back into standing conventions in which risk is subordinated to protecting reputation against failure, or value is otherwise diluted by self-interest. The clarity in the globalization experience of the last two decades cannot, however, be denied. Owners must act like owners. Someone must challenge management and serve them with an expectation for value-added performance.

The caring for value and the willingness to lead with risk will more readily transfer from small enterprises to the deployment of mega-capital in the near future. An entrepreneur's willingness to set aside ego for the sake of a good deal will more often be replicated in the behavior of corporate contributors from the mail room to the board room as this decade ends and the new century gets underway.

Why will this be possible? There are numerous waves of change coming ashore on the global business landscape: raw capitalism in emerging markets, the use of alliances and JVs to create enterprise units among multinationals, a shift in the investment community to EVA models, information technology delivering owners timely and precise performance information, fewer degrees of freedom in ownership mobility among institutional investors, and the willingness in corporate governance to establish genuine enterprise units in place of subsidiaries under a corporate veil.

Ronnie Chan, chairman of the $5.5 billion (USD), family-held Hang Lung Development Company, Ltd. and Morningside/Springfield Group of Hong Kong, delivered a speech in Tokyo on March 23, 1997, to the Trilateral Commission. It was entitled "Asia Pacific Community Building: Political and Security Trends and Challenges."

In the speech, Chan speaks of where he sees China and her billion-plus market of consumers, saying, "What is the situation in China now? Raw capitalism is no longer found in any of the Trilateral countries. Yet it pulsates in China. In some ways, the Chinese economy is more market oriented than most Western European countries represented here. As a percentage of GNP, the government in China is smaller than much of Western Europe!"

In other economies, including much of the Overseas Chinese communities whose 55 million people create a virtual national economy ranking third in the world only to the U.S. and Japan,[1] capitalism is less fettered than in developed societies. Developing and emerging economies from Eastern Europe to the Pacific Rim, are boldly capitalist—to the point at times of being opportunistic and exploiting.

The impact is that entrepreneurial firms in these economies will emerge to the marketplace with sleek, responsive organizations. Many of these firms will have the latest in technology given their recent capitalization. The inherent advantage to the entrepreneurial approaches of these new competitors will need to be matched in developed societies. For the foreseeable future, you may face head-to-head competition with raw capitalism.

This does not mean that raw capitalism will prevail in the long haul. Exploitation in the market place can devolve to preying on itself, or elicit political backlashes. The recent economic shifts in the Asia-Pacific area evidence just this point. Nonetheless, the exploiting will likely continue for some time, as it is the dominant pattern.

The use of alliances and JVs to create enterprise units among multinationals and between multinationals and local partners produces several advantages. One is size. An alliance or JV tends to be smaller. The numerous and diverse product lines often produced by mergers and acquisitions are not found in alliances and JVs. Alliances and JVs tend to have narrow charters, at least at the onset when partners are just getting together. Until the courtship is complete, investment is limited and this keeps the play smaller.

Another entrepreneurial advantage is flexibility. Alliances and JVs take on entrepreneurial flares when they organize to keep overheads under control. In place of paying their share of allocated overheads as an affiliate or subsidiary might, alliances and JVs purchase only what they need from an owner. In many cases, they may outsource with a third party who is a more competitive provider than one of the owners.

An additional entrepreneurial advantage is closer alignment of rewards to value-added performance. Not only is it clearer to see the relationship between effort and results, but the complexity caused by history in compensation policy is washed away with the new venture's charter to streamline, and not be caught up in past practice.

Still another advantage is that risk is delegated close to people who make things happen. Finally, we will point out that multiple owners tend to impede corporate interference. If one party does it, others will encroach. As a result, everyone watches to prevent meddling and imposition from corporate.

More and more of the investment community are shifting from accounting models to economic value-add models. The comparative benefits of the latter are better correlation with market value, an indication of capital deployment and better tools for aligning rewards. Legg Mason Wood Walker Inc. enjoys a prominent position among fund managers and one of their key indicators for examining complexity is economic value-add.

Information technology permits the largest businesses to provide comprehensive information about performance. From the smallest detail to comprehensive summaries, information technology can dissect, analyze, assemble profiles, and otherwise report performance. The advantages of the entrepreneur to be real-time or near real-time in financial reviews, and put their arms around the business can now be had by managers and owners of large firms.

Not long ago, we watched an entrepreneurial procurement system demonstrate the capability to move to a national system with a nominal cost increase. The leverage available for accessing discounts in procurement and inter-linking customer databases for group purchase was staggering.

Institutional investors have grown so large, they frequently cannot move interests without selling to one another. The profit-taking of moving in and out quickly in stock ownership is not over. The opportunities are sharply narrowed by the largest players. As a result, institutions will likely stay longer with a company. New SEC rules permit communication among major players holding the same stock. This facilitates concerted effort to influence management behavior.[2]

In multinationals, statements about subsidiaries are made carefully. No one wants to mistakenly penetrate the corporate veil for these wholly-owned or majority-owned companies. Significant tax and liability risks exist. The reality of conduct can be a different matter.

Subsidiaries are not necessarily independent and function more like a division of a company than an independent entity. Capital is held up and decisions are not made because the parent is consumed with other businesses.

Alliances and JVs established as enterprise units have the pressure of other owners. Decisions tend to get made—in part from fear that the other side will delay on their side in the future—or delegations are made to the partnership. Either way, the entrepreneurship of the relationship is encouraged.

In all strategic relationship dynamics, there needs to be an owner sponsor—an executive with decision-making authority, the sponsor moves things along inside his or her organization. A sponsor often serves as a board member, provides coaching to the joint effort, and is the primary contact for other owner parties. The nature of the relationship should be like that of an outside director. The sponsor should be kept informed on a timely basis in a fully transparent manner. Skills in mentoring can be important to sponsors. They can influence business direction by educating and coaching players in the joint venture.

Mike Hudson, president of Allison Engine, advocates that senior managers on all sides should draft principles of agreement. These principles are then given to the individuals delegated to put together the detailed rules of engagement. Within the details, mutually agreed upon metrics and performance targets should be set for shared stewardship. For Hudson, the task of senior management does not end here. Senior management must assign good people and continue to show an interest.

Hudson estimates shared ventures mean another 15–20% of management time must be invested. Good people will reduce this requirement which is driven by the overlap in stewardship among partners.

Hudson further advises that good people are essential to obtain continuing support within the sponsoring firm. If the venture leader's job is not valued, the support will wane. The leader must also be encouraged to perform, and feel that there is a home base worth returning to when the joint venture job is done. The venture leader must walk a precarious line between serving the venture and fulfilling the fiduciary role to the owner. When it comes down to it, what is best for the owner must count first and foremost.

Joint pursuits, according to Hudson, are not places for the soon to retire, trainees, or irritants. If the wrong people become involved, you may soon wonder why the partnership isn't working.

Finally, in investor relations, we will address the growing interest in owner audits—sometimes called strategic audits, performance audits, and strategy evaluations. Whatever the name, these are third-party studies for owners of the alliance or joint venture. These studies are important to benchmark, gauge progress, and search for creative alternatives. The owner audit may engage the joint effort contributors in the process or be a stand-alone, independent report.

Gordon Donaldson writes in the *Harvard Business Review,*

> Board members, seeing the number of stockholder lawsuits and the escalating cost of directors' and officers' liability insurance, are feeling pressure from their increased risk as well. Even more important is the pressure from holders of large blocks of stock (pension and mutual funds), from judicial and regulatory authorities, and from the financial press—all of whom are calling for boards to be more active.[3]

Donaldson is a proponent of establishing formal processes to help directors review strategy without undermining a CEO. We join in this recommendation. Our template for building an effective audit is the intensive business review template found in Chapter 7.

Owner audits validate strategies and educate senior management in both methods for managing complexity and the nature of the business landscape. Specific areas of executive development brought forth in owner audits include financial engineering, cultural integration, alliance and JV management, value chain optimization alternatives, and complexity management.

Properly conducted, owner audits facilitate the introduction of board expertise and outside consultants. Conservative managers must confront the reality of what their choices are doing and not doing. Presented as guides and prompts, the owner audit results can be orchestrated to accomplish management buy-in and improved understanding of the business landscape.

Leadership

Every nuance of leadership has been explored in the volumes of books on the subject ranging from what to do in one minute, to the several best habits of leaders, and to Ghengis Khan's preferred methods. For us, leadership is a human process. It is essential to setting the right patterns in implementation.

Some Genes Are Tight, Others Are Not

There is probably not a leadership gene but there are traits associated with leadership that can be biologically influenced. Just as developmental psychology research with children indicates there is probably a shyness gene, it is also believed that there is one for assertiveness. Clearly, leaders are more likely to feel comfortable with assertion. People suffering anxiety from interaction will not find leadership comfortable.

In adulthood, those not afflicted with an extreme influence by their biology are able to determine how they want to behave. Some may have to learn more, prepare more, or dedicate more energy to be a certain way than others for whom the behavior is typical. For those choosing leadership roles in the implementation of strategic business relations, there is a criteria for self-assessment (see "SBR Leadership Attributes" on page 221). It has potential for guiding the selection and development of talent to lead SBRs.

The Power Politic

Leadership is a power base. Inherent to the use of power is a politic. From the leader's view of things, the politic can influence reward and recognition, and access to future opportunity. From the follower's view, the same dynamics apply, but there can be a question as to the intent of the leader. Does the leader lead for self, those he or she leads, or both?

The political nature of leadership is a two-edged sword. It can move people to support a leadership direction. It can dilute backing of the leader simply to compliance and foster resistance.

Leadership, as a process, can play out in the initiative of a peer to move the group a certain way, or it can be vested as a role responsibility within a hierarchy, offering command of resources and talent. A wide variety of leadership configurations can be designed and made to work. What we see as most important is the capacity to make a decision and have it acted upon.

SBR Leadership Attributes

NEED

- ❏ Able to Provide Focus Among Competing Priorities & Choices
- ❏ Team Leader
- ❏ Systems Thinker
  - • Strategic Intent
  - • Renaissance Knowledge of Business; Commercial, Technological, Organizational
- ❏ Integrates Expectations
- ❏ Belief in Mission
- ❏ Persuasive to Bankers (sound investor relations)
- ❏ Persistent in Vision
- ❏ Bias for Open Communication & Able to Dialogue
- ❏ Able to Leverage Multiple Disciplines
- ❏ Fully Leverages Information Technology
- ❏ Facilitates Conflict Resolution Across Groups
- ❏ Excellent Time Manager
- ❏ Manages Upwardly with Success
- ❏ Connects Well to Sponsors & Champions
- ❏ Pursues Mutual Benefit without Dominance
- ❏ Reputation for Honest & Integrity
- ❏ Willing to Support Another in a Pinch
- ❏ Able to Manage Contingencies
- ❏ Advocate of Total Quality & Continuous Improvement/Innovation
- ❏ Permitted to Offer Continuity
- ❏ Effectively Manages Transitions

Commercial decision-making is mostly a knowledge function after power and ego are set aside. Leadership, as remarked earlier, can evolve to a co-dependency in which others rely on the leader to leverage the leadership vantage point and make smart decisions about the market. As we proceed more into the next century, the need for broad input and participation to the decision making will expand. Regardless, you hope your leader has the understanding and insight to match the leader's power and authority to act on the marketplace.

Moving people in a direction is a vector of choices and degrees of freedom for leadership. Autonomy is not determined by what choices you have but how you use them. Leaders rarely have the freedom of limitless choice. The regulatory environment, the conventions of business, and the norms of the firm set parameters.

What choices there are must be fully utilized. Most of the influence internal to the firm is the power to distribute reward, recognition, and access to career opportunity. External to the firm, the power lies in decisions about direction, capital deployment, customer responsiveness, and partner relations.

A leader's internal influence by and large depends on the leader's credibility and character. Credibility functions with business decision-making results. Smart picks in the market place earn respect. In most organizations, hierarchical control correlates with commercial success. That is, more power and influence are granted to people who are capable of making things happen. This is how we confound subject matter expertise with leadership competencies.

Some will catch on by trial and error and acquire leadership competencies. Others who are already advanced to leadership catch on a little and struggle to be directive in style. Still others do not catch on but create patterns of control and dominance to force their way. A few leaders fail outright because they have no skill to orchestrate an agenda for action.

Character is not without influence. It does tend to be valued after business acumen. Take this into consideration. Do you hire surgeons for their personality? Is "fun-loving and cheerful" on your criteria for selecting a lawyer or tax advisor? Is your favorite basketball star noted for civil conduct? This is not to excuse behavior, but to point out that if you are really good at something, your character means less. So it goes in the century culminating in optimization.

As business relationships determine more about value-add, the subject of character will mean more. In place of singular, hierarchical control, there will be shared responsibility among partners. Having value tied to someone without character does not make sense. They cannot be counted upon and they represent potential for trouble. They may directly undermine your value position to optimize their own.

The settling-in effect of globalization and the clarity in behavior revealed by broader transparency in business, posits character will mean more. As the executive from Exxon, Jim Lowe, commented about prospective partners, you want to associate with someone who is a "straight shooter . . . no sharp tactics." Strategic business relations are based on trust.

The Spin on Integrity

In closed systems like work organizations, we very much want to trust our leaders. They are important to our destiny. Their trust is more important to our lives than public officials and political leaders. If they make a mistake, our economic well-being as individuals is at stake.

We coach leaders aspiring to 21st century high performance to build strategic relations. This includes their capacity to present a *prima facie* case for integrity and trustworthiness.

Rosabeth Kantor of Harvard completed extensive research on alliance dynamics and coined her eight "I's" that create success in alliances. Take note of the eighth "I."

- Individual Excellence
- Importance
- Interdependence
- Investment
- Information
- Integration
- Institutionalization
- Integrity[4]

In the 20th century, leadership has not always embraced integrity. The choice of late is integrity or spin. Integrity is supplanted by spin under two conditions: collusion and denial. Transparency defeats collusion by making the covert known. Transparency confronts denial and reveals reality.

Integrity is predictability. The capability to predict others' choices is a requisite for trust. The boldness in integrity is faith in the person and belief in the person's message.

Leaders are responsible for the firm's implementation of work atmosphere choices. Prominent among the choices are the building blocks for trust. Leaders can create transparency, sponsor learning, promote civility, and envision the future. Trust, as defined by these building blocks, is not wholly the responsibility of leadership. They make the choice as to whether trust has a chance to flourish in a firm.

WAR STORY

The Integrity Roulette as a Wheel of Fortune

There are countless stories about how integrity pays off in business. Many, though, still treat integrity as a revolving door. When things get tough, integrity gets going—out the window.

We encountered a striking example of virtue in leadership and how it paid off for an individual. This is in sharp contrast to any flight from integrity. Alan Raymond, president of the newly created Shell Energy Services Company, now leads one of the most exciting start-ups in the energy sector. His agenda is to embark Shell on a venture to sell electricity and natural gas directly to homes and businesses. How he got this choice role is the story.

Alan has a reputation for being an outstanding performer and innovator. Alan is known inside and outside Shell for his integrity. We saw this in how he led his organization and in relations with business partners. In a difficult situation with partners, he told the whole truth, not a corporate qualified version of reality—nor a spin on bad news that one can encounter with executives in multinationals. His honesty bought him and his team credibility, and they were rewarded with partner support on a position benefiting Shell.

(continued)

WAR STORY *(continued)*

This is what the man is about, but it is not yet the story of focus. It begins when he was a product manager in Shell Chemicals. As Shell Chemicals was repositioning, for the good of the firm, Alan was proactive in transferring to another part of Shell. Top performers like Alan were more attractive to other businesses in Shell. His willingness to be flexible brought Shell Chemicals a smoother transition, and transferred critically needed skills to a new venture elsewhere in Shell. Alan did what was best for the firm, confident in who he was. If he had any hesitation, he took comfort that if his risk were to go against him, he would somehow succeed.

When Alan's new corporate home would later undergo its transformation, he found himself in the same boat as before. This time the integration brought another oil company into a joint venture. Even more flexibility would be needed by the firm for the transition. Alan worked diligently on expediting the integration planning—yet another example of his diligence.

An offer for Alan to be involved in the new business as the number-two player came forward. The thought process was to bring someone from the industry in as president. Alan responded with a "No." His integrity this time was to himself. He knew he would not be fulfilled and challenged. He was ready to lead a business—though the decision put him at risk to the turbulence of his home organization's integration of large numbers of executives into a competitive enterprise unit.

In time, Shell saw the wisdom of the key role holder being familiar with innovation and owner relations with Shell. They needed a motivated and capable leader. Alan was appointed president. His courage to serve firmly and to say what was the best use of one's talent is impressive. Integrity is honesty to self as well as to the firm. This is what we meant earlier by seeing more in win-win than just in winning. Win-win is life, and in this vitality there is the potential for growth—more than just the first win. Shell's decision to place Alan in the role of president is their gamble that they will win more than one time.

Implementation Czar

Implementation is complex and involves the need for an individual or group to be well-informed and capable of making decisions. We look to leaders to understand and act on the business landscape. The pace of implementation, the resiliency of the implementation in dealing with crisis or customer complaint, and the investment of energy and resources are largely the choice of leadership.

Listed below are what can be debilitating distractions for partnering. Expect leaders to be able to understand and mediate, if not eliminate, the distractions.

DEBILITATING DISTRACTIONS FOR SBRs

- Litigation
- Reorganization
- Owner Transition
- Economic Performance Slump [actual or currency-based]
- Major Initiative [expansion, facility turnaround, new product/service launch, capital project]
- Disruption to Work Flow [supply, manufacturing, distribution]
- Environmental Challenge
- International Customer Relations Challenge
- Nationalism
- Failure to Understand Laws of Other Sovereignties
- Product Acceptance

There are events which can surface on the business landscape that cause dilution of value. Again, expect leaders to understand and act on the events and choices noted below before they impact:

WATCHOUTS FOR SBRs

- Limited Preparation
- No Business Purpose
  ⇒ No Customer
  ⇒ Customer Not Ready
  ⇒ No Backers

WATCHOUTS FOR SBRs *(continued)*

- Incomplete Response to the Market
    - ⇒ Missing Link in R&D, Marketing, Engineering & Manufacturing, Distribution, Administration & Services Dynamic
    - ⇒ Failure to Satisfy Customer
- Applying Traditional Organizational Structure (e.g., Function)
- Failing to Select Effective Advisors in Accounting, Law, Facilitation, Technology
- Taking a Short-Term Return & Tactical Pursuit of the Association
- Cultural Differences
- Poorly Prepared Leadership
- External Interference—in Particular, From Owners
- Poor Sponsorship
    - ⇒ Funding
    - ⇒ Advice/Guidance
- Dysfunctional Group Dynamics

Leadership is not an illusion, and it is not the sole determinant of what happens. It is very important to value. In 20th century optimization, hierarchical command and control was the cornerstone of leadership. The transition that began in the last quarter of the century has been a shift from the directive to participation. The 21st century opportunity is for leadership to serve the firm as a catalyst and to provide facilitation.

Offering new ideas, sponsoring others, and guiding the learning and relationships to make things happen, are the next leadership competencies. Catalysts and facilitation contend with the uncertainty of global business. From leadership's sponsorship, patterns for increasing returns emerge to benefit the firm. There are people who can make a difference.

We recently read the following inscription, "*Coach* n. one who possesses the invaluable gift of treating people not as they are, but as they can be." A twist on the insight for leaders of strategic business relations: 21st century leaders in partnering will possess the invaluable gift of managing shared responsibilities not as they are, but as they should be.

The Mosaic Worth Having

Making strategic business relations work can be dramatic. The highest drama is creating value. Value is a part of sustaining life and enabling survival, success, and sophistication. A life worth living is more than style, money, and choice. It is making a difference for yourself, your loved ones, and others. It is a process requiring constant attention to remain vital.

A life worth living emerges from the mosaic of implementation, and the willingness of others to join in. Implementation tones the firm and is the architect for autonomy. The resonance within implementation is the glue that holds it all together. Resonance among parties also builds hope. In all, implementation is a leadership career pursuit. The 21st century sparkle for executive careers will not be the deal, but the ability to extract value for the strategic business relations created by the deal.

Not long ago we met with Fouad Alghanim, a highly successful businessman from a leading trading family in Kuwait. At the end of our discussion of possible joint business ventures, he reminded us of the ancient Arab saying to capture the importance of partnering in business, "What is the sound of one hand clapping?" The silence is deafening.

REFERENCES

1. "Overseas Chinese Businessmen and the Global Century," a speech by Ronnie Chan delivered October 2, 1996 in Los Angeles.

2. Pozen, Robert C., "Institutional Investors: The Reluctant Activists," *Harvard Business Review,* January-February 1994, p. 145.

3. Donaldson, Gordon, "A New Tool for Boards: The Strategic Audit," *Harvard Business Review,* July-August, 1995, p. 99.

4. Kantor, Rosabeth, "Collaborative Advantage: The Art of Alliances," *Harvard Business Review,* July-August, 1994, p. 100.

Index